Planning
Human Resource
Development

Planning Human Resource Development

EDUCATIONAL MODELS AND SCHEMATA

ST. JOSEPH'S UNIVERSITY   STX
LB2846.D26
Planning human resource development;

3 9353 00038 7231

Russell G. Davis

Center for Studies in Education and Development
Harvard University

LB 2846
.D26

81688

RAND M^cNALLY & COMPANY   **CHICAGO**

RAND MᶜNALLY EDUCATION SERIES
B. Othanel Smith, Advisory Editor

Copyright © 1966 by Rand MᶜNally & Company
All rights reserved
Printed in U. S. A. by Rand MᶜNally & Company
Library of Congress Catalogue Card Number: 6619441

IN DEFENSE OF NUMBER

EDUCATING HUMANS AND PLANNING FOR THEIR EDUCATION ARE TWO quite different bits of business, and we can only be glad of that. Education by the numbers is grotesque; planning on the basis of numbers is a necessity. We can sympathize with the cry of Bernanos, that a world dominated by Number is ignoble; that "the abject tyranny of Number is a slow infection which provokes no fever." But everything depends on how pervasive one allows number to become. A teacher does not work with a statistic or a classroom full of data, but rather communes, mind-to-mind and soul-to-soul, with an individual or a group of individuals. Working at some remove from this scene the planner must reduce this rich dialogue to a manageable array of symbols and numbers, and unless he be the fiercest kind of technocrat he is aware of the aridity of this. But, unless the planner is the wildest of romantics, he is also aware of the futility of trying to devise models and statistics that will reflect the true richness of the teacher-learner communion.

Teachers and students are organized into classes, and the classes into schools with principals to direct them; and the schools are grouped into systems. The planner did not decree that this be done, but this indeed is the way that it is. Nor is this wholly the work of the modern state and its administrators; the first step was taken when classes increased from one to two members. The result was a group, and the tutor organized it into a class. As classes grew into schools and schools into systems, decisions had to made on the basis of less intimate knowledge of what really went on at the heart of the matter—the confrontation of teacher and learner. Decisions, reached in ignorance of the essentials, could only be implemented in terms of the broadest and least obtrusive statements of policy, backed by the gentlest and least irksomely detailed directives. Even so they were decisions, and though they could not be based on perfect knowledge, they had to have some rationally derived basis. The planner provides the decision maker with that rational basis.

The planner, with schemata and statistics, marshals the hum and buzz of reality into some imperfect replica of the system and its components. With aggregate and average, relative frequency and ratio, the lineaments of the matter are shown—palely, darkly, imperfectly, but without malice. To reduce one child with all his perfections and imperfections to one counting number and to describe a group of them with one statistic may be a high crime in epistemology, but it is not an immoral act as those galled by Number sometimes maintain.

If the administrator is to make a decision that will affect persons and situations which he cannot see, and if the decision is not to be purely autarchical and arbitrary, he requires some image and likeness of what exists in the domain. He can be supplied with a thousand pictures of 10-year-old students, read a thousand or 10 thousand words written about them, or scan a table of a thousand numbers used to characterize them on some basis. There is nothing inherently evil in one mode of representation over the other. Decisions will be neither more nor less oppressive because they are based on numerical summaries. And the number will give the best characterization along one dimension —order of magnitude. As to quality and essence, numbers, words, pictures, physical analogues, all are equally unavailing. The planner will operate with numbers because he has no better alternative when order of magnitude is at issue. And in educational operations, magnitude is at issue.

Summary tables lack flavor. They lack savor which only direct confrontation could bring. But direct confrontation is limited by the time allotted to man, and in worlds of vast compass only a bit can be experienced.

TO THE MEMORY OF

NORA WINIZKY DE LIFSIC

ACKNOWLEDGMENTS

THIS MANUSCRIPT WAS PREPARED WHILE I WAS A MEMBER OF THE CENter for Studies in Education and Development of the Harvard Graduate School of Education. The Center was created and sustained during these years by a grant from the Carnegie Foundation. To both the Carnegie Foundation and the Ford Foundation, I owe acknowledgement for support of this work.

Some of the routines and methods were worked out or borrowed during the course of planning operations and are difficult to credit to published sources. Lot Cooke, William Charleson, Noel McGinn, Richard King, Edward Mackin, Cristobal Espinosa Aragón, Susan Vogeler, Chai Hon-Chan, Ato Tafara Wondimagenhieu, Mariano Ramirez, Richard Durstine, Adolf Wilburn, Corrine Holman, and Srimaung Thavisakdi have worked with me and contributed. Specific contributions by Lot Cooke and David Williams are acknowledged in the text. The fillip, intellectual and personal, provided by my colleagues, Adam Curle, Director of the Center, and C. E. Beeby has been enduring and significant.

Lois Masor, Sol de Lenhof, and Susan Hayward helped prepare the manuscript. My wife, Mary Elizabeth Davis, bore the brunt of long hours of travail.

Contents

INTRODUCTION

MODELS, SCHEMATA, AND METHODS
FOR HUMAN RESOURCE
DEVELOPMENT PLANNING

THERE IS AS YET NO GENERAL MODEL OR SET OF MODELS WHICH DE-scribes, explains, or predicts how a society develops its human resources by educating and training its members.

Even in the 'simplest' cultures the phenomena that might be characterized as education are so elusive, and the methods for observing and characterizing them so insensitive, that results are seldom precise. In more complicated societies, statistics—demographic, cultural, and economic—are based on vast aggregates that often mask significant differences. So, there are great problems of status assessment and mere description. When the data are used as bases for estimates of the future, as they must be to serve planning models, the operation may produce meaningless or even harmful conclusions.

Yet, in developing countries, the need to generate educated and trained people is so pressing and the resources so exiguous that not a moment or a penny can be wasted. This cries out for planning so that mistakes can be minimized. Planning entails some general models for associating the data so that relationships can be observed and estimates made about the future probable state of the system.

It would be pretentious to talk of developing a model that would be sufficiently general to explain how all knowledge is acquired and transmitted in a society, any society. Here, the problem is limited to transmission. Second, only the more formal modes of transmission are covered. This restricts the analysis to agencies and institutions that specialize in education. Third, only the more formally organized agencies, i.e., schools, yield suitable data for analysis. Policies have to be adopted with respect to other less formal institutions (libraries, museums, cultural and industrial productivity centers), but they are not handled under the schemata treated here.

The job at hand is to develop schematic models that will serve a limited but extremely useful purpose, i.e., the planning of the growth of educational and training enterprises, primarily in developing countries.

Although the approach and methods of planning illustrated here have come primarily from work in developing countries, the models and schemata may have relevance for the planning task ahead in the United States. As the U.S. federal government moves more vigorously into education and general social development, programs must be planned with broader strokes to cover a wider domain. State, regional and even national programming can profit by the planning approaches sketched out in this book.

There are systems which by purport are general educational planning models. The Correa Tinbergen Bos model is one. Moser, and Redfern and Stone have also developed models that are supposed to cover the total educational process. But all of the general models are addressed to only part of the educational planner's task. Manpower schemata set the educational targets for the economically active portion of the population. But there is still the rest of the population. In Iraq, women make up only slightly more than 1 per cent of the economically active population; yet if the culture is to develop, and even if the economy is to prosper, the mothers of workers may have to be educated in future years, whatever their workforce participation rates may be.

Even if a model set requirements for the total population (and some modification of the Orcutt simulation models might be made to do this), it has only covered one part of the problem of human resource development. There must be models, or at the very least schemata, for assessing and forecasting resources to meet the requirements. There must be schemata and routines for allocation of resources to education and training, rather than to other socially beneficial or productive uses. There must be models for allocating to some levels and kinds of program within education, rather than to others. There must be routines for associating inputs of men and treasure with outputs of trained people. In terms of these routines, the program (curriculum and teaching-learning situations) is arranged.

There must also be models for associating program inputs and outputs in a sequential fashion. There is a long lag between an input to education and a higher-level output; and if the sequential nature of decisions and strategy are not accounted for, the system will not produce the right number at the right time. Handling humans by the numbers, as graduates or teachers, is a distasteful business but it must be done if large-scale decisions are to be made effectively.

Rather than to try to concoct one general model, this book examines the models, schemata, and subroutines for handling the general components of human resource planning. The offering here is neither a mathematical treatise on planning models nor a handbook on educational administration, but it has some of both features. Good mathematics would in some cases require that we break contact with reality and create systems of equations which have variables and coefficients impossible to evaluate with present data. A good administration handbook would require attention to fine detail impossible in the space provided here. Educational programs should not be bent to fit the simple forms provided here without the background knowledge of how school systems actually work; and that cannot be provided by any one book, but must come from long and intimate experience in the business.

The book is, in short, a hybrid, for the field to which it has relevance is that way too. The world cannot always be sorted out according to the departmental structure of a university.

This book is by and for those who do human resource planning in developing countries. In this field, the economist has dominated. His terminology has become the meta-language of the field, and his methods have prevailed. At the same time, very central problems of economic conceptualization, definition, measurement, and analysis have to be glossed over if the planner is to produce any meaningful result in any finite period of time. The true costs and benefits of education and training, as the economist might like to see them handled, receive short shrift in most planning operations, and this book reflects that fact perhaps even more starkly because the writer is not a professional economist.

All would be well if the writer could feel that he satisfied professional educators, already somewhat restless with the literature that is issuing in the name of the economics of education. But there is no space for detailed treatment of many of the topics dear to the hearts of professional educators. The theory and method of planning curriculum development, teacher training and supervision, measurement and guidance, and school construction are very briefly treated. Fortunately, the reader may choose from among several excellent existing works for more detailed information about such specialized subfields. This volume attempts to create the general frames (models and schemata) within which all of these programs can be planned comprehensively instead of in isolation as is now the case. To the American professional educator, accustomed to local instead of national systems and to relative plenty in human and fiscal resources, the problems singled out for attention here may seem unreal. But those who have taught and planned in the educational systems of developing countries will recognize the situations and problems as live ones.

The material in Chapter V is least satisfying. Linear programming models and operations research techniques are not familiar ground for most educators, or even for all economists. Originally, the models in Chapter V were introduced with spurious data and worked examples. This made the section run to inordinate length and implied that the methods had much more immediate application to educational planning than is the true case. Hence, the material was cut back to a critique of the methods and models. Didactically, the section is not now satisfactory and can be skimmed or skipped by those who do not wish to go to other sources for a more painstaking introduction. Throughout the book, there is an attempt to push just a bit beyond currently useful techniques.

Finally, demographers and samples applications and census specialists will find their fields worked over with shallow furrows.

The offerings here are educational planning to the professional economist, economic planning to the professional educator, and the combination of both to the statistician.

There are eight chapters:

    I. General discussion of human resource development and the part played by the formal educational system. Present status of the field of human resource planning in developing countries with illustrations of the schemata used. There is a smattering on the economics of education and its relevance to human resource planning.

    II. Schemata and formulae for estimating educational requirements for the economically active and total population.

    III. Demographic analysis and estimation routines for projecting populations.

    IV. Flow and output of educational systems. Strategies for maximizing the output of educational systems through sequential moves. Estimating the flow and output of educational systems. Norms and sampling applications.

    V. General models that may be useful for setting output targets and allocating resources to education. This sketches out, but does not develop in full, possible applications of optimization routines and operations research technics to educational planning. It goes a bit beyond current planning methodology, presupposes some knowledge of rudimentary matrix algebra, and can be skimmed by those who have no taste for such things.

VI. Cost formulas and the planning of quality in educational programs, present, and future. Common routines and methods for costing inputs to education, covering conventional components (teachers, books, and classrooms) and some newer gadgetry.

VII. Schemata for educational outlays and receipts. National accounts and the estimation of resources and revenues in future years.

VIII. Nonquantitative planning and prognostication. Guesses about future trends in higher education.

At the outset, a word on the distinction between human resource development planning and educational planning. The first is not merely a more pretentious synonym of the second. Educational planning covers the arrangement and ordering of school programs and the more formally managed in-service training courses. Human resource planning has a wider domain. First, it may cover the establishment of standards of nutrition and sanitation and medical care that reduce morbidity and mortality to levels where the population can use whatever education and training it has to produce. The planning of these preconditions is not part of this work. Second, human resource development planning can cover all of the institutional and individual ways in which a population acquires and improves knowledge and skill for social, political and economic development. Much of this goes on privately, in the minds and hearts of men, unamenable, fortunately, to observation, characterization, and control. Formal education is a large part of human resource development, but not all. Planning one will often involve planning the other, but not in all cases.

The terms 'developing' and, sometimes, 'underdeveloped' are applied freely to the countries for which this work on planning has relevance; and the assumption is that elaborate characterization is not necessary, that the terms are generally understood. Insofar as any general typology can capture the myriad differences that prevail, the Harbison and Myers schematic, for countries in Level I (underdeveloped) and sometimes in Level II (partially developed) will serve. The countries have predominantly agricultural economies, with people engaged in subsistence activities, the product of which does not come through the cash market; and insofar as the aggregate means anything, the per-capita GNP is $200 or less. Populations are rural, agrarian, and traditional;

and political structure can vary from dynastic absolutism to egalitarianism. There may exist one city which has some light industry and urbanization. The school systems have been typified by Beeby and Sizer. In Beeby's terms, they are at dame-school level and beginning to acquire formalism in the more efficiently run institutions. In any given country, different areas may be at different stages of development.

HUMAN RESOURCE DEVELOPMENT AND EDUCATIONAL PLANNING: SOME GENERAL PERSPECTIVES

A SOCIETY DEVELOPS ITS HUMAN RESOURCES BY EDUCATING AND TRAINING its members. There is as yet no general model or set of models which describes, explains, or predicts how this is done. Much less is there an idealized model of how this can best be done. Psychology offers some explanation of learning and teaching, surely the central components of the process of human resource development. But in moving from the rat learning the maze under conditions of deprivation and reward to the individual student learning algebra, much is lost. The matter is further confounded when the individuals associate into ordered groups and societies which must be treated in the round. How and why do societies, or at least substantial numbers of individuals in them, learn the rudiments of the germ theory of disease? Or Fermi-Dirac statistics? Perhaps more significant—how are they motivated to work long, work well, and turn the fruits of their work into productive investment and wholesome consumption?

In those societies, which in Doob's (1960) terms "appear to be simple," and which tend to be small, absolutist, and formal, the trained anthropologist may characterize fairly comprehensively the way in which values, manners, and arts are transmitted from older to younger members. At least the apparent aim and the outward aspects of the bush school, the initiation class, and apprentice training in crafts and household arts can be observed and described. Reasonable predictions can be made of how these will transform the future behavior of individuals. The working of the system as a whole can be evaluated by observing whether or not societal stability is maintained, manners and morals are conserved, and arts and crafts endure. The odd deviant will flunk out of the school and society and go rogue, or transcend the system to produce Lascaux cave paintings, Homeric poetry, or Ife bronzes. But the system stays in balance and seems simple to observe. Is it?

Even in traditional societies, long before there is an accumulation of scientific and technical knowledge there comes an increase in the division of labor, which Smith (1930) regarded as the onset of technological progress. The lore to be transmitted multiplies and becomes more specialized, and few are the sages who can master it all. Responsibility for transmission of some part of the lore may pass from the family to specialized surrogates, i.e., teachers or masters. These teachers may federate into companies or schools. The family may retain responsibility for transmitting manners. A priesthood may take over the teaching or inculcation or morals. Masters may take over training in the arts and crafts. And the sages may provide access to the stored wisdom of the past, perhaps vastly increased by the development of a system of graphemic storage. Schools must also provide modes of seeking and accumulating new knowledge. Even at this simple stage of development, a model which covers the entire system and predicts likely results is not as easy to formulate as the observers of traditional societies make it appear.

The lore to be transmitted may be packaged and labeled *trivium* or *quadrivium,* but comprehensive coverage of learning-teaching is difficult. Vast segments of essential learning are transmitted in the family or acquired in the market, church, forest, shop, or field. No curriculum plan or formal school program covers it or provides hints on how to evaluate—or even observe—it. Scientific and technical knowledge accumulates, and the process of accumulation accelerates. The lore fragments into a vast technology with cells endlessly subdividing and proliferating. Substrative to this, a structure of science takes shape.

It would be pretentious to talk of developing a model which would be sufficiently general to explain how all knowledge is acquired and transmitted in a modern society. The job at hand is planning for transmission rather than acquisition, although the two are closely related. A modern society increases and enhances its science and technology even as it transmits it. Educational and training agencies are engaged in both research and teaching, and one cannot be readily separated from the other. But one aspect, i.e., transmission, of what may be the same underlying process can be selected for analysis.

Second, only the more formal and observable modes for transmission are covered. This restricts the analysis to agencies and institutions that specialize in training and education. The formal educational system may transmit only a fraction of a society's science and technology, to say nothing of its values and aesthetics. But planning is usually limited to this fraction that can be observed.

The task at hand is to develop schematic models that will serve a limited but useful purpose, i.e., the planning of the growth of education and training in a developing society. A true model of the cultural transmission system would define its elements so that they could be observed; observe dimensions of these elements and characterize them for state and magnitude; map the relationships in such a way that the status of the system can be assessed and predictions about probable future states made. Here the aim is no more ambitious than the development of a rationale for getting maximum educational yield, given the restrictions that exist within and outside the educational system of a developing country.

Psychologists map the ways an individual learns. When learning binds individuals into societies and cultures, the anthropologists and sociologists are there to chart the ways, abetted by the historians. On these bases, the educator must plan the specifics of school curricula. But implementation takes place in a political and economic context that controls the commitment of men and money to system-wide programs. The planner provides comprehensive analysis of the educational system through models that cover, but do not detail, the central aspects of curriculum planning. The best schemata provide only frames for a general decision. A host of specific decisions must follow. Even to provide this much of a basis requires comprehensive and detailed analysis.

CURRENT PRACTICES IN NATIONAL EDUCATION PLANNING

To date, models for planning educational growth provide no such general coverage. The usual approach is to work from objectives which describe the expected, or, at times, the hoped-for output of the system. Almost all of the Latin American countries, for example, have laws on their books which state that a complete primary education (six years) will be provided to *all citizens of school age, under state control and at state expense.*

The law is a statement of what the society and its government wish the educational system could do. Reality may be quite different. After a hundred years, the system may still serve less than half of the school-age children. It may not be free, and it may not be wholly under state control. In such a situation, the planner must undertake the task of reducing, often very gradually, the difference between reality (what the system is doing) and the goal (what the state would like to do).

How the goal itself is warranted is another matter. It may be a national aspiration based on political, social, or moral grounds, e.g., all children who are educable have a fundamental right to a complete six years of education. The planner takes the law as it stands and makes a very simple approach to shaping the system to conform to it.

A. The number of school-age children is established by count or estimation.
B. The number of school-age children enrolled in schools (private and public) is established.
C. B is subtracted from A and this represents a gap for the system to fill.
D. The cost of filling the gap is estimated, either by calculating a rough per-pupil average cost and multiplying it by the number that must be educated, or by dividing the number to be educated by some assumed ratio, e.g., 40/1, to establish the number of teachers and classrooms that must be provided. The cost of teachers and classrooms is then estimated and totaled, and sometimes the costs of furnishings, equipment, teaching materials and supplies are added.

In many developing countries, even these crude calculations are sufficient to indicate that the country does not have the resources to fill the gap immediately. The planner must program a gradual satisfaction of the goals over a period of years. The major, but by no means only, determinants of the program will be: resources, in the form of government revenues and private subsidies that will be available; the population to be educated, which in all cases will be increasing; the requirements of teachers, classrooms, and educational materials (again, increasing); and competing demands on available revenues for other kinds and levels of education and other goods and services.

The schema for this is most simple, as the example from a Latin American country shows, in Table I.1.

Table I.1 is minimally useful, even for the limited purpose of scheduling public investment in the primary and secondary schools of the country. The need and investment are based on the population estimates in column (1) which have these weaknesses: census is carried forward 13 years; vital rates based on inaccurate registries; assumption of unchanging vegetative increase is questionable; and assumption that population will conform to 1950 proportions in rural-urban and age distribution, more so.

TABLE I.1

Investment necessary in the education program of a Latin American country, 1964–65 to 1972–73

Schools	(1) Total	(2) Enrolled[b] Age 7–14	(3) Not enrolled	Classrooms (4) No. required[c]	Classrooms (5) Average cost[a]	Classrooms (6) Total cost
Primary						
urban	240,250	165,314	74,936	1,499	$6,000	$ 8,994,000
rural	720,750	93,217	627,533	12,551	1,000	12,551,000
Secondary (high schools & normal schools)	51,076	16,219 *Age 15–16*	34,857	697	8,000	5,576,000
	1,012,076	274,750	737,326	14,747		27,121,000

Schools	Furniture & Equipment (7) Cost per classroom[e]	Furniture & Equipment (8) Total cost	Teachers (9) No. required[f]	Teachers (10) Annual salary[g]	Teachers (11) Total cost	(12) Total cost of classrooms furniture and equipment, and teachers' salaries[h]
Primary						
urban	$360	$ 539,640	1,499	$1,000	$ 1,499,000	$11,032,640
rural	30	376,530	12,551	1,000	12,551,000	25,478,530
Secondary (high schools & normal schools)	500	348,500	697	2,000	1,394,000	7,318,500
		1,264,670	14,747		15,444,000	43,829,670

SOURCE: Primary School Extension (prepared April 1962)

[a] Based on 1950 census, with total population brought forward to 1962 by vital rates (birth & death.) Total population in 1973 estimated from a vegetative increase rate of 0.02993 calculated on years 1956–60. Rural-urban population and numbers in 7–14 age group calculated on basis of proportions which existed in 1950.
[b] Estimated on the basis of present enrollments and future possible enrollments, given existing teachers and classrooms.
[c] Classroom need based on student/classroom ratio of 40/1, with 25% of classrooms being used for double load.
[d] No basis for these average costs in actual construction experience in the country.
[e] No basis. [f] Assumes one teacher to one classroom. [g] Assumes no salary increases in eleven years.
[h] All values expressed in U.S. 1962 dollar equivalents.

A sounder projection for the 7–14 age group, for example, would have been made by concentrating on the vital rates and registries to make them more accurate; by constructing a life table, calculating surviving children aged 11–13 in 1973 on the basis of births in 1959–61 and, with age-specific fertility rates, estimating births in 1962–66 and surviving children 7–11 in 1973.

More adequate demographic procedures than this are possible; but for the moment the techniques are not so much at issue as is the general point that with all education needs being based on population estimates any such scheme for educational planning requires higher quality demographic analysis as its base. Furthermore, it is not clear why the total population 7–14 should determine educational needs in the primary schools in 1973. If progress through the primary school were normal (low rates of retardation and dropout), most children 13 and 14 who entered a six-year primary school at the age of seven would have finished it six years later and graduated. However, inasmuch as progress is decidedly not normal and dropouts and retardations are high in this and many other similar countries, the actual school population will be made up of many students over 14. So, the base 7–14 is not appropriate. A sounder procedure would be to assess the current age-grade distribution of the school population and set a policy that would either progress over-age students through the schools within a given time or provide another program for them, separate from day elementary schools. The other program would be planned separately.

Column (2) is equally weak, inasmuch as it is based on an estimate of future school capacity which provides no wastage factor for teachers who will retire, die, or for other reasons leave the service, or for classrooms that will become totally useless during the 11-year period. Column (3) is based on column (1) and column (2).

In column (4) computation is based on student/classroom ratio of 40/1, and an allowance is made for the fact that some classrooms can be used to handle a double load of students. In the case of rural schools, the assumption is that 25 per cent of the classrooms can be put to double use. The population concentration in rural areas and the lack of roads and transportation service make this assumption an absurdity.

Columns (5) and (7) have no basis whatsoever in actual costs in the country. They are guessed average costs. In column (9) it is assumed that there will be one teacher necessary for each classroom which is not so in secondary school and unlikely even in primary. In column (11) no salary increases are provided for in 11 years. It is unclear what meaning column (11) has. Seemingly it is the current cost of providing teachers' salaries for additional students in one year, 1973, rather than total outlay on salaries over the period.

The total cost is meaningless. It lumps current costs for teachers' salaries (to take care of additional students for one year) together with capital costs for classrooms and furnishings. The programming of teaching costs for future years is better separated and handled under two rubrics: the cost of training the teacher (which is a government responsibility in most cases) and the costs of paying their salaries when they teach. Increases in instructional staff will also increase expenditures for administration, supervision and supporting service. The total also seems to be expressed in plan-year dollars, without taking into account changes in costs and prices over the 11-year period.

The entire scheme rests on the assumption that 100 per cent of primary and secondary school age children should be, or can be, educated in the country. The textual material accompanying the tables does not explain why this figure should be set or how the children should be educated, any more than it offers an adequate estimate of what it will cost and how it will be financed.

It is profitless to criticize the schema further, but it is significant to point out that this is typical of the general efforts in educational planning that are produced in many countries. No account of the kind and quality of education appears in the general planning schema. There are general descriptions of school programs and curricula in the regulations produced by the Ministries of Education, but these are not related to the numbers to be educated and the probable costs. Yet, the probable cost is surely a function of the kind of education to be given.

In the schema, in very general terms, education for a year is presumed to consist of 1/40th of a teacher (training level unspecified) and 1/40th of a classroom minimally furnished. There is no provision for books and materials for elementary students, or for laboratories, supplies, libraries, and shops for secondary students. The plan covers only the formal educational system and only two of the three levels at that. (In this country, post-secondary education is also a charge of the state and absorbs a fixed percentage of the national budget.) The plan, further, pays no attention to the fact that private education handles 15 per cent of present primary enrollments and over 50 per cent of secondary. Presumably the total bill will belong to the state.

A simpler and clearer approach, to the problem, from another Latin American country, is shown in Table I.2. The data bases for this plan are not much better than the first one, but at least the result is simpler and easier for officials to understand.

TABLE I.2
Educational needs (teachers and classrooms)
of a Latin American Country, 1963–1972

| | No. of additional students to be enrolled— | | | No. of additional |
| | *to cover* | *because of the* | | *teachers and class-* |
Year	*the deficit*[a]	*natural increase*	*Total*	*rooms required*[b]
1963	46,000	80,600	126,600	2,532
1964	46,000	83,100	129,100	2,582
1965	46,000	85,600	131,600	2,632
1966	46,000	88,400	134,400	2,688
1967	46,000	90,800	136,800	2,736
1968	46,000	93,500	139,500	2,790
1969	46,000	96,400	142,400	2,848
1970	46,000	99,000	145,000	2,900
1971	46,000	102,200	148,200	2,964
1972	46,000	105,300	151,300	3,026
Total	460,000	924,900	1,384,900	27,698

[a] The deficit as of 1962 is estimated at 460,000.
[b] Based on a student/classroom ratio of 50/1, and one teacher per classroom.

TABLE I.2—METHOD

1. Enrollment was subtracted from school-age population (9–16), and this represents the deficit.
2. The deficit was scaled down by subtracting students who would be taken care of in private schools, and students who could be handled by present staffs of teachers and in present classrooms, assuming better organization. The result is a deficit of 460,000.
3. The annual natural increase of the population is estimated (excess of births over deaths).
4. The deficit is divided into 10 equal parts and each part is added to the natural increase component for that year and this total is divided by an assumed pupil/teacher and pupil/classroom ratio of 50/1.
5. The result is the number of classrooms (and teachers) necessary to cover the deficit and handle the increase.

A more finely spun routine for estimating primary school targets, outlined in Appendix I, is taken from an evaluation of the Mexican 11-Year Plan. Chapter V offers a model for a similar approach to planning.

MULTI-NATIONAL MODELS FOR PLANNING

The aid agencies (UNESCO, AID, the Alliance for Progress) have sponsored international meetings (Bogotá, Santiago, Punta del Este,

Addis Ababa) to encourage underdeveloped countries to formulate educational plans. The underlying model for planning covered three elements:

1. Goals were set in terms of the numbers of children who have a fundamental right to be educated.
2. A time period was established within which the goals are to be met.
3. A price tag for the education was calculated on the base of very rough, and sometimes imprecise, estimates of unit (per-pupil) costs.

Under the Alliance for Progress, the participating Latin American countries pledged themselves to the goal of universal primary education within the Decade for Progress (1960–1970). This goal has been the law of many lands for a hundred years, and the only new element was the setting of a time span for accomplishing it. In countries with 80 per cent of their school-age population already provided for, such a goal is reasonable. In countries with teachers and facilities for only 40 per cent of the school-age population, the goal is almost impossible. Ironically, the countries with the scarcest resources have the largest gaps to fill.

Whatever the goal set at the international level, each country must face its own problems and deal with them within the limits of its own resources. The amount of aid that will come in from East, West, or international agencies is extremely small in comparison to the need. In the Kenya Development Programme, the statement was made, "In the last resort, the total size of the educational programme depends on what the country can afford, not only in respect of the initial cost of building and equipping new schools, but also of subsequently maintaining them."

International goal setting has served well as a needed fillip, arousing countries to the necessity of setting some kind of human resource development targets. It has served less well from the standpoint of offering countries models for planning programs that are fiscally and technically feasible. To this task the efforts of the International Institute for Educational Planning (UNESCO) are currently addressed.

UNESCO has encouraged the setting of general goals and justified the provision of an elementary education to all as a fundamental human right. This may be so, but it is unhelpful for planners in a country which simply does not have the wherewithal to guarantee this right, save at the expense of other levels of education and other meritorious social and economic development programs. UNESCO (1962) has estimated that to reduce the number of adult illiterates in the world by half, the requirements would be those shown in Table I.3.

9

TABLE I.3
UNESCO Literacy Cost Estimates

New Literates	Cost Per Literate	
Africa: 70 million	$7.00	$ 490 million
Asia: 230 million	$5.25	$1,208 million
Latin America: 30 million	$6.15	$ 185 million
Totals 330 million		$1,883 million
$660 million would also be required for teaching materials.		

Individual countries are encouraged to plan their literacy programs in terms of these general data. But in one Latin American country, the cost of producing a literate—by even the simplest standards—is $18 (including instruction and materials), about twice the cost estimated here. Curle (1964) has made a penetrating analysis of the problems and possible costs of a world literacy program.

Per-pupil cost calculations, even for such seemingly straight-forward enterprises as literacy campaigns, are more difficult than Table I.3 makes them appear. There are no standard definitions of what a 'literate' product is, or what a literate person can do that an illiterate can't. In some countries the standard is the number of years of schooling completed, without respect to any achievement measure. In other countries, a given number of years of schooling successfully completed makes a literate. Often this is set at four grades completed, for no apparent reason and without respect to the kind of primary education offered in the different countries. Other countries set the completion of a series of readers as a standard, sometimes with achievement tests and sometimes without. One country counts the number of literates it has created by the number of literacy kits (books and charts) distributed. When countries adopt goals that are beyond their capabilities, the result is often a sham, a game of numbers in which the true educational yield is slight.

Country Resources for Meeting Requirements

To plan any program of human resource development, from literacy to university education, developing countries must follow a model which provides an estimate of the numbers to be accommodated in the program. This model must permit the country to program a balance between what it would like to do and what it can and must do. What most countries would like to do, if they could, is offer universal education through primary school and sometimes through secondary school. What most countries must do is produce sufficient numbers of educated and trained people to staff government and private institutions and man the economy.

What most countries can do is strike the optimal balance between aspirations and resources. The first step is the planning of educational programs that will produce some meaningful result. The second step is determining the minimal unit costs of these programs. But the minimal unit cost is not one that provides a result so substandard that no meaningful result is achieved; it is rather one that yields a product at some standard. That standard is assessed by measurement of achievement and performance. When the quality and the cost of the program are set, it is appropriate to assess the resources that will be available and thereby determine the numbers that can be accommodated. If this number is smaller than the number minimally required, greater effort and larger resources must be provided, or the social and economic development aspirations must be scaled down. But the educational product should never be diluted to reach mere number goals.

Goals must be realistic and attainable, and the sacrifices entailed must be meaningfully presented to the masses of people who will be called upon to struggle to attain them. The models that will follow in this book attempt to provide programing toward medial and feasible goals.

Universal education through primary and secondary school may be the only appropriate ultimate goal, but the models will be addressed to medial and attainable goals. The models are meant for technicians. They are offered with full sympathy for politicians who may still be forced to go on with public promises of universal education, even when they know that their country does not have the resources to provide it.

Education has an almost universally accepted value; so much so that in some countries planning has proceeded on the basis that too much of a good thing is impossible. Hence, countries have accepted goals of universal primary education, only to face the problem that satisfaction of such goals depletes fiscal and human resources to such an extent that other vital areas of education (secondary and university) have to be shortchanged, to the detriment of the country's economic and social development.

Education at all levels, from literacy to university programs, contributes to social and economic growth; but developing countries cannot plan on so simple a basis as 'The more education, the better.'

Overproduction of graduates unequipped to work and contribute to the progress of the country, let alone pay for further educational development, is already a fact in some underdeveloped countries. Already, West Africa is developing surplusses of virtually unemployable elementary school graduates with high expectations but no training to join the work force except in crowded clerical fields. There are no places for these primary school graduates in the secondary schools, and work as agricultural or industrial laborers offers no incentives. India's teeming universities—the enrollment in Calcutta is in excess of 120,000—will pour out graduates faster than the economy can suitably employ them.

In Latin America there has been a chronic surplus of lawyers, at least relative to shortages in other professional fields, with the result that lawyer-generalists swell government bureaucracy and at times fill, through default, jobs for which they have no technical training and less professional commitment.

Not so obvious is the fact that there may soon be a surplus of certain kinds of professional engineers (civil, primarily) in some Latin American countries. Large enrollments of engineering students are appearing, perhaps as a counter movement away from law studies. Presumably these engineers will be employed in the industrial expansion which is expected to come with development. But the technicians who should be supporting these engineers, and the estimate is variously that this support ratio should be anywhere from 1/2 to 10/1, are not being trained in corresponding numbers. Nor are the skilled industrial workers in chemical, electrical, and machine trades appearing.

A study of engineering education in Mexico showed that professional- (college-level) engineers were being trained in sufficient numbers for Mexican industrial development of the present, but the highly trained engineer-scientist types and the engineering technicians to support them were not being produced in sufficient number to man the research and development activities that Mexico will need to create new industries and markets for the future. Davis (1964).

In recent times, countries have become far more preoccupied with the problem of economic development and growth and the part that planning can play in marshalling scarce resources to support development programs. Education, as a prime agency for human resource development which in its turn is a basic necessity for economic growth, has come under more searching scrutiny. Some education and training programs, rather than others, seem to be more likely to promote economic development. Some kinds of education programs that have merely been allowed to grow, seemingly not only do not contribute to growth, they may even inhibit it. Growth has, of course, been measured primarily in economic terms. Hence, planners have sought newer models in which human resource development is related to economic development and the output of educational and training establishments calibrated to the needs and the capacity of the economy.

THE ECONOMISTS AND HUMAN RESOURCE DEVELOPMENT PLANNING

Economists dominate development planning, and increasingly their theories and methods have been extended to cover human resource development and its formal aspects of education and training which were once the exclusive preserve of the psychologist, sociologist, and professional educationist.

Not all of the interest of the economist in education has been recent, nor has it been stimulated only within the context of economic growth and development. Economists have, from the time of Adam Smith, been interested in education and have been much exercised by such questions as to whether the expenses of education should be met by the government or by the individuals receiving the education. Adam Smith, as Vaizey (1962) reminds us, attributed "the superior intelligence, and the providential, orderly habits" of the Scottish people to the early and widespread education that they received. Most economists who followed Smith acknowledged the importance of education but tended to leave it aside when developing their theories of economic growth, until Marshall again attempted to relate education to the study of economic change. Marshall, moreover, was one of the first to concern himself with the return to education and he included as a mathematical appendix to the *Principles of Economics* (1908) a schema for calculating such returns.

The importance of education or training has been implicit rather than explicitly formulated in the work of many other economists. Schumpeter (1947), for example, made the role of the entrepreneur central, indeed, but did not specify how this epitome of progress and growth was synthetically produced by education and training. To the present time, economists have made much of the contributions of innovators and entrepreneurs, but without offering detail as to how these movers and shapers are identified for nurture and development by education and training.

In the early days of North American industrial development many of the innovators seemed to be natural noblemen—although this would be a strange term applied to some of the early entreprenuers—little shaped by formal education and training. In modern and complex technologies, however, the innovators seem more likely to come from the ranks of research and development specialists, who must have formal training and education even to qualify for entering the field. Certain kinds of education and training may be more effective shapers of such talent, but neither the economist nor the psychologist has helped much in specifying how this is best done. Everything from strong dosage of formal science to creative play activity is recommended—and sometimes works.

Superficially, the innovator-entrepreneur seems one strongly driven to accomplish, undaunted by the fact that this may require the treading of new ground, and equipped to arrange facts in new permutations from which emerge conclusions that were not obvious to others. Another way of saying it is that the innovator is highly motivated, creative, and able to set and solve nonroutine problems. But this says almost nothing. What cues motivate him and what paths beckon to his latent creativity? and, What enables him to shape problems in a fashion that yields possibilities of solutions? Economists have not gone deeply into the literature on creativity, although their own discipline has produced creative men.

Polya (1957) and the mathematicians have emphasized the way to lay out the problems in modes that are amenable to solution, i.e., the heuristic. Getzels (1962) and his associates have attempted to distinguish the highly intelligent from the highly creative individual. They suggest that conventional IQ tests do not single out the creative individual and that other measures are needed to evaluate divergent and unconventional thought. Economists seem only now to be catching up with the IQ test and realizing its possibilities for classifying large populations and perhaps selecting the most 'gifted' to be the beneficiaries of education in a situation where resources are scarce. Yet, it may be the creative, rather than the conventionally intelligent, individuals who will provide thrust to an economy by innovation and entrepreneurship. The IQ test may select only those students who will be good at being students. Whether the cute, and often trite, writing that the Getzels group scores as "creative" is any better predictor is debatable. All but the most routine thought processes mask themselves and resist observation and measurement. From Piaget (1953) to Bruner (1960), the paths of cognition have been charted, using as models everything from lattice algebra to question games.

McClelland (1961) has concerned himself with how people are motivated to achieve and has attempted to relate "need achievement" to economic development and growth. There are formidable problems in establishing reliable and valid measures of creativity and need achievement. The measures are subtle in mode to the extreme. The test stimuli are ambiguous—pictures with cues that may suggest different things to different viewers; and the responses are buried deep in linguistic and kinesthetic webs that are difficult to untangle and score objectively.

If measurement is difficult, the stimulation and nurture of creative thought are even less well understood. Nonetheless, motivation and creativity are the mainsprings of human growth and development and the economist has been correctly concerned with what education and training can contribute to the performance of all tasks, creative as well as routine, which enhance productivity.

In the great emphasis that has been placed on economic development during the years following the end of the Second World War, there has developed a theoretical and practical awareness of the significance of a suitably trained work force. The early estimates made by the U.N. of the amount of capital required in underdeveloped countries were modified as awareness grew that the absorptive capacity, i.e., capacity of the country to make use of new capital in an effective manner, was limited by the nature of the labor force.

In the same period, the notion grew that all people had a 'right' to education. The two forces enormously increased the drive toward education in the newer countries. Education was viewed as not only desirable for its own sake and as a means for stimulating economic growth, but was also considered a prerequisite for human dignity. There was consequently a demand for education that was far greater than anything previously known. Countries were faced with the problem not only of deciding how much to spend on education but also whether to spend for one kind of education rather than another. Economist-planners were presumed to assist in these decisions.

Lewis (1955) points up the dilemma of the low-income country which must provide education that both contributes to its development and meets consumer demands for increasing amounts of it. Individuals demanded education; work forces required it; and whole populations were said to have a right to it. Individuals sought education for its own sake, as an intrinsic good—as well as to enhance their means of earning a livelihood. Politicians set goals to respond to this demand, and planners sought the best means for satisfying it.

Lewis makes the statement that most countries have no difficulty in deciding that all educational facilities which directly increase output are worth expanding to the limit. The early literature of educational planning in most underdeveloped countries does not completely bear this out. Early treatises on planning view education as a social overhead cost, burdensome but still necessary because people want it or have a right to it. The amount programmed for vocational and technical education is small in comparison with the vast outlays for general education in the primary schools. In those few countries where manpower requirements or development needs are related to education, there is some attempt to balance the two.

Lewis' assertion that literacy is desired "not as an investment but as a consumer good" holds for some countries only. Increasingly, even in countries where the development effort is stronger in agriculture than in industry, planners tie minimal levels of literacy to the productive aspect of education. At the very least, literacy is human resource infrastructure, the parallel to roads, harbors, and power facilities on the physical side. It establishes conditions for growth. Community development and rural extension service tie fundamental education—which is literacy with practical content—to increased production in rural areas.

As yet, there have been few attempts to measure the minimal literacy needs in major economic activity sectors. The data indicate that the requirements are higher in industry than in agricultural and service sectors, but they have been analyzed only on the most superficial descriptive level and checked by the most simple correlational comparisons. In Central America and the Dominican Republic, the argument for universal literacy in the active labor force is based squarely on an assumption—as yet untested—that it will increase productivity.

Svenlinson (1962) and others of the OECD economists offer a slightly different description of education from that of Lewis. They refer to the 'production aspect' and 'consumption aspect of education. They point out that education is not a current consumption good but rather an investment in 'a durable consumption asset.' During the recipient's lifetime, education serves as a key to further learning and satisfaction and promotes sounder habits in the consumption of other goods. Tinbergen (1958) makes a distinction between general education and specialized education and training, the latter being more closely tied to economic development. General education, in his terms, also contributes to development but is desirable for its own sake. Tinbergen, Schultz (1963), and others have emphasized how much of development and economic growth are accounted for by human resource improvement, presumably through education, rather than by the increase of capital, land, and other classic factors in a growth function.

Increasingly, too, economists have contributed to studies of the costs and methods of financing education. Vaizey (1958) and Benson (1961) have studied costs and the means of raising revenues to finance public education in the United Kingdom and the United States. Some of the theories, methods, and findings are applicable to lower-income countries. Schultz (1960) and others have tried to account for "direct" and "indirect" costs of education. Estimates of the amount of income foregone by full-time students are included in indirect costs. Harris (1962) has tried to estimate future costs and means of financing higher education in the United States. Several OECD economists have developed schemes and models for projecting educational expansion and future costs.

Brand (1961) offers this comment on economically based models for educational planning:

> There is as yet no systematic and integrated model which would enable the problems in the field of education and manpower to be viewed in their entirety. One element in such a model could be the net marginal productivity which different training possibilities offer to persons of various abilities now and in the future, and the effect of this productivity when the number of people with different kinds of training background is changing. Another approach could be the construction of a model, or various models, with different assumptions, projecting the probable evolution of the structure of the economically active population on the basis of the expected pattern of domestic and external demand for goods and services and of the composition of employment in the various branches of the economy, considering foreseeable technical and organizational changes.

MANPOWER AND FISCAL BASES FOR PLANNING

The result of the applications of economic theory and method have been rationales and schemes for educational planning which rest on two fundamental data bases: (1) the resources, primarily fiscal, which the country can mobilize to support the accomplishment of education and training goals; (2) the country's need in general education and specially trained human resources. When overly simplified—and they often are—these approaches are said to be based on budget and manpower data.

One sort of data, rather than another, may dominate the goals set and the subsequent planning. More often, the fiscal restrictions dominate. Most countries can make rough estimates of resources likely to be available for public outlay on education. The simplest model for doing this entails projection of total and active population; assumption of productivity per active person; multiplication of active population by productivity to yield gross product or total resources available; estimation of the value of imports which when subtracted from resources equals national income. Application of tax rates and savings rates gives an estimate of the revenues likely to be available for public outlay, and education will claim some share of these.

Such a procedure may sound simple to someone who has not had to get the data and warrant the assumptions involved. A commoner and simpler way of estimating the likely availability of fiscal resources is to project revenues available for education as a fixed percentage of an assumed growth in national budget or gross national product. Countries participating in the Alliance for Progress program committed themselves to raising educational expenditures to 4 per cent of gross national product during the Decade for Progress. It was estimated that this level of expenditure on education would insure that countries could provide universal elementary education and still support other educational programs at the secondary and university level. Whether either of these two figures, the 4 per cent for expenditure and the 100 per cent educational target, were based on calculations of even the roughest sort has never been clear. None have ever appeared.

When revenues projected on the base of national income or budgets are compared to rough cost estimate for educational programs needed, it usually appears that the poor country has little hope of meeting its educational goals. When the gap between need and resource is as great as it is in some countries—projections in one country in Latin America indicated that an outlay of $70 million in 10 years would be required, when likely educational revenue estimates were for no more than $30 million—the future may be so depressing as to discourage planning, or paper plans may be spawned and no efforts made to realize them. Plan estimates are used only to show how hopeless the task is in the foreseeable future.

Country needs in trained human resources have played a lesser role in setting educational planning goals than have fiscal restrictions. The most notable attempt to plan in terms of manpower or human resource goals was the work of the Ashby Commission (1960) in Nigeria. Here goals were set in a very general way on the basis of skimpy data and large assumptions as to similarities in the structure of Nigeria's trained manpower and that of Egypt and Ghana. Puerto Rico (1957) made projections of manpower needs which were based on income, productivity, occupation, and educational structure, and work force participation rates in various sectors of the economy. The central assumption was that Puerto Rico in 1975 would reach "approximately" the same levels of productivity as the United States in 1950. An outline of the basic tables used in the Puerto Rican scheme appears in Appendix A. Whatever the results, the method is worth studying.

Both the Nigerian and the Puerto Rican planning efforts were valuable pioneering efforts, although deficient in respect of the data on which they were based. General plans for human resource development (*Perspectives of Educational Development in Asia: A Draft Asian Model.* Paris: UNESCO, 1965.) still appear, however, with very little attention given to relating manpower requirements to educational targets. Some of the early manpower advocates appear to be souring on the method and advocating a return to back-of-the-envelope calculations.

Resource limitations and manpower shortages interact, or will, when a country's economic and social growth is planned over time. The country's fiscal resources will depend on its product, which will depend on productivity, which in turn is related to development of human resources. The training of human resources will be restricted by financial resources available to meet the costs; and, like so many things in development, the process is circular: Poor countries have limited fiscal resources because they have untrained human resources, and they have untrained human resources because of limited fiscal resources.

In the short run, human resource shortages may be more serious than fiscal limitations in restricting the educational and training goals which can be reached in a developing country. The most compelling example is that of teachers. In educational development, large numbers of trained people, who must be' employed as teachers, become rather like the intermediate products in the economist's input-output analysis model, i.e., their time, talent, and training are used up to produce more educated people, rather than in production. This become especially acute in the matter of teachers of technical and scientific subjects who are also in high demand for industry. Two alternatives are usually possible, neither of them very successful. Untrained people are used as place-holders on the instructional staff. This allows quantitive expansion but at great cost in quality. A second possibility is to import large numbers of trained teachers from abroad. These expatriates are expensive.

In Latin America, part-time and untrained teacher practitioners are used at all levels. At primary level they are called *empiricos;* at secondary and higher, *profesores de tiempo parcial*. The use of sometime professors may permit the university to take in larger enrollments and relieve political pressures, but it is not at all clear that it increases the output of graduates, even quantitatively. Between 1951 and 1961, enrollments increased from 2,824 to 5,447, or 93 per cent, in the University of San Carlos de Guatemala. Graduates increased from 115 to 139, or 21 per cent. During 11 years, more students were taken into the University, but a truer measure of its output is the number of graduates. Some of the increased enrollments represent not gain but mere loss for the country's workforce in wages foregone.

Human resource restrictions take longer to satisfy than shortages in plant and equipment, and programs to meet trained-teacher demand have to be planned further ahead—in the case of university teachers, about 12 years beyond general primary level. For this reason, systems output models which show the sequence of attainment of levels by years are outlined in Chapter IV.

In countries where secondary school populations are inflexibly divided into vocational and preparatory streams, the career die may be cast in the seventh year of schooling. This problem underlies one of the most serious deficiencies in the use of manpower models for educational planning. The approach tends to lead the planner to prescribe undue specificity and inflexibility in the face of future uncertainty.

The manpower approach often is boiled down to a simple demand-supply balance: What does the work force require? What are educational and training institutions supplying? Presumably, at least, current demand can be set by an assessment (sometimes by census data and sometimes by a survey of establishments) of present employment in sectors and industries within sectors. The supply side is filled by assessment of the product of educational and training programs. When the two are in balance the educational system is meeting the requirements of the economy, and presumably the society. In educational planning there are at least two major hazards to the approach:

1. Present workforce demand may bear little relationship to future demand. Economic planners may set priorities and growth goals for sectors of the economy, but rarely is it possible for industries to be specifically identified as certain candidates for future growth. The educational system may have to train people for employment in industries which have not been established.

Furthermore, with technological progress, the pattern of occupational requirements and specific educational and training qualifications may change over time. A U.S. Department of Labor Study (1954) showed that educational requirements at the higher levels did not change much, *quantitatively* (percentage of work force requiring higher education), from 1940 to 1950. This does not mean, however, that different kinds of higher educational preparation were not required in 1950. Nor does it mean that there would not be a quantitative change over the next decade, 1950 to 1960. Planners may project general growth in the industrial sector and identify food processing as a major candidate for expansion. But during the time the industry is being established and developed, the occupational requirements may change from the need for a substantial number of semi-skilled machine operators, with basic literacy and some mechanical training, to a few experts on programming servo-mechanisms and highly skilled machinists and electronic workers to repair and replace machine parts.

2. A second major problem is that the relationship between occupation and education is sometimes a tenuous one, even in the highly skilled and professional levels. Men are educated as mechanical engineers but work as restaurant managers. Less frequently, men work as engineers with seemingly no formal education for it. A U.S. survey (1954) showed that 21 per cent of the work force classified as engi-

neers did not have the formal professional training normally associated with this position. The pattern can become a crazy-quilt affair in some underdeveloped countries. In one country the Minister of Education was a pharmacist, the Minister of Agriculture a schoolteacher, the Minister of Public Health a lawyer, and the head of the Supreme Court a medical doctor. This would not be serious if the officials at the working level were career officers, but these career officials—i.e., career during the tenure of whatever friend happened to be minister—were usually from equally inappropriate backgrounds.

Even if the occupational structure of the economy could be determined, there is no easy way to translate this into educational and training requirements. A vast amount of specific occupational preparation takes place outside formal systems; and in many countries the formal requirements for the job are disregarded in favor of family or political connections. Proponents of manpower planning point out that this is how it is, but not how it should be, and that the approach itself serves to alert people that there should be some relationship between preparation and occupation.

Problems in the manpower approach highlight the fundamental need to maintain flexibility and corrigibility in an educational system which has to fit its output to an unknown future demand in the labor force. Models and schemata for planning this educational output must permit this flexibility. Flexibility in the model should entail flexibility in the educational system itself, in the sense that when educational preparations begin to diverge at the secondary level there should be provision for shifting from one stream or program to another.

In a situation of considerable state control over individual career choices, this shifting can be done by fiat and *en masse*. In the case of most countries, however, it can only be effected indirectly by educational and vocational guidance, scholarship incentives, expansion of places in one study program rather than another, and wage incentives and worker benefits in the labor market. It is a common phenomenon in underdeveloped countries for teacher training institutions to turn out graduates who never work at the profession. Given the salaries and benefits that attach to teaching, these people never had any intention of becoming teachers but took the only educational opportunity that was offered to them, i.e., normal schools and teacher training programs. The economists might say that this output of trained teachers who do not teach represents no loss because the education contributed to increased productivity in other work. This is in part true, but it does represent a loss insofar as:

1. The training given was so narrowly vocational and professional that it is in part wasted when put to other ends. One may indeed suspect this to be the case in teacher training programs.

2. Trainees, by not entering the teacher force, create shortages which slow the production of future educated people. Whatever else the teacher does, he does multiply the number of educated people more rapidly than any other professional. This is in the nature of his work.

Educational and training opportunities may be offered for the purpose of increasing the numbers in a given profession. Yet, the profession may offer no prestige or money incentives to practitioners. People will take the education and duck the profession, and the result is large numbers of people trained for one job but working at another. Teaching is the notorious example.

CURRICULA FOR A LIFETIME OF WORK AND LEARNING

A curriculum to prepare all men for all things does not exist. In the primary school, to reading, writing, arithmetic, and physical science, must be added social studies, art, music, and, some would say, second language training. In the intermediate grades, all of these subjects would be carried forward, and it would be helpful to add a general prevocational experience to acquaint students with the world of work through manipulation of laboratory equipment, art equipment, shop equipment and tools and computing machines. In secondary school all of the verbal and symbolic disciplines must be deepened and some students must be equipped with entry level skills for the work force. Here lie irrevocable commitments to specialization that may soon be outmoded, and here lies the significance of the statement that no education can be terminal, that all curricula must prepare people for a lifetime of learning and training.

Education can not be planned in one-to-one correspondence to work force requirements. The relationship between education and production is too indirect. Education may increase production, lower it, or be irrelevant to it; and education does more than merely enhance a man's productive behavior. Educational planning in terms of work force requirements provide some minimal estimates which are useful for planning, but work force requirements can never control all educational target setting.

II

THE SEARCH FOR OBJECTIVE CRITERIA:
SOCIAL GOALS, MANPOWER TARGETS,
AND RATES OF RETURN

A COUNTRY CAN EMPLOY ITS RESOURCES (HUMAN AND FISCAL) TO PRO-
vide education and training according to a set of political and social goals.
Chapter I provided some examples of this, and Chapter V offers a model
for shaping the plan objectives quantitatively. Examples of simple goal
statements are: All children within a specified age range will be given
a complete primary education; certain portions of older age groups will
be given education and training at secondary and tertiary levels; certain
portions of the adult population will be made functionally literate . . .

The problem consists in determining how many people are to be
provided a certain kind and amount of education. *Kind* introduces the
problem of quality which is at the heart of educational planning. Defer-
ring consideration of quality in order to sketch out the main lines of the
approach, kind is then related to amount to yield unit cost (years in
program), as in Chapter VI. Unit costs are multiplied by the numbers
to be educated to provide estimates of total cost. Inasmuch as the objective is to provide a plan for future years, the exercise can be taken
a step further to provide estimates of how many there *will* be to educate
and what the cost *will* be for providing the kind and amount of education envisaged. Even in this crude schema there are objective criteria
for planning decisions. The obvious one is that the estimate of total cost
when compared with the estimate of likely resources may demonstrate
that the program translation from the goal statements is not feasible.

This information feeds back to the planners and administrators who scale the program down to fit resource limits.

The weaknesses of this rude schema are many, but the paramount ones are:

1. The goals themselves are not set up or evaluated by any objective criteria, but are taken as givens. The warranty for the objective is based on propositions that do not yield readily to rational analysis and decision.
2. The evidence that feeds back is largely negative, i.e., the program cannot be accomplished, given the imbalance between resources and the requirements for resources. However, because the goal is stated before the assessment is made, the objective is allowed to remain on the record with all this fact implies in political and social frustration.
3. The planning criteria are so crude that quality and real output may be sacrificed to a sham program in which mere numerical quotas are filled in schools. Educational program quality may dip below a meaningful level. This is particularly likely in the national, centralized systems of many developing countries where mere numbers games are played back at the Ministry while schools languish.
4. Planning becomes a Procrustean exercise in which individual programs are lopped off without attention to effect on the total system. The result may be school buildings without teachers or materials, or upper level programs without sufficient sources of student feed from below.

The rejoinders to these criticisms are based on facts from the real world. Most developing and many developed countries do their planning this way. The controlling decisions are often politically and socially inspired, and not necessarily rational; and the most objective arguments can be swept away by the unbearable pressures that politicians face. The exigencies of time, lack of trained people and adequate data, and the pressure that comes from the fact that schools are open and running long before planning starts, all conspire to make this approach the most practical first approximation to planning. The analysis methods are, by admission, crude; but the same problems are found at the heart of more sophisticated and elaborate models where only passing attention is given to quality under the heading Technology of Education. More elaborate and general models only push the problem of rational decisions up to another level, although economists would argue that if the planning of education and training can be related to and incorporated into general growth models of the economy some gain is made, even if basic social and political values are not necessarily made more amenable to quantification. Furthermore, the crude schema never eludes the imposition of economic criteria, for considerations of cost and resources must enter at some point.

ECONOMIC BASED MODELS: MANPOWER REQUIREMENTS AND RATE OF RETURN

The economist seeks models which will relate the planning of education and training to general economic growth and development and provide criteria for estimating the costs and benefits of education so that they may be compared to other possible investments. It is customary to view manpower and rate of return schemata as different and even conflicting approaches to human resource development planning, but there are more similarities than differences. Both approaches bottom on an assumption that can be schematized in this nondescript function:

$$P_j = f(HR_{ij}, CI_{ij}, Z_k) \tag{1}$$

This may be taken to state that Product in any sectior j of the economy is a function of Human Resources, HR, Capital Investment, (plant, equipment, etc.) and Z, other institutional conditions (social and political). The literature of economics should be scanned for a more adequate handling of the problem, but for the moment the main notion is that the way in which human resources of type i (usually defined in terms of education and training) are employed with other factors in a sector of the economy j will influence the product of that sector. Few would care—or bother—to argue about such an inconsequential statement. Economists have demonstrated some residual contribution to production from education; and Z covers about everything else under the sun that cannot be readily measured or quantified.

A more straightforward statement of the manpower-cum-education approach may work off an equation of this sort:

$$^jx^i = {}^ja^ip^j \tag{2}$$

This states that the number x in the work force of sector j with education or training qualifications i is directly proportional to volume of production in the sector. This is, with very minor modifications of notation, identical to the first equation of the Correa Tinbergen Bos model (1965) for relating educational development to the general development of the economy. If growth of product can be projected for future years, then, with a series of linear equations that relate product to edu-

25

cational attainment in the work force, enrollments in the educational system can be derived. More detailed treatment of these models is offered in Chapter V. Further on in this chapter, more conventional schemata for relating work force demand will be discussed.

The bold assertion of relationship between educational attainment and product may cause some uneasiness. Educational attainment, when defined in crude levels and without respect to field and quality, may have a positive, a negative, or no effect on product, may be a cause or result of increased output; and the form of the relationship over any period may be best described by a function that is decidedly nonlinear. In most examples of application of the model, the function is treated as linear, increasing, monotonic. The model builders, Tinbergen and Bos (1965) are working toward refinements and disaggregations to meet criticisms leveled at earlier and simpler versions of the model.

Conventional schemata for relating educational demand to manpower requirements through occupations are described in detail further on in this chapter. If manpower requirements could be estimated and expressed in simple educational equivalencies, a straightforward solution to this problem of predetermining educational enrollments, at least for the work force, is possible. Using three levels of educational enrollments (x_i) and three classes of labor (l_i) and transitions from one state to the other (x_{ij}), a set of equations can be written which relate manpower demand to educational enrollments. Large numbers of school enrollees receive their education and never enter the work force, and unknown numbers will jump in and out of educational and work-force status, and students and workers will die and retire; but these possibilities are left out of consideration for purposes of the exposition at hand. Moser and Redfern (1964) have developed a more comprehensive model and closed the system, i.e., defined all states and transitions over time; their work will be examined in the next chapter. In this simple situation, we show:

$$x_1 - x_{11} - x_{12} - x_{13} = l_1$$
$$x_2 - x_{21} - x_{22} - x_{23} = l_2 \qquad (3)$$
$$x_3 - x_{31} - x_{32} - x_{33} = l_3$$

x_i is the enrollment in level i, x_{ij} is the number going to level j from level i, and l_i is the number of graduates of level i needed in the labor force. The first equation merely states that the enrollment at Level 1 of the educational system minus those staying in Level 1 and those going on to Levels 2 and 3 is equal to the number with education Level 1 in the labor force. If labor force requirements can be set, then educational enrollments can be determined by a simple manipulation of matrix algebra.

Using coefficients a_{ij} and class size x instead of the transition numbers x_{ij}, we would have:

$$(1 - a_{11})x_1 - a_{12}x_2 - a_{13}x_3 = L_1$$
$$+ (1 - a_{22})x_2 - a_{23}x_3 = L_2 \qquad (4)$$
$$\text{etc.}$$

Here, a_{11} would be the proportion of people staying in Level 1 and a_{23} would be the proportion of people with education Level 2 going onward to Level 3. In matrix notation, (4) would be:

$$(I - A)X = L \qquad (5)$$

By inverting the matrix it is possible to solve for X (enrollments):

$$X = (I - A)^{-1}L \qquad (6)$$

In this solution, given the manpower requirements expressed in educational attainment terms, the planner can solve back for the original enrollments necessary to meet the labor force demand. Or can he?

First, the labor requirements are those of a subpopulation, the work force, and the enrollments refer to the general population, without respect to present or future participation. The two might be made to coincide through forced labor, but that does not seem an appetizing or realistic policy alternative in most countries. Or, the model could be enormously extended and closed, as in the Moser-Redfern work, by taking into account all of the possible states of working, loafing, death, and retirement into which school enrollments could go. Adjustments could be made in the coefficients so as to reflect death, retirement, and nonparticipation, or a number could be added into the requirements to take this into account in some crude fashion. A more adequate treatment of the problem is reserved to the next chapter.

There are other problems. The planner must secure estimates of the manpower requirements in the first place. Application of the schemata to be discussed later in this chapter could provide them. But the problems of estimating present, and future, work force requirements will prove to be formidable.

Even if the labor requirements, present and future, could be accurately and precisely estimated, translation of these requirements into educational equivalencies is a formidable task. There is, demonstrably, a poor fit between educational preparation and work force job classifications. Any given job in the work force may be filled by people with a given education and training. Also people with a given education may work in a wide variety of jobs. One way around this problem of variability is to use very general categories. The three levels (x_i) used in the example could refer to primary, secondary and tertiary enrollments. Requirements (l_i) in the work force could be expressed in the same terms. But the numbers at each level may not be as useful for planning as data on the mix of fields within levels. The planner's dilemma may be briefly stated: Refined catgories yield results that are more useful and seemingly precise; but they may also be more inaccurate.

The planner still has no basis for programming the output of educational and training programs except on the basis of a fit between preparation and occupation that is known to be loose in the first place. The matter can be put into linear programming form in a standard activity analysis schema. For the rudiments of the method, several standard references are available. The notion is that the planner sets out to optimize the output of various educational or training activities (xs):

$$\text{Optimize } x_1 + x_2 + \ldots x_n \tag{7}$$
$$\text{Given all } x \geq 0$$

The xs which represent educational training activities could be classified by levels (primary, secondary, tertiary) and also kinds of programs within levels (technical, teacher training . . .). The activities cannot operate at minus levels (i.e., produce negative numbers of graduates).

The relationship between educational program flows and labor requirements can be schematized as before; by showing a column of labor requirements expressed in educational terms which must be equalled or exceeded:

$$a_{11}x_1 + a_{12}x_2 + \ldots + a_{1n}x_n \geq l_1$$
$$a_{21}x_1 + a_{22}x_2 + \ldots + a_{2n}x_n \geq l_2 \tag{8}$$
$$\cdot$$
$$\cdot$$
$$\cdot$$
$$a_{m1}x_1 + a_{m2}x_2 + \ldots + a_{mn}x_n \geq l_m$$

The solution of the system of inequations is determinate. In linear programming terminology, the basic and feasible solution that solves the body of equations is also the optimal one. The dilemma is that this is an optimum, rigged on the basis of a fit that either must be too general to be useful or too complicated (all flows possible) to be manageable.

Simple input coefficients, which purport to express the relationship between educational attainment and work force requirements, often mask the considerable elasticity that exists in reality. Various combinations of education and training are possible in any given work force post and depend in part on the technology and resources that prevail. Furthermore, the classification rubrics used in both education and work force are crude ones. Later, we will examine certain technics of multi-varaite analysis which may offer possibilities for solving the problems of classification that plague both manpower and rate-of-return approaches to planning.

Rate-of-Return Approach

Rate-of-return technics have been increasingly applied to educational planning in order to permit a comparison of investment in education with investment in other developmental enterprises, e.g., increase of plant and equipment for industry and provision of necessary physical infrastructure (roads, harbors, power . . .).

Essentially, rate-of-return calculations are based on simple accounting technics or tactics, although there are complications in educational planning where returns in future years are highly variable and difficult to estimate. When benefits are measured on the basis of increments in income presumed to have been generated by increments of education, and this assumptive net must be cast ahead many years, the rate-of-return approach becomes just as imprecise as the education-occupation slippage encountered in manpower planning. Becker (1964), Mincer (1962) and Schultz (1963) should be consulted to supplement the rudimentary treatment to follow.

Very simple criteria can be applied for ranking investment in education with respect to other possibilities, but the measurement and the calculations are not always simple or satisfying. In a simple payback method, the ratio of the investment cost to the annual cash flow, assuming the flows evenly distributed over the years, can be used to compute the number of years for payback of the investment:

$$\frac{\$100,000 \text{ investment}}{\$20,000 \text{ annual cash flow}} = 5 \text{ year payback}$$

Or the ratio can be reversed:

$$\frac{\$20,000}{\$100,000} = 20\% \text{ rate of cash flow}$$

The problem of the payback routine generally is that it does not take into account the productive life of the investment; but the problem of it when applied to the evaluation of an investment in education is that, except in the case of a private school enterprise run for profit, there is no ready route for computing the cash flow in the denominator.

Present value calculations and computations of rates of return handle the general problem by taking into account the life of the investment, but they don't solve the problem of measuring costs and benefits in education. Present value calculations permit the planner to reduce the future cash flows on the investment to present value, thus making it comparable to the cost which is in present terms. The cash flows are discounted at an interest rate which accounts for risk and return on the investment. There are tables for computing present value, based on the formula for $1 invested at interest rate i for n years:

$$\frac{1}{(1+i)^n} \tag{9}$$

The notion is that the dollar received in the future year is not equal in value to one in the present year. If $10,000 were to be received five years hence, and the interest rate of 12 per cent were the appropriate discount rate to apply, then the calculations would be:

$$\$10,000 \cdot \left(\frac{1}{(1.12)^5}\right).$$

In a table of present values, the second factor would be .567 which when multiplied by $10,000 would yield $5,670. Conversely, $5,670 invested for five years at 12 per cent interest compounded annually would yield $10,000.

When applied to evaluating investment alternatives, where education is one of the possibilities, present value calculations permit the planner to compute and compare internal rate of return on the investments. For this computation the planner must have the investment cost and the annual cash flows of each alternative. The internal rate of return is the interest rate that makes the algebraic sum of the present values of the positive cash flows (returns) and the negative cash flows (costs) equal to zero. There are no major calculation problems if the investment consists of a one-shot proposition in the first year and the inflows are known and equal for each of the future years. If the life of the investment is known, the internal rate of return can be solved for in approximate terms from a table of present values of $1 received annually for n years. If the investment is $36,000 and if this produces an annual return of $13,000 for 30 years, a simple ratio can be computed and the table can be entered and the internal rate of return solved for:

$$\frac{\$36,000}{\$13,000} = 2.769.$$

Entering the table with this ratio at the 30-year line, the internal rate would be between 35 and 40 per cent, approximately. Internal rate-of-return comparisons could then be used to compare investments in education with other investments, if the costs and benefits of education could be readily assessed. Investment in some productive possibility could be readily assessed, but what is the situation when rates of return are applied to educational programs?

When internal rate-of-return calculations are applied to the educational situation, e.g., to evaluate the pay-off on investments in two different kinds of educational programs, the estimated net earnings streams of the graduates of the programs are discounted over their estimated work life. Net earnings are earnings reduced by the direct and indirect costs for the education in the years of attendance, and this is the counterpart to the investment cost shown in the simple example above. The indirect costs take into account the earnings foregone by the persons while they are attending education or training programs. The net earnings (earnings reduced by direct and indirect costs during training periods) of graduates of program x^1 can be compared to graduates of programs x^0 (next-lower level) by discounting the difference in lifetime (l) earnings to present value with an appropriate interest rate (r).

The present-value comparison of the two net earnings streams would be shown by:

$$\sum_{t=0}^{l} \frac{x^1 - x^0}{(1+r)^{t+1}} \qquad (10)$$

Becker uses internal rate-of-return comparison, which is the rate that equates the present value of the differences of the two net income streams:

$$\sum_{t=0}^{l} \frac{x^1}{(1+r)^{t+1}} - \sum_{t=0}^{l} \frac{x^0}{(1+r)^{t+1}} = 0 \qquad (11)$$

Present value and rate-of-return technics provide the planner with an objective and quantitative basis for ranking investments in human resource development.

Rate-of-return calculations, as well as manpower analysis techniques, have formidable problems of measurement that affect both the precision and accuracy of the results they furnish. Theoretically, the rate-of-return results should be applicable to two general kinds of situations. In the first, the planner attempts to relate and perhaps rank investment in education and training with investments in other enterprises and projects that will enhance the development of the total economy. In the second, the planner uses present value or rate-of-return criteria for allocating optimally to one level or kind of education, rather than to another, given the general parameters for the total allocation to education.

In the first situation the rate-of-return approach has some severe conceptual limitations, apart from the problem of measuring the costs and benefits associated with education. Danière (1965) has pointed out the difficulty of using rate of return criteria in general optimizing models in developing economies. The country may have a very small stock of educated people. A large and nonmarginal increment to this stock must generally be planned. Future benefits are estimated on the basis of the income streams of this large increment of educated people, even when it is unlikely that the same income structure will prevail in the distant future.

The income differentials that prevail for the small group of educated people who exist in a developing country before a plan period begins may be a poor basis for estimating the differences that will prevail when large numbers of educated people are added to the stock in future years. Some plans call for a doubling or tripling of stocks over a 10- or 15-year plan period, and optimizing models which get their signals from small and marginal moves do not seem useful for this situation.

Rate-of-return or present value technics have more meaning in the suboptimizing situation exemplified by the model in Chapter V. Here the problem is to allocate resources optimally among several educational activities (e.g. various university and secondary programs, engineering, normal school training . . .). The present value of the net income streams associated with these programs can be used as a C coefficient for weighting the objective function in a linear programming model for resource allocation (cf. Chapter V).

Beyond the measurement problems, which are formidable, one is left with the feeling that there is in the nature of the game a dilemma to face. Do differences in income, associated with differential educational attainment, reflect the productive contribution of education or the selective and classificatory artifact? To cite the fact that the increased education is antecedent to increased earning and that this implies causality, in one sense smacks of *post hoc ergo propter hoc* reasoning. At base, the rate-of-return approach suffers from the same weaknesses as the manpower approach. In the manpower approach, the relationship between preparation and occupation may be a weak one; in rate-of-return approaches, the relationship between education and output, when measured through income, may be even weaker.

When dealing with large aggregate populations, there may be a correlation between education and production that shines through statistically; but as one moves toward more precise suboptimizing situations this might be less stable a criterion. Presumably, the search is for utility rather than artifact. The question is not how is it or was it done, but how can it best be done. In the U.S., university-educated salesmen earn more than technicians; therefore the rate-of-return signal comes up: Allocate to university. And the manpower signal comes up: Educate salesforce at university. In the general case, the absurdity is equal. In the developed country, education functions as a social selection device; in a developing one as a device for maintaining social stratification. But the evidence is still unclear as to how it functions in purely economic terms and, until the evidence is in, econometric models, manpower, and rate-of-return, will have glaring shortcomings. Perhaps that is why the political decision is still the controlling one.

SETTING HUMAN RESOURCE REQUIREMENT TARGETS FOR FUTURE YEARS: POPULATION AND WORK FORCE SCHEMATA

In human resource development planning, manpower schemata (some might call them models) have many difficulties. There is the notoriously poor rationale that underlies the fitting of educational attainment to occupational requirements in the work force. Secondly, the so-called requirement targets or 'demand' data generated for educated and trained people reflect, *at best,* work force demand, or the economic demand for educated and trained people. The population studied is the economically active population, or work force, and there is no routine at this point for generalizing work force educational requirements to the total population. The numbers of educated and trained people in the total population will reflect social and political objectives that cannot be readily incorporated into econometric schemata for setting requirements.

The situation faced by the planner is sketched in Figure II.1. The work force, or economically active population, is defined in the Handbook of Population Censuses (1958, p. 4):

> all persons of either sex who furnish the supply of labor available for the production of economic goods and services. It includes both persons employed and unemployed during the time reference· period adopted in the census.

The work force block in each case has occupations in the ordinate, and economic activities on the abcissa; each resulting cell would show a fine structure of education and training levels.

With limitations soon to be examined, educational attainment tar-

FIGURE II.1
Human Resources in Population, years *x* to *n*

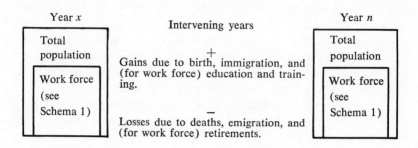

Year *x*	Intervening years	Year *n*
Total population Work force (see Schema 1)	$+$ Gains due to birth, immigration, and (for work force) education and training. $-$ Losses due to deaths, emigration, and (for work force) retirements.	Total population Work force (see Schema 1)

gets for the subpopulation—economically active or work force—can be set. The targets may cover only 75 per cent of the males and 25 per cent of the females in the total population over 10 years of age in a developing country. Educational attainment targets can be generalized to the total population, but there is as yet no rationale for doing this. In the free, developed, and affluent country, education and training are provided with no guarantee beforehand that the recipient will turn them to economically productive ends. In the developing country, the strategy might have to be very different, and exiguous resources may have to be employed primarily to educate and train the work force. One would not propose going to the extreme of programming no education for those who do not enter the work force—even if this could be known beforehand. This might be poor welfare economics in the long run; it would certainly be short-sighted social policy and perhaps dangerous politics. Correa (1963), when modeling an educational and work force system on a Markov chain, assumed no education for those not entering production, just as he assumed that work force participation or nonparticipation was an absorbing state (people did not move in and out), but this was done merely to satisfy the restrictions of the model, not to suggest likely policy.

To the extent that it provides useful, rather than illusory or deceptive, guidelines, the use of work force requirements to set educational and training targets has merit. If it provides requirement targets for a substantial portion of the population, and if it demonstrates that these minima must be met if the development plan is to be feasible, it has served. Once the economic-requirement minima are established, the targets can be expanded to take into account social and political demand, insofar as they can be estimated. Further, the knowledge that certain high-level education and training goals must be met if the country is to develop as assumed or projected may postpone a program of universal primary education until the resources of a country will bear it.

The Simplest Approach to Educational Attainment Target-Setting

The accuracy and precision of educational attainment targets depend on the existence of valid and reliable data—above all on a base-year census which classifies the work force by occupations and educational levels, occupations and economic activities, and occupations by age. The simplest approach to target setting is the one taken by 'the flying manpower man.' The flying manpower man is in great demand over wide areas and has, in his best week, only a few days to spend in any given country. His notion is that targets are set arbitrarily anyway, and the less fuss the better. This being so, the matter can be most easily worked out on the back of an envelope as the plane circles for a landing. (The author has been and sometimes is a flying manpower man.)

The flying manpower man has reason on his side in many cases. When the data are foul, the needs vast, and the potential output of educational and training facilities meager, why not the back of an envelope? But, then, why not simply mail the envelope—assuming first a quick check on the educational level of postal employees in the country—and save travel time?

When the data are better, the needs smaller, and the output in education greater, the matter can be taken beyond the back-of-the-envelope calculations. The schemata and routines for doing this are crude, but the exercise has at least three virtues. First, it takes time. This means that the expert may be pinned down long enough to learn something about the educational system, and perhaps the economy too. More important, his local counterparts may learn right along with him. Second, the great yawning holes in the tables suggest that better data are necessary, and ingenuity is taxed to provide them. Last, the exercise provides useful general guidelines for human resource development planning.

Other Simple Approaches to Target Setting: The Schemata

Setting targets through the schemata is simple enough. This approach, or variants of it, had its first full field test in Puerto Rico (1957). The basic tables are sketched out in Appendix A. The approach is criticized by U.S. experts at home—and widely used by their students and assistants abroad. When the going is good, the routine requires two to three weeks for a rough run-through. The Platt, Loeb, Davis study in Chile (1964) is a fair example of this. Almost everyone can see the holes in the scheme, and that is one of its chief virtues.

The essential moves are to project employment for future years by sectors of the economy, to distribute occupational composition in the sectors, and, in turn, to set educational attainment levels within the occupations. The result is the so-called stock of educated and trained people required in the workforce in the target year. When the stock existing in the base year is wasted for death and retirement during the intervening years and subtracted from the stock in the target year, the result is the so-called deficit, or the targets which must be filled by educational and training programs. It is also sometimes called the economic demand on education and training.

EMPLOYMENT PROJECTION (STEP ONE)

1. Product has been projected from base year to target year by sectors in over-all development plan.
2. $\dfrac{\text{Product}}{\text{Workers}}$ or product p.c. is analyzed in base year and previous years. On the basis of past trends or future expectations of increase or decrease in sectors, rates are projected for the product p.c. from base to target year.
3. Employement is then projected by sectors for target years, by division of: (1)/(2). (Work force is computed from employment by estimating unemployment and adding it.)

The simplicity of the first step of the schemata is shown in the following symbols. The aim is to project employment from year x to year n. This is symbolized $_ne_x$. The simple relationship used is:

$$_ne_x = \frac{_np_x}{_np(p.c.)_x}. \tag{12}$$

This is done for each sector. Product for each sector is taken from the national development plan. Product per head is a rate computed from past performance, or assumed on the basis of estimates about development in the sectors, or borrowed from one or a group of other countries where the history of economic performance is known.

From the outset, the results depend on how well the national development planners have estimated product in sectors for the future year. This is the crucial projection which underlies the schemata, as it underlies almost all other attempts to derive educational demand from the economy, including application of the Correa Tinbergen (1962) model. The difficulties in dealing with vast aggregates such as Gross National Product, National Income, and the like are discussed in Chapter

VII and need not be detailed here. The point is that the adequacy of any work force projection along this route depends on the adequacy of the product or income forecast.

In (2), Product could be inappropriately aggregated in past years as well as poorly estimated for future ones. Work force could be inaccurate depending on the basic data (census or survey) from which it is taken. If the resulting ratio is projected on the basis of a trend observable in past years, the adequacy or representativeness of the base years is in question. If the ratio is pushed forward on the basis of what might happen in the sectors and assumptions about probable effects, the adequacy of these assumptions must be examined. The homogeneity of the units in which the product is expressed can also be troublesome. Monetary values may have to be adjusted to a base year; and when this is difficult and no indexes are available, the product may have to be expressed in terms of physical units.

Census data will usually furnish the basic numbers in the work force, employed and unemployed. The census data may have to be brought forward to the first year of the plan by an establishments survey which covers new employment. Surveys of employment, usually on a sample basis, may be used to derive an estimate of the total of employed and unemployed in the entire work force.

The establishments survey may also be designed to get management's best estimate of likely expansion and future employment. Hence it may furnish one basis of work force estimates for future years.

In rapidly developing countries, the establishments survey will have shortcomings as a basis for future year estimates. It covers only existing industries. Some industries may not exist or even be possibilities in the first of the plan years. In areas like the Guayana in Venezuela, planning may have reached the stage where most major industrial possibilities have been studied. Employment for these future industries may have been estimated through feasibility studies which also cover sources of raw material, investment and financing, production problems and market and sales forecasts. On the basis of these studies, employment can be estimated for future years.

Planners may use the general sectoral ratio previously shown to derive first approximations of employment, but usually they must go beyond this and work on estimates for individual industries or groups of industries within the sector. A general ratio of product to product-per-worker may be used as a first estimate of employment for an entire heavy industry group. Then, detailed employment estimates may be constructed for each individual industry, and the results totaled and compared.

Product may be derived from investment ratios, or estimated on the basis of market demand, minimal effective size of the plant and assumptions about the percentage of capacity at which it will operate. Product for one industry may be derived from another, e.g., oxygen from steel.

For light industries and in the service and commerce sectors, employment may be derived from a ratio or rate to the total population that is projected for the area, e.g., so many bakers per 10,000 of population. The U.S. Industry Fact Sheets (U.S. Department of Labor: Bureau of Labor Statistics. *Economic Forces in the U.S.A. in Facts and Figures,* 1960) compiled by the International Cooperation Administration is a useful guide for setting ratios and rates. From the size of the population and the effective market, an estimate of the required output can be made; from this the U.S. Fact Sheets can provide employment estimates under varying assumptions about the scale, technology, and desirability of following a U.S. model in the first place.

All of this detailed information may be summed into the general employment estimates for target years.

The result of the first step, however it is taken, is employment in the target year by industries and sectors of economic activity.

When the data are put into the schemata tables, several check ratios can be applied. Employment can be expanded to population economically active by estimating unemployment and adding it in. The number in the total workforce as a percentage of the total population can serve as a control check. This participation rate can be further broken down for age groups, education levels, and sex, and compared with experience in the past and with data from other similar countries. The percentage distribution of employment by sectors can also serve as a check, e.g., the percentage in services as compared to the percentage in industry. Gross overestimates and underestimates will show up. The percentage of work force in primary, secondary, and tertiary sectors is also a possible check.

WORK FORCE DISTRIBUTED BY SECTOR OF ECONOMIC ACTIVITY AND OCCUPATION (STEP TWO) In the second step, work force (base year and target year) can be distributed by occupation as well as by sector. This requires that base year census data be available, in which the work force is classified by occupation and sector. If these data are available, either from a census which is current in the base year or brought forward to the base year, the rest is simple. Occupations and/or activities (as sectors) can be classified by one or more digits. The finer the classification the greater the detail in the final result, as shown in Schema II.1.

SCHEMA II.1

Distribution of work force by occupation and sector (base year x and target year n) of Economic Activity

Occupation	Total No. x	n	Total % x	n	Agriculture, % x	n	Mining, % x	n	Manufacturing, % x	n	Services, % x	n
0 Professional												
1 Administrative												
2 Clerical												
3 Sales												
. . .												
5 Farmers												
. . .												
7 Artisan-craftsmen												
8 Operators												
9 Service Workers												
. . .												

A. Industry or economic activity (columns of the matrix.) In *Principles and Recommendations for National Population Censuses* (1957) Industry, called also 'branch of economic activity,'[1] is described:

> Industry refers to the kind of establishment in which the person works (or worked if unemployed). For purposes of international comparability, it is recommended that countries adopt the International Standard Industrial Classification of All Economic Activities (ISIC) most recently approved by the United Nations, or that they tabulate their statistical data so that the categories can be regrouped in accordance with the Standard Classification or at least with the divisions (one digit) of this classification.

The ISIC (United Nations Statistical Office) provides a taxonomy for classifying economically active civil populations. It has eight major divisions or sectors and a supplementary one (for 'other,' unknown or unemployed) grouped under a one-digit code. The eight divisions are divided into 40 or more major groups (two-digit code) and more than 100 subgroups (three-digit). In actual practice, the basic or standard classification will generally be modified for any given country. Government may be added as one of the main divisions; Manufacturing may be broken into more than one main division. Classification may be restricted to divisions and major groups (two digits), to cut down the tabulation necessary. In some countries a system modified from the basic ISIC classification may be developed by the Ministry of Economics or the National Revenue Service, Income Tax Division.

In the U.S., the Bureau of the Budget has developed the Standard Industrial Classification. An industrial classification system developed by the Bureau of the Census is similar. In developing countries, one of the standard classification systems may be used as a model, with appropriate modifications, according to the nature of the country's economy. There are disadvantages when a country departs too widely from one of the standard classifications, as Mexico seems to have done in its 1960 census. Comparability is difficult and retabulation may require going back to the original census schedules, a difficult and expensive task. Still, simplification of the categories may be necessary because of deficient data. A simple three-sector breakdown (industry, agriculture and services) may be all that is possible.

B. Occupations (Rows of the matrix). The United Nations' *Principles and Recommendations for National Population Census* states:

> Occupation refers to the kind of work done by the person employed (or performed previously by the unemployed) irrespective of the

---

[1] Commonly called 'sector' when one-digit general classification is used.

branch of economic activity, or the status (as employer, employee, etc.) in which the person should be classified. For purposes of international comparisons, each country should provide for the necessary subdivisions of its occupational classifications to make possible the classifying or reclassifying of the data in conformity with the latest edition of the International Standard Classification of Occupation (ISCO).

ISCO classes civil populations economically active into nine major occupational groups, plus a supplementary group not classifiable. The major groups of ISCO are subdivided into 70 minor groups (two-digit level) which are subdivided into 200 unit groups (three-digit level). Unit groups can be broken down further if the gain in precision warrants it. Other systems of occupational classification are used. The U.S. Bureau of Labor Statistics has used a classification (1963) based on the Dictionary of Occupational Titles (1949). The Inter-American Statistical Institute, on the basis of the 1950 census of America and the ISCO, worked out a classification scheme for the 1960 Census of America (COTA-1960). In an actual country situation the basic system is modified according to the prevailing occupational structure. Some country systems tend to follow the original model too slavishly. In the Dominican Republic a two-digit activity code space was reserved for hunting, trapping and repopulation of game supply, a trade that would not be too modish in such a place.

Occupational classifications tend to become dated rather quickly, as new technologies and administrative hierarchies develop and new job classifications and occupational titles are created to fit the situation. Not only the nature of the work changes; but the educational requirements— and these are the two main bases for occupational classification—also change. The change is almost always upward, i.e., more training and education are required. In the United States, the *Occupational Outlook Handbook* (1966–67) is designed to keep new workers and guidance counselors informed about recent and possible changes in demand for workers, new work patterns and new education and training requirements. Over 700 occupations are analyzed in the 1963–64 edition, and the compilers state that some of the information will be out of date before the edition appears in print. The *Dictionary of Occupational Titles* (1965) is the best reference for complete coverage.

In step two, the percentage of workers in each occupation and each activity is set for the future year. This setting is almost completely based on experience, opinion, and percentage distributions in the work forces of other countries. The census furnishes the base year distribution of occupations by activities. The simplest procedure is to assume that these same base year percentages will hold in the target year. Usually, however, the planner takes into account the growth projected for the different sectors and activities from base to target year, the expectations of changes of inputs in labor and capital, and the experience of other countries, in order to set a reasonable distribution for the target year. The planner may also take into account the change in occupational structure in past years in the country and its influence on output. The major guidelines come from expected growth in certain key sectors, as assumed or projected in the over-all plan. If growth is planned for the manufacturing industry, the percentages of Professional (0), Administrators (1), Artesan-Craftsman (7), and Operators (8) might be raised in the Manufacturing column. How much would they be raised? There is no sure answer to this. It would depend on how high the existing percentages are for the country in the base year and how high they are in other countries that have similar outputs or industrial structures. Again, it is common practice to select a more developed country and to move the percentages up toward this target.

Distributions of percentages in occupations have been published for various countries. Parnes (1963) has summarized some of these in his appendix tables. *The Yearbook of Labor Statistics* (1963) has data on both occupations and activities, but (until 1964) the two are not cross-classified. A collection of these tables is one of the basic working tools for those who would run the schemata (cf. Appendix 0).

In step two, as in step one, it is important to realize that the upgrading of occupational percentages for the target year depends on a series of assumptions and guesses.

The concluding move in step two is to multiply the percentages (occupational distribution set) in the target year by the employment projected in step one. A one-cell example will suffice (Schema II.2)

SCHEMA II.2
Number in a given sector, by occupation, in target year n

Occupation	Total No., year n	Sector, %, year n	No. in sector year n
0 Professional	1,000,000	.60	6,000[a]
.	.	.	.
.	.	.	.
.	.	.	.
			(TOTAL)

[a] .006 x 1,000,000

The result is a table showing the numbers of workers in each occupation for the target year.

EDUCATION AND TRAINING OF WORK FORCE (STEP THREE). The aim in this step is to distribute the target-year work force according to educational attainment. The educational classifications used depend on the relevance of different kinds and amounts of preparations and training for the occupations and industries. A typical matrix might be like Schema II.3, in which educational attainment (levels and type) are classified against occupations for the base year.

The educational attainment percentages for the target year are then set for the various occupations. Again, this is an operation without hard and fast rules. The general strategy may be to raise university and college attainments in the first two occupational categories, and to raise technical secondary school training attainments for craftsmen and operators. For example, if the professional group having university graduate preparation in the base year is 5 per cent, the strategy might be to raise this to 7 per cent for the target year. This is a substantial raise and will create a large demand on the educational system, inasmuch as the professional work force in the target year will be a much larger base number on which to levy the increase. This is so because the total population, and usually the work force, will almost certainly be growing during the plan period and the percentage of professionals in the work force will have been raised in step two.

Educational attainment coefficients are given for many countries. Some care must be exercised in choosing comparative models. Educational attainment levels may be the fruit of high work force productivity, rather than the cause. The equivalence of educational attainment, measured in years completed and programs fulfilled, may be very difficult to establish between countries. There is no standard educational attainment unit, although years completed is most often used. The measurement of true product in an educational system is a lengthy process and is discussed in another section. It cannot always be based simply on an analysis of curriculum content, as it is described in Ministry of Education bulletins. The curriculum guide represents the ideal and not the reality, which may only be measurable by massive achievement testing. Standards for comparisons of curricula are difficult to apply across systems, inasmuch as the objectives may be quite different. Also, things can change. Many European and U.S. writers in the manpower field— and, unfortunately, some planners—are still ignoring the revolution in science and mathematics teaching that took place in the United States in the late 1950s and is still in full vigor.

The route to occupational efficiency may be quite different in different countries. One country may require much more formal education for a comparable occupation. For a U.S. model, see Appendix N.

SCHEMA II.3

Educational attainment by occupation in base year (x)

Occupation	Col. 1 Total	Col. 2 University Graduate Studies complete (19 yrs.)	Col. 3 First Degree level University (17 yrs.) Professional and Higher normal	Col. 4 Sub-professional (15 yrs.)	Col. 5 Tech. complete (12 yrs.)	Col. 6 Secondary general	Col. 7 Lower Normal complete (12 yrs.)	Col. 8 Primary complete (6)	Col. 9 Literacy Grade 4–6
0. Professional No. %									
1. Administrative No. %									
2. Clerical No. %									
. . .									
7. Artisans No. %									
8. Operators No. %									

Note: Educational levels are cumulated.
Col. 2 includes all who finish through 19th grade.
Col. 3 includes all who finish 17th through 19th grade.
Col. 4 includes all who finish 15 grade sub-professional.
Col. 5 includes all who finish only 12th grade technical training plus the proportion of those who finish this track and attend higher education (Both sub-professional and professional, i.e. lines 3 and 4).
Col. 6 includes all those who finish only 12th grade general preparation plus those who go on to higher education from this track.
Col. 7 includes all those who finish only 12th grade lower normal plus the proportion from this track who go on to higher education.
Col. 8 includes all those who finish primary, plus those who finish grades 7 up to 12 (in the secondary tracks) plus the totals of 5, 6, and 7.
Col. 9 includes 8, plus those who finish at least 4 grades but less than a complete 6 years of primary.

Alternate settings may be used for the target year. In one set, the educational attainment coefficients of the base year may be maintained into the target year. Even when the coefficients are unchanged, the target year requirements will be larger absolutely, for the reasons given before. Two or three, or more, sets of educational attainment coefficients can be applied to yield an equal number of alternative projections. Before coefficients are raised to some optimistically high level, the consequences for demand on educational output should be checked against the capacity and likely revenues available for expanding the educational and training facilities (cf., final section in Chapter IV). Planning is the interweaving of the necessary, the desirable, and the possible; and there are no easy analytic solutions.

The final operation in step three would appear as in Schema II.4, which is not a final demand table because no allowance has yet been made for wastage or in-migration of educated and trained people.

Step three yields the target-year stock of educated people required in the work force. This comes from summing each educational level down the occupations, and there will be a different total for each educational level according to which of the alternative hypotheses is chosen.

WASTAGE OR IN-MIGRATION OF EDUCATED WORKERS DURING PLAN PERIOD (STEP FOUR). In this step the work force, in the base year, is wasted by outflow rates over the plan years. The most direct route is to calculate wastage rates for groups classified by educational attainment levels, but usually it is necessary to work through occupations and then education levels. The outflow rate is made up of two components: death rate and retirement rate. These are usually age-specific rates, i.e., computed for age groups. In order to apply them, the work force in the base year should be broken down by age groups (10–14, 15–19, etc.). Because the outflow rates will be different for occupations (depending on base year age structure and work life), the work force in the base year may be cross-classified by occupations and age groups. The outflow rates that will prevail during the plan years are estimated and applied in five-year steps. The mechanics of this life table method are treated later in the chapter.

The procedure is sketched in Schema II.5. During each five year plan period a certain number in the occupation leave through death or retirement, i.e. w_1, w_2, etc. These numbers are summed over the plan period. Outflow by occupations can be converted to outflow by education levels, using the educational attainment by occupation coefficients of Schema II.4. These outflows are then added into the final demand table shown in Schema II.6.

SCHEMA II.4
Educational attainment by occupation in target year (n)

Occupation	Univ. Grad. Studies Complete (19 yrs.) Hyp. I	Hyp. II	First Degree Level University (17 yrs.) Hyp. I	Hyp. II	Sub-Professional...... 15 yrs. Hyp. I	Hyp. II	Literacy Grade 4-6 Hyp. I	Hyp. II	TOTALS[c]
0 Professional (Total = 100,000)	5,000[a]	7,000.							100,000
1 Administrative									
. . . . . .									
7 Artesans									
8 Operators									
. . . .									
TOTALS[d]									

[a] .05 × 100,000
[b] .07 × 100,000
[c] Hyp. I = Hyp. II = 100,000
[d] Hyp. I ≠ Hyp. II.

SCHEMA II.5
Application of Outflow Rates to an Age-stratified Occupational Group
(Base Year x to Target Year n)

Occupation: 0 Professional

Age Group	Stock,[a] x	Outflow Rate, x to $x + 5$	Outflow, x to $x + 5$	Stock, $x + 5$	Stock, ... n
30-34	3,000	0.0282	85[b]	2915[c]	
35-39	5,000	.0375	188	4812	
40-44	6,000	.0625			
45-49	7,000	.0915			
.					*Note*
.					Repeat process from
.					$x + 5$ to $x + 10$,
.					$x + 10$ to $x + 15$,
					until year n is
					reached.
70-74	500	.5081			
75+	120	.6429	w_1[d]		w_2

[a] fictitious

[b] 0.0282×3000

[c] $3000 - 85$

[d] Outflow for occupation from $w_1, w_2 \ldots$

Note: The Outflow by occupation can be converted to wastage by educational attainment levels because the educational attainment for the occupation is known in year x.

SCHEMA II.6
Demand for Education and Training (Hypothesis I)
Educational Level: University Graduates
Studies Complete (19 yrs.)

Occupation	No., year x	No., year n	Difference	Outflow, x to n	Total Stock Increment, x to n
0 Professional	10,000	20,000	10,000	1,500	11,500
1 Administrative					
.					
.					
.					
.					
.					
.					
TOTALS					

If the period between x and target year n is sufficiently long, it is also necessary to apply wastage rates to the new entrants to the work force during these years. Entrance rates are first applied to the age groups, and then these entrants wasted with a second difference. Usually, some rough allowance is made for this, unless the plan period is very long. In Venezuela and Chile, demographers have constructed life tables for the economically active population. The tables appear in standard life-table format, except that both mortality and retirement rates are applied to reduce the original cohort.

DEMAND FOR EDUCATED AND TRAINED PEOPLE (FINAL STEP). The final step would yield the demand table shown in Schema II.6.

In some countries, no substantial inflow of people already educated and trained is assumed; but such situations occur and where they do the final table may have to account for additions to the stock as well as wastage from it. In some African countries, large numbers of highly trained expatriates may have to be scheduled for replacement before their normal work life would end. Some countries might cut down political and social friction by having an expatriate wastage schedule concocted before they bring educated outsiders in to take choice jobs.

Comparison of Targets to System Output:
Historical and Comparative Checks

Application of the schemata yields the stock of educated workers required in the target year. The next step is a comparison with the output of educational and training institutions, present and projected, to determine the deficits or surpluses of educated and trained people in the work force at the end of the planned period. The methods for carrying out these projections are detailed in Chapter IV. The sum of the outputs from year x to year n is subtracted from the requirements targets and represents the gap or deficit for the system. If the output targets seemingly can't be reached, the assumed product of the economy may have to be restudied and scaled down. With the output of the economy scaled down, the income available for education and training will be reduced; and, unless larger proportions of revenue can be allocated to education or assistance can be provided from outside the country in the form of trained people to fill the targets or money to train the local population, the gap may continue to be formidable. Hence the setting of targets, however crudely, may touch off a series of adjustments in economic and social development plans.

More directly relevant for the educational planner are the adjustments which such sad news must touch off within the educational system itself. Resources may be insufficient from all sources to reach targets by traditional routes which are often insufficient in their yield with respect to cost and time. The option, then, is clear: Cost and time may have to be reduced. Yet, there is a limit to which cost and time can be reduced and still yield the same educational attainment. Unless standards are maintained, planners are merely playing with numbers. In a crude way, this game is played in countries which decree universal primary education without having the resources to insure it. Numbers of enrollments increase but the educational attainment in the levels drops drastically, and nothing very much is gained.

Very careful measurements may have to be made to insure that, if cost and time are reduced, the education still has some quality. Often, in the primary level, the inputs are so minimal that no reduction in per-head costs are possible, and, in fact, increased expenditure may yield more of actual value, i.e., well trained graduates.

Cost and training time can sometimes be reduced markedly in university courses with small yield. Professional programs may be reduced to subprofessional and, instead of full-fledged doctors and engineers, greater numbers of semi-professionals may have to be turned out. Against this is opposed the whole weight of educational tradition and standards and some sorry experience with professional half loaves which are not markedly better than none. Still, in the face of absolute need, the prospect may have to be examined.

Formulas for Scaling Requirements to Past Output of the System

The output of the system in the past provides some guideline for scaling requirements down to realistic limits. When data are available on the output of various levels of the system for a past period, the rate of growth in the various levels and kinds of educational program serves as some check on requirements. The limits are imposed by the present state and size of the system and its capacity to accelerate growth—while still maintaining minimal quality standards. If the system has only been able to grow, within a given level, at a rate of about 2 per cent cumulative annually, there is no reason to suspect that it can reach targets which would imply a sudden acceleration to 10 per cent annually. There are some data, the last table in Chapter IV, which indicate, in free-hand fashion, the possibilities of growth at various levels in an educational system.

Estimation Routines in Target Setting

Underlying the schemata are a variety of subroutines for estimating the component parts. All of them are essentially simple and, beneath an occasional facade of algebra, very similar. The schemata and variants require fundamentally that product, product per head, occupational composition in the work force, and educational levels within occupations be set or estimated. The sources and methods available for doing this are:

1. Arbitrary assumption of growth in product and product per head and the raising of corresponding occupational and educational levels.
2. Borrowing of product and product per head performance figures from another country, and fixing of occupational and educational attainment structure to correspond.
3. Derivation of the relationship of output to occupation and education from a regression analysis of a number of other countries where data are available.
4. Extrapolation or curve-fitting on the basis of past performance within the country for which the estimates are being made.
5. More often, the use of a combination of these sources.

PRODUCT ESTIMATES. Product for future years may simply be set both for the economy as a whole and for the sectors. Planners may simply say, and piously hope, that product will be x million at the end of the plan period. Or, planners may assume an annual cumulative percentage increase applied to the known base year:

$$p_n = p_x(1 + r)^t$$

Here p_x is the product in the base year, r is the assumed annual growth compounded over t years, the term of the forecast; and the result is p_n or product at the end of the plan period.

The setting of r is not often purely arbitrary. It might be derived from the performance of the economy between two time periods in past years:

$$(1 + r) = \sqrt[t]{\frac{p_x}{p_{x-t}}} \tag{14}$$

Here p_x is, as before, product in present year; and p_{x-t} is product t years previously. The root is one plus the past growth rate over t years. If the root $(1 + r)$ turned out 1.07, and if the planner assumed that this annual growth rate of 7 per cent would continue over 10 years of the plan period, given a base year product of 12 billion:

$$p_n = p_x(1 + r)^t = 12(1.07)^{10} = 23.6 \text{ billion.}$$

The growth factor $(1.07)^{10} = 1.9672$, can be looked up in compound interest tables. (*Growth Factors: Compound Interest Tables,* Stanford, 1963).

The rate may be pushed up on the basis of growth observed in another, presumably similar, economy. Or it may be based on knowledge of future likely investment, capital output ratios, the establishment of new industries, the opening of new markets, and the country's likely share and earnings.

The analysis may be incorporated into a macro-economic growth model of formidable appearance, in which a massive algebraic superstructure serves to divert attention from the spindle-shanked data which support it. Or, the rate may be based on shrewd guesses made by experts who know what the growth potential is in various industries and sectors. Sometimes, the product estimated on the basis of guesses about employment may at some later date be used to derive employment for the schemata. Around and around they go.

The future product may be borrowed directly from some other economy, without fear, favor, or arithmetic. Or it might be the average of a group of countries. Or it might be derived by fitting some exotic growth curve to the past of the home country and extrapolating. Development economists seem to prefer compound interest functions, exponentials (with $b > + 1$), and fits to a regression line. These functions trend onward and upward, spiritually upbeat as a development planner should be. The functions are simple and easy to work with, because there are either tables or simple computational routines; and things do seem often to behave in this way—perhaps, because the data have been beaten into this shape for so long, they are cowed.

PRODUCT PER HEAD FORECASTS. Product per head is handled in much the same way as product, with assumptions about employment policy and the relationships among labor, capital, and technology thrown in.

OCCUPATIONAL COMPOSITION AND EDUCATIONAL ATTAINMENT. The percentages and numbers of work force members in occupations in future years are set in a variety of ways. But they are *set,* and the process is not free of pure guesswork. In the simplest situation, the percentages are merely raised for the higher and skilled occupations in the sectors which are marked for growth. One occupational class may simply be raised arithmetically, e.g., from 3 to 5 per cent. Or the percentages which prevail in the same sector in another country may be taken as a target toward which percentages in the plan are raised.

Two crude methods are used to estimate numbers in a specific occupation in some future year:

$$1.\ \frac{pa_n}{pa_x} \cdot o_x = o_n \qquad (15)$$

Here the number in the occupation in the base year (o_x) is increased as the work force increases from year x to n, i.e., if the work force doubles the number in the occupation doubles.

$$2.\ o_x \cdot (1 + r)^t = o_n \qquad (16)$$

Here, the number in the occupation is raised according to the cumulative increase in product assumed or estimated over the t-years between x and n. Neither method has any rational basis, especially (16), although the notions can be put together, as will be shown.

The same considerations hold for the educational attainment coefficients. There is even less adequate information on the relationship between educational attainment in the work force and economic performance. Education (when measured on the basis of years of formal schooling completed), may enhance economic performance, inhibit it, or have no effect on it whatsoever. When measured in a country such as the U.S.A., it may reflect the results of economic performance rather than the cause. Yet, simple linear relationships between educational attainment and performance in the U.S.A. are computed in the form of coefficients and inserted into development plans for other countries. Appendix N gives some ratios.

Combinatory routines which assume simple relationships between product and work force requirements, and derive one from the other in a set of equations are, at base, exactly the same. The essential relationship assumed is:

$$p = f\!\left(\frac{o_j}{n}\right) \tag{17}$$

Performance is a function of the ratio of the number in the work force in some given occupation to the total number in the work force. If this is accepted, the number in the occupation from year x to year n can be derived, if the performance can be estimated. Also, at some point in the proceedings, the exact coefficients relating performance and proportions in the occupation are borrowed from another source. The following routine is typical.

To project occupation o from year x to year n: $_no_x$

$$o_n = o_x e^{it}$$

    o_n = number in occupation in year n
    i is the exponential rate of increase
    t is the time between year x and year n (18)
    o_x is the number in the occupation in base
        year and is known
    e = 2.71828. . . base of natural system of logs

The rate to be evaluated is i, and it depends on the relationship assumed in this question:

$$\frac{o}{n} = k\!\left(\frac{p}{n}\right)^{\theta}$$

    o = number in occupation
    n = number in work force
    p = Product or output   (19)
    k = constant
    θ = coefficient

Equation (2) is transformed so that the rate of increase of both variables is shown as:

$$s = \theta r$$

    s = rate of increase of $\dfrac{o}{n}$ (20)
    r = rate of increase of $\dfrac{p}{n}$

$$s = i - q$$

    i = increase of occupation o (21)
    q = increase of work force (n)

$$r = g - q$$ g = increase of product (p)   (22)

Substitution then gives:

$$i - q = \theta\,(g - q) \tag{23}$$

$$i = \theta\,(g - q) + q \tag{24}$$

$$i = \theta\,g + (1 - \theta)\,q \tag{25}$$

When i is solved for, expression (18) can be evaluated. The number in the occupation in year x is known; the number of years of the forecast, t is known; and e is a constant. But to solve for i in expression

(25), the coefficient θ must be obtained. This coefficient is s/r, or the rate of increase in the occupation over the rate of increase in product. (The common denominator is the number in the work force). This rate θ is usually not available in the country for which the plan is being concocted, but it is available in the land of plenty, and only slightly used; so it is borrowed from the U.S. and slapped into the formula:

$$s = 3.5 \qquad\qquad \theta = \frac{3.5}{2.4} = 1.46 \tag{26}$$
$$r = 2.4$$

Assuming that the annual growth rate envisaged for the country over a 10-year period is 6 per cent and the growth in the work force is set at 3 per cent annually, the evaluation of i would be:

$$i = .06\,(1.46) + (1 - 1.46)\,.03 = .0738 \tag{27}$$

$$o_n = o_x\,(e^{.074\, x\, 10}) = o_x\,2.0959 \tag{28}$$

If the number in the occupation in year x were 5,000

$$o_n = 5,000 \cdot 2.0959 = 10,480 \tag{29}$$

When the planner has run through all the algebra and evaluated $e^{.074 \times 10}$ in a table of exponential functions, the matter turns on whether or not there was any warrant for borrowing the coefficient from the U.S. The routine, which is as useful as any other model or method, illustrates the fact that coefficients are often borrowed from the U.S. economy— not because this is the best or even a reasonable model but rather because they are available.

ESTIMATIONS BY SIMPLE CURVE FITTING:
EXTRAPOLATION AND REGRESSION

A linear trend can be extrapolated from past data to estimate increase in product, work force, or productivity. Simple extrapolation is not often recommended, but is very commonly used.

Product over past years is simply graphed; a line is fitted to the points, and extended on the assumption that the trend will continue. With product on the Y axis and years along the X, the line can be extended into future years on the assumption of a continuation of the same linear trend. The calculation is straightforward and the method is available in any elementary statistics text. Figure II.2, taken from actual country data, illustrates the simplicity of the assumption and perhaps should suggest the danger.

In addition to fitting to the line by $y_c = a + bx$, which may first be smoothed with a moving average, a second degree curve $y_c = a + $

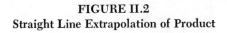

FIGURE II.2
Straight Line Extrapolation of Product

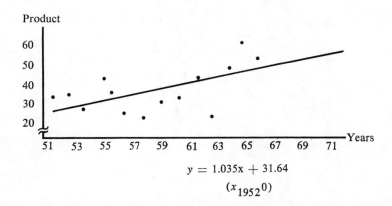

$$y = 1.035x + 31.64$$
$$(x_{1952}0)$$

$b x + c x^2$ or a logarithmic adaptation (Log $y_c = \log a + x \log b$) of an exponential are common forms for extrapolation exercises because the normals (derived equations in which the data from the problem can be directly substituted in order to solve for the constants) are known and results can be readily computed. Fitting to such curves is simple enough to be worth the trouble, but dangerous in the extreme when the poor and inadequate historical data of most developing countries are used, without other checks, to shoot the estimation far into the future. Extrapolations do offer useful checks for estimations based on other routines. After the schemata have been run, it is useful to check results against some form of curve function. The extrapolation routine illustrated in Figure II.3 can be used with product, or product per head, or even numbers in occupations, or education levels in the work force in past years.

A simple bivariate model is also used to estimate the value of one variate (e.g., employment of members of a specific occupation) from another (e.g., product or product per head) through regression. Figure II.3 shows a typical example of this. The dots in the scattergram represent the bivariate distribution (from 40 countries) of data on the relative frequency of engineers to total workers graphed against total production over total workers.

The objective would be to estimate X_1 (percentage of engineers) from X_2 (product per head expected in the sector) by the linear equation $X_1 = a + bX_2$. Given the expected production and work force of the sector for some future year and using the values of the constants

FIGURE II.3
Sector *j* (or industry)

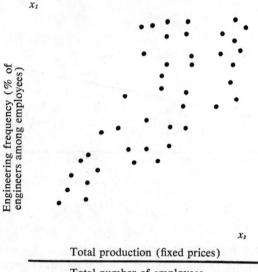

Total production (fixed prices)
—————————————————————
Total number of employees

computed on the basis of the 40 countries, the percentage of engineers in the firm, industry, or sectoral work force can be estimated. The simplicity of the logic underlying the models provokes a slight queasiness. Why should a conglomerate of industries and countries yield—through simple linear regression—a magic answer? And what is the significance of choosing this one aspect of human resource education and training (relative frequency of engineers in the work force) and this one estimate of 'productivity'.

Nor will multiple regression solve the problem completely. One could envisage this model:

$$Xc_{1.23} = a_{1.23} + b_{12.3}X_2 + b_{13.2}X_3 \tag{30}$$

Here, various mixes of human resources can be used to estimate productivity or various factors of productivity can be used to estimate some human resource requirement. But which mixes? And which factors?

Multivariate Models

Both productivity and human resource composition should be explored through multivariate analysis before any meaningful simple relations could be set up for investigation.

This is work for economists, but one first approach to the problem might begin in this fashion. Observations and measurements covering the two general aspects of the problem (human resource mix and output) are made on 50 establishments engaged in the same or similar enterprise, but with varying sizes, locations, and mixes of humans and other factors of production.

FIGURE II.4
Human Resource-Output Analysis Format

| | *X* Variates | | | | | | *Y* Variates | | | | |
| | *Human Resource Mix (Measures)* | | | | | | *Output (Measures)* | | | | |
Firms	A	B	C	D	E	F	Q	R	S	T	U	V
1												
2												
3												
.												
.												
50												

To simulate reality we could give some examples of the measures proposed:

Human Resource Mix[1]

A = Educational attainment (grades completed, mean)
B = Relative frequency workers with tertiary education
C = Relative frequency workers literate
D = Relative frequency workers with higher science-technology
E = Relative frequency workers middle technical-vocational
F = Relative frequency workers in-industry training

Output Examples[2]

Q = Product per worker hour
R = Product per unit fixed investment
S = Product per unit power (KWh., etc.) (cost)
T = Product per unit expenditure on R & D
U = Product per unit raw material (cost)
V = Product per head potential market

[1] Educators or training specialists could choose better ones.

[2] Economists or engineers could choose better ones.

The first step would generate two correlation matrices (based on 50 firms):

| | HUMAN RESOURCE | | | | | | | OUTPUT | | | | |
	A	B	C	D	E	F		Q	R	S	T	U	V
A	1	xAB	xAC	xAD	xAE	xAF	Q	1	yQR	yQS	yQT	yQU	yQV
B		1	xBC	xBD	xBE	xBF	R		1	yRS	yRT	yRU	yRV
C			1	xCD	xCE	xCF	S			1	yST	ySU	ySV
D				1	xDE	xDF	T				1	yTU	yTV
E					1	xEF	U					1	yUV
F						1	V						1

57

Sundry possibilities are open for the next step in analysis. A principal components analysis could be carried out on each side in order to throw light on the validity of the constructs 'human resource' and 'productivity'. More than one component or factor is possible for human resources. The next step might be to compute a canonical correlation between the transformed variates of both sides to establish the strength of the relationship between human resource and output. From this point on, a more searching analysis of relationships between various pairs of variates might be revealing. After examination of the results of a general analysis, one could see the point of picking out components for more searching study through pair comparisons.

Analysis through partial correlation, in which various product and human resource factors are held constant while others are allowed to vary, also provides a way around the problem of interaction among components that gets masked in the simple regression model. Multiple stepwise regression is better. A multivariate analysis of variance among the human resource factors, with output the criterion variable and with other factors of production used for covariance adjustments, is yet another way into a more searching analysis of the problem. More detailed procedures are beyond the scope of this book and out of the field of competence of the author, but the general point should be made that if manpower planning is to go beyond its present limitations it must get away from simple regression analysis based on statistical relationships that may exist for reasons quite irrelevant to productivity.

RESEARCH PREREQUISITE TO MANPOWER PLANNING

Manpower planning is as yet weak; obviously so when the simple schemata are used, and less obviously so when the basic weaknesses are nested within the algebra of more ambitious models. Some basic problems of definition and classification must be cleared away. Both jobs and the characteristics of the people who fill them are crudely defined and too simply categorized. To plan the output of a number of people characterized as 'secondary school graduates' to fit a number required in a job characterized as 'machine operator' doesn't accomplish much. Considerable research is necessary to refine classification schemes used in manpower and education planning. Here, researchers in the field of guidance may have more to offer than economists.

Only the outlines of the approach can be offered. The guidance man attempts, among other things, to effect the best fit between the individual's characteristics (including education and training, but also including general capacity, special aptitudes and motivation) and the requirements of a given occupation. He views the problem as one of assessing the probability:

$$p(\mathrm{H}_i \cdot S_i | x) \qquad \begin{array}{l} H_i \text{ is the statement, This} \\ \text{individual is a member} \\ \text{of group } i \text{ (occupation)} \\ S_i \text{ the individual succeeds} \\ \text{in this group} \\ x \text{ is a score combination on} \\ \text{a set of predictor vari-} \\ \text{ables (measures of achieve-} \\ \text{ment, capacity, aptitude,} \\ \text{motivation)} \end{array} \qquad (31)$$

The guidance counselor then attempts to assess the probability that, given a set of scores which characterize the individual, the individual is a member and succeeds in a certain group (which may be an occupational or further education group). Tatusuoka (1957) has shown that the probability can be evaluated by: $p(H_i | x) \cdot p(S_i | H_i \cdot x)$, i.e. the product (32) of the probability that the individual is a member, given the scores, and the probability that he is a success, given that he is a member and has a certain score combination.

The manpower researcher must take a slightly different approach. The performance and characteristics of practicing members of occupational groups can be used to define and classify the occupational groups themselves.

Levin, Martin, and associates (1963) have made an approach to this in the basic health sciences through their functional criterion analysis. The original work should be consulted for the detailed procedures, but the essentials of the approach were:

1. A sample of practicing scientists and technicians furnished information on the characteristics of themselves and their jobs. The sample was split into two.
2. A principal component analysis of the responses yielded nine major factors which accounted for most of the variance found.
3. Factor scores were obtained for the individuals in the first sample and submitted to a hierarchical grouping on the basis of similarity of profiles of factor scores.
4. The nine natural groups found from grouping process were examined in order to find the basis on which individuals clustered into groups.
5. On the basis of the dimensions that seemed to differentiate

most, rules could be adduced to reclassify both samples of the individuals into seven groups.

6. A discriminant analysis was run to test the extent to which the groups separated from each other.

7. Individuals were assigned to groups on a probabilistic basis by factor scores, and the predicted membership was compared to the actual to test the accuracy of the classification procedure.

8. On the basis of the extent of overlapping and misclassification, two groups were combined, cutting the number of groups from seven to six.

9. A second discriminant analysis was run, and the six factors that contributed most to distinguishing membership were examined and interpreted.

10. Again individuals were assigned and there was a marked improvement, i.e. reduction in misassignment.

11. Groups could then be described and distinguished and, to a certain extent, more effectively defined.

In its later steps, the study needs clearer exposition and more imaginative description. If the study could be carried further it is possible that it might provide a much better basis for classifyng manpower. Educational programs could be better fitted to work force requirements. Misclassification of manpower could be minimized and training programs could escape rigidity and maximize corregibility by taking into account group similarities and hence transfer possibilities among jobs.

The poor fit between preparation and occupation may be partially caused by poor definition and classification. It is easy to criticize manpower planning. Its defects are obvious. It does seem possible, however, that some of the deficiencies can be cut down by better research into taxonomy and classification. Alternate technological possibilities will still leave some slackness in manpower planning, but some of the difficulties of the schemata could be cut down by better classification systems.

A Note on the Spin-Off of Trained Workers

Converse to the proposition that educated and trained people contribute to production and development is the fact that the production process contributes training and education to the workers. This training is not limited to cooperative and continuation arrangements between firms and schools, or even formal in-industry training programs. Some of it comes through direct association with a machine technology in which a scientific and technological *Weltanschaung* is acquired by workers who have seemingly little formal education. Nor is informal learning limited to the acquisition of manual skills from direct work experience with tools, machines, and laboratory equipment. Through experimentation, inquiry, and even self-study, workers may also acquire knowledge of basic scientific principles and laws. One recalls many years ago meeting a master mechanic in an African shop who referred to the "engine juju," the "machine tool juju," and other jujus. One would think that his notion of internal combustion engines and electric motors might be slight, but this was not the case. Deeper conversation revealed that he understood the principles perfectly and used 'juju' as an enclitic for 'gadget' because he had learned the nomenclature that way from his first European boss. Over the years he had listened and observed, and buttressed this with sessions in which his literate son had read to him from technical manuals and diagrammed things in the sand.

Education and training through spin-off cannot be readily handled in formal models and schemata, but they should be taken into consideration when one is translating educational and occupational coefficients from a more developed country to a less developed one. The rather large gaps in education from one worker group to another with near-equal productivity may be explained by this covert process.

The case for spin-off, however, does not weaken the argument for formal education and training as important prerequisites to growth and development. Because a man of high natural endowment wins through to an understanding of science and technology with little formal schooling does not mean that he might not be all the more productive if his high talents had been identified early and shaped through formal education and training. Education and training should never be underestimated in their screening and selection capacity as well as for their more commonly recognized formative contribution. It is education as a maturing and screening agent, rather than a training mode, that determines much of the preference given to job candidates with high formal education in the United States. The dropout is often shunned because he is a dropout, rather than because he lacks general education and specific skills that school completion might have given him. Hence, a better measure of educational attainment in a developing country might be deviation from the average attainment, because that marks what is possible, rather than mean attainment. There is no question that the person who completes a basic program which makes him literate has a basis for acquiring vast amounts of informal education and training through spin-off.

Nathaniel H. Leff (*Brazilian Capital Goods Industry*, doctoral dissertation, 1965) has made a study of the effects of educational spin-off in the development of the capital goods industry in Sao Paulo, Brazil.

Schemata Targets

Targets set through applications of the simple schemata can do no harm as long as they are not treated as though they had precision and finality which they do not in fact have. Furthermore, the schemata must be applied through successive iterations which only gradually approximate useful results. In setting targets for the Guayana, six iterations were run on the schemata within one year. Each stock shot produced by running the schemata provoked the general economic planners to revise and reprogram their output targets. When these targets were reset, a whole round of adjustments was necessary and a new application of the schemata was in order. When product or productivity are moved up or down in the heavy industries, the work force and the population estimates will move up or down, and this will affect employment in the service sectors. The process moves through successive approximations, and hopefully it coverges—if not toward some 'true value,' then at least toward a value with which a majority of planners can agree.

Parnes (1963) uses a scheme which shortcuts the schemata process in the third step, where educational attainment levels are set for the work force. Parnes groups occupations into four broad categories, according to the amount of education they generally require. Class A occupations, by this typology, require a university education or advanced degree equivalent. The move saves one table and a few steps, because once occupational distributions are determined they can be converted directly to educational requirements. This takes target setting one more remove from reality, because it assumes a closer relationship between education and occupation than the data from most countries show. On the other hand, it may save the planner from cooking up precise recipes for specific training programs.

Countries in the early stage of development show wide variations in educational attainment within occupations, with some surprisingly low levels shown in the professional and managerial categories, which would be Parnes' Class A. Many managers and executives reach their posts by routes which do not appear in data on formal education. In some countries almost a quarter of those classified by the census as professional have an elementary school preparation or less.

A Coda on the Utility of the Manpower Approach to Educational Planning

Manpower projections could fall quite wide of the mark and still serve a useful purpose. If the target figures motivate political decision makers to provide resources to education and training in order to insure future economic growth, then the manpower approach is not in vain, no matter how abysmally projections may fail in statistical precision. The history of educational expansion in some of the developing countries suggests that this is so. Laws providing for universal education have been in existence in Latin America for over a century. And yet, provision for implementing the law has never been made, even in Venezuela, a country that has not in modern times lacked resources. Other motivations have entered into the failure to provide for education, but, with the exception of the outright dictators deliberately withholding resources, the major reasons are inertia, indifference, and the failure to view education as anything more than a burdensome social overhead. Most planners have had the experience of using the manpower game as a lure for higher allocations to education. This is not to say that manpower planning is pure farce. Rather, it is an approach that has two purposes and two payoffs, and the target numbers it furnishes are only one possible return from the approach.

III

Demographic Analysis
and Target Setting

Application of the manpower schemata and variations depends on demographic as well as economic data and analysis. The projection of the total population lies at the base of most general planning models. In certain cases, the population is projected first and the work force derived from it by assumed or projected participation rates; or the product or income may be derived from the population, with certain assumptions about per-head contribution. In the schemata, the base year work force is wasted by outflow rates that have death and retirement as major components. The work force is also replaced by birth and entrance rates and retention within the system. The human resource planner need not be an expert demographer, but familiarity with the rudiments of census operations and demographic analysis underlying projections enables the planner to work with censal and vital data and understand—as in the case with national account statistics—the hard and soft points in the routines.

However human resource targets are set, reaching them will depend on:

1. Human resource stock in the base years.
2. Attrition of this stock during the plan years.
3. Replacement and addition to the stock from the output of educational and training institutions within the country or by importation or in-migration of trained people from outside.

Classification and enumeration of the population in the base year according to age, sex, education, and training; the wasting of this stock through death, emigration, and retirement; projection of increase to the population and work force by births, immigration, and raised participation rates—these are standard censal and demographic chores. Replacement of the human resource stock by projection of the output of educational and training programs is educational systems planning; and the setting of future year requirements depends on political, economic and social analysis. The bulk of this section will describe the planner's use of census and demographic methods for assessment and projection.

CENSUS AND PROJECTION METHODS

United Nations and U.S. Bureau of Census publications provide handbooks on the methods of designing and conducting population censuses and tabulating and analyzing the results. Special attention is given to the handling of data in developing countries, so that precision and accuracy are maximized by correcting for under-registration of births and deaths and for biased reporting, e.g., digit preference in age classes. Also, for other less ingenuous evasions, e.g., under-reporting of income. The U.S. Bureau of the Census has prepared an excellent set of training materials, using a case set of data based on a fictitious country, Valencia, which takes the student through the entire exercise from design to analysis of a population census.

In theory, the educational planner is not responsible for working up census data or carrying out projections of the population. In fact, he often must be involved, if not in the design and basic tabulation then at least in further analysis of the data. The planner is a consumer of census data, rather than a prime producer, but a basic understanding of the possibilities and limitations of such data is useful. The planner may often be lucky enough to get his projections full-blown from a demographer who is working with a general planning group. Or the planner may have to run the projections himself, or at least check those done elsewhere.

In the general case, census data provide the base from which projections into future years are run. The base data and the projection tables are almost always expressed in terms of age groups, e.g., 0–4, 5–9, . . . Census data can be brought forward to current date and projected into future years by a variety of methods, some more reliable than others. In developing countries, the method used will depend on how speedily answers are required and the existence of data which can be used to get them.

Short Methods: Extrapolations

A quick and rough estimate can be made by extrapolation based on arithmetical or geometric rates of increase that are either assumed or based on analysis of past growth. In the arithmetical case, if the total population increased by 100,000 over a 10-year period in the past, an average annual increase of 10,000 is projected. In 20 years the new total is 1,200,000, if the population base were 1,000,000.

The standard compound interest formula is also used for determining the increase

$$p_n = p_0(1 + r)^t \tag{1}$$

Here, p_0 is the population at the beginning of the period, t is the time in years over which the forecast or updating goes, r is the annual rate of increase, and p_n is the total population projected at the end of the period. The rate of increase can be calculated on the basis of two past censuses, p_1 and p_2:

$$(1 + r) = \sqrt[t_1]{\frac{p_2}{p_1}} \tag{2}$$

or more directly:

$$p_n = p_2 \left(\sqrt[t_1]{\frac{p_1}{p_2}} \right) t_2 \qquad \begin{aligned} t_1 &= \text{intercensal} \\ &\text{time interval.} \\ t_2 &= \text{post-censal} \\ &\text{interval.} \end{aligned} \tag{3}$$

A more commonly used procedure is extrapolation based on a second or third-degree polynomial:

$$p_x = a + bx + cx^2 \tag{4}$$

Results of three past censuses are required for a second-degree polynomial:

$$1940 \text{ population} = 1,000,000 = a + o.b. + o.c. \ (x = 0)$$
$$1950 \text{ population} = 1,100,000 = a + 10.b + 100c \ (x = 10)$$
$$1960 \text{ population} = 1,500,000 = a + 20.b + 400c \ (x = 20)$$

$a = 1,000,000$:

$$10b + 100c = 100,000$$
$$20b + 400c = 500,000$$
$$c = 1500$$
$$b = -5000$$

To estimate 1970, where $x = 30$:
$$1,000,000 + (30)(-5,000) + (900)(1,500) = 2,200,000$$

Very often, use of a parabola of the second degree has little warranty, other than that it is a convenient form for casting the existing census data of the past in order to get a rough estimate of the future. That is, no examination is made of the data, or the major influences on population through births, deaths, and migration, to see if such a curve function is likely to fit. When long extrapolations are made, the population may be seriously overestimated or underestimated.

More elaborate growth curves (Pearl-Reed, Gompertz, or Yule) can be fitted to multiple census results so that future totals can be extrapolated. The Pearl-Reed curve can be expressed in the form:

$$y = \frac{k}{1 + e^{a + bx}} \qquad \begin{array}{l} \text{IN THIS APPLICATION:} \\ y = \text{projected population} \\ x = \text{interval value (in years from origin)} \end{array} \qquad (5)$$

This is not formidable to evaluate once k, a and b are obtained. However, these constants are usually based on averages of nine census results, more than are generally available in developing countries.

All of the methods, in addition to having the usual weaknesses of extrapolation, will only furnish general totals. Subtotals for age groups are required for human resource development planning. To project the output of educational institutions an age-grade matrix is necessary, and the number of six-year-olds who will be entering the system in future years (if that is the entrance age) must be estimated so that wastage (or retention) rates can be applied and the output at various grade levels estimated. The same procedures are applied to the work-force data, as base year stock is wasted for death and retirement over plan years.

When one of the quick methods is used to estimate future total population, it is usual to assume that the base-year proportions in the age groups will hold in the future years (e.g. 25 per cent of the total population will be in 0–4, 22 per cent in 5–9, . . .). There is no reason to assume this over a long period, but it is customary to do so. Arithmetical smoothing operations, or adjustments to extreme ends of the age groupings may be made. The 0–4 age group always requires special attention. Some of the adjustments are little more than guesses or assumptions, i.e., about birth and death rates, digit preference, registration and reporting.

Projections can be made almost as rapidly and more accurately by component analysis. The three components which influence future populations are mortality, fertility, and migration. With rates established, the population can be carried forward in steps (periods of years, often five) with the population aggregated into corresponding five-year age groups (0–4, 5–9 . . .). Life tables for the country, or for similar countries, or model tables can be extremely useful in the analysis.

Minimal data, usually available or obtainable in developing countries, are:

1. Reasonably current census data, with population classified by sex and age.
2. Life tables for male, female, and total populations, or mortality data so that abridged tables can be constructed or model tables used.
3. Fertility data which can be used to estimate age-specific fertility rates and hence future-year births.

Migration is often insignificant in projections of the total populations of developing countries. When the populations of subareas of the country must be projected, internal migration rates may be highly significant and projections are quite difficult to bring off with accuracy in smaller regions and provinces. Tarver (1959) discussed the problem of making subarea projections, using the standard components of population change, i.e., births, deaths, and migration. In general, assumptions are made that death and fertility ratios of the subarea population to the total population will prevail into the projected period. Migration may be estimated as a residual between two past censuses, after population changes from births and deaths have been taken into account. Only methods for projecting total national populations are covered here. One routine for projecting subnational area population is outlined in the Stanbery formula in Appendix D.

PROJECTIONS BASED ON UNITED NATIONS MODEL LIFE TABLES

With a base year population and specifications on changes in fertility, the planner can use United Nations model life tables for population projections. The most useful of the tables is Table V in United Nations Manual II, *Methods for Population Projections by Sex and Age*. This is a table of survival ratios (p_x) at birth and in the age groups 0–4 up to 80 +. The tables are arranged by levels according to mortality conditions assumed or calculated for the countries to which they will be applied. At level 0, life expectancy at birth ($^0e_0$) is 20 years, and at level 115 of the table the life expectancy at birth is 73.9 years.

To enter the table at the appropriate level, a demographer must have an estimate of the mortality conditions in the country for which he wishes to make the projection. Once he has this, the projection is reasonably automatic, assuming that fertility rates and base year population are available. Estimating the mortality and fertility components is not an easy or automatic process but discussion of the methods will be deferred so that a simple runthrough of the projection methodology can be presented.

Table III.1 outlines the hypothesized fertility rates that underlie

TABLE III.1
Hypothesized Fertility, 1960–1970 (rates per 1,000 women)
according to Hypothesis II(a)[a]

		Hypothesis I(a)		
Woman's Age	*1960*	*1965*	*1970*	*1975*
15–19		84.4		
20–24		223.3		
25–29		260.4		
30–34		198.7		
35–39		139.0		
40–44		64.9		
45–49		15.8		

		Hypothesis II(a)		
Woman's Age	*1960*	*1965*	*1970*	*1975*
15–19	84.2	81.3	78.4	75.7
20–24	223.3	214.3	206.7	199.4
25–29	260.4	251.3	242.2	233.6
30–34	198.7	191.5	184.9	178.3
35–39	139.0	134.0	129.2	124.6
40–44	64.9	62.6	60.4	58.3
45–49	15.8	15.2	14.7	14.1

[a] Hypothesis I(a) assumes that the fertility rate in 1965, 1970, and 1975 remains the same as in 1960.

the projection. In Hypothesis I (a) the same age-specific fertility rates are assumed to prevail over the period 1960 to 1975. In Hypothesis II(a) the rates are declining over the period 1960 to 1975.

To use model life table survival ratios to project the population, the planner must have:

1. The population base. This may be from a current census or a census brought forward with vital data (births and deaths) and migration, or an old census brought up to date as part of the projection itself.
2. The mortality component. The planner must have hypotheses on mortality in order to enter at the proper level of the table and in order to move to different levels during the term of the projection. Mortality is built into the survival ratios which appear in the table.
3. The fertility component. The planner must have fertility rates. He may have a general rate or age-specific rates.

4. The migration component, where this is relevant. This might be the most difficult component to establish, but in most developing countries external migration is not a significant matter and for simplicity the problem will be deferred.

Assume that for the base year the planner has a current population classified into age and sex groups.

TABLE III.2

Basic Data and Components

Base Year Population (1965)			*Mortality Component*
Age-Group	*Male*	*Female*	Having studied the vital data and con-
0–44	475,291	459,374	structed an abridged life table, we con-
5–9	402,120	392,669	clude that our survival ratios will move
10–14	314,449	340,742	according to the U.N. Model Life Tables:
15–19	302,190	315,684	65–70 70–75 75–80
.			Level 80 Level 85 Level 90
.			($^0e_0 = 57.6$)
.			
85–89	2,582	4,030	*Fertility Component*
90+	1,093	1,718	Hypothesis II (a) Table 3A
External Migration			65–70 70–75 *and on*
none			1965 column 1970 column
			Birth Ratio for Sexes
			Male = .5089 Female = .4911

To illustrate, the projection will be run on part of the female population for the first period, 1965–1975, sketched into Table III.3.

TABLE III.3

Partial Projection Table

Age-Group	*Base Population (65)*	P^1	*Pop. 1970*	P^2	*Pop. 1975*
0.4	459,374	0.9708		0.9765	
5.9	329,669	0.9909	445,962	0.9924	
10.14	340,742	0.9900	389,096	0.9914	442,573
15.19	315,684	0.9848	337,335	0.9871	385,750
.	.	.	.	.	.
.	.	.	.	.	.
.	.	.	.	.	.

[1] *P* values taken from Level 80 of Model Life Tables (p. 81).
[2] *P* values taken from Level 85 of Model Life Tables (p. 81).

[1] The appropriate table for survival ratios is Table V found on pages 80–81 of *Methods for Population Projections by Sex and Age*, United Nations, 1956.

The group that is 0–4 in the base year multiplied by the survival ratio (459,374 $\times$ .9708) equals 445,962, the number that will be 5–9 in 1970. This can then be multiplied by .9924 to give 442,573, the number 10–14 in 1975. All of the numbers below and to the left can be filled in for all ages and future years. To get the numbers above, e.g., the group that will be 0–4 in 1970, we must use the fertility components to estimate births. For this we will need the women in child bearing ages (15–49) and the age-specific fertility ratios of Table 1. We will, for illustrative purposes, cover only the births between 1965–1970, i.e., the group that will be 0–4 in 1970. Again we will work only with females, but to include males requires only two more columns and the same routine. Note also that we would have had to fill in projection Table III.3 completely, in order to get the women in child bearing ages in 1970.

TABLE III.4
Births and Survivors 1965–70

Age-Group	Average of Women in Group 65–70[1]	Fertil-ity[2]	Births	Female[3]	Surviv-ing[4]	Male	Surviv-ing	Total
					(0.9070)			
15–19	326,510	.4065	132,726	65,182	59,120			
20–24	300,298	1.0715	321,769	158,021	143,325			
25–29	263,735	1.2565	331,383	162,742	147,607			
30–34	223,715	.9575	241,207	118,457	107,441			
35–39	199,583	.6700	133,721	65,670	59,563	(Total, male-female born		
40–44	175,226	.3130	54,846	26,935	24,430	and survived goes into		
45–49	145,662	.0760	11,070	5,436	4,931	0–4, 1970)		

[1] This is the average of the number of women in the age group in 1965 and the number that would be projected for 1970 if the first table had been completely filled out. There will be slight discrepancies because the calculations were not carried out and an approximation was used.
[2] This results from multiplying the rates in Table 3 by 5 (to get five year rate), e.g., .0813 x 5 = .4065 . . .
[3] Total births multiplied by .4911 to get female births.
[4] Births multiplied by birth survival rate taken from level 80 of U.N. Model Life Tables.

Male births would be computed the same way, and male and females added to give the number in the 0–4 age group in 1970. The same operation would be carried on to get the 0–4 group in 1975, 1980. . . .

The projection methodology is repetitive, and we need not spin out all the numbers in this example. The age groups are survived into the next higher age group five years ahead and all the groups can be filled in at once, except the 0–4 group which must be calculated from births by women, ages 15–49. If the projection goes beyond 15 years (beyond the year 1980 in the example), the survivors of the female births in the first five years (Table III.4) will be the women in the child-bearing group 15–19.

The Components: Fertility and Mortality

The major components of mortality and fertility require skilled demographic and sociological analysis before they can be set out as they are in Table III.2. Demographic and social analysis will yield varying hypotheses on the way the fertility rates will move in the years ahead.

In Table III.1, Hypothesis I(a) is that they will remain the same over the 15-year period. Hypothesis II(a) may be based on analysis of past trends which show a decline over a period of years. Or, the rates in II(a) may be set on the basis of assumptions about the way concomitants of lower fertility will affect births in the future years. Shifts from rural to urban living, from agricultural to industrial employment, from less to more education, and the spreading of information and assistance on means of population control, all tend to lower fertility; and the demographer takes this into account in his analysis. Generally, as countries develop economically and socially, the rates tend to fall slightly. Mortality rates also tend to go to lower levels with development and the introduction of disease control and improved medical services.

Demographic analysis also yields alternate assumptions about the way mortality rates will go in future years. Again, shifts from rural to urban, improved sanitation and social services, and increased medical attention will tend to lower morbidity and mortality rates. On this basis, the demographer reduces mortality or increases survival rates. This is work for the skilled demographer with experience of the country and its data, and, like handicapping horses, it is an art and science in itself, and only the superficial features of it are examined here.

Constructing Abridged Life Tables and Using Model Life Tables

If life tables are not available they can be constructed, if there are mortality data available. In many developing countries the data are available from death registries. First, age-specific death rates are calculated:

$$m_x = \frac{d_i}{p_i} K \qquad (5)$$

where d_i is the number of deaths during the year in the ith age group and p_i is the mid-year population of the same age group; K is usually 1,000

Infant death rate is almost always computed separately:

$$_1m_0 = \frac{d_0}{B}$$ where d_0 is the number of deaths below age one registered during the year, and B is live births same year. (6)

Once these rates are available for all age groups an abridged life table can be generated. Reed and Merrell associate m values with q values by equation (7). Once the death rates (m) can be related to the probability of dying (q), the table can be readily generated:

$$_nq_x = 1 - e^{-n \, _nm_x - an^3 \, _nm_x^2}$$ (7)

The constant a was empirically derived as .008, and the equation was then used to generate a table of values. Given m values, q values can be read from the table. Usually, individual tables are shown for single years up to 5. The other columns of the table can be readily worked up, beginning with the imaginary cohort of $1_x = 100,000$, multiplying by the probability of dying $_nq_x$ and then subtracting. This yields the column $_nd_x$ which in turn yields $_nL_x$, T_x and e_x. The relationships are straightforward, but some work with tables is requisite before the symbols mean much.

Vasquez first constructed the abridged life table that appears in Appendix C on the basis of mortality data in the Dominican Republic. On the basis of the mortality patterns revealed in the table, life expectancy at birth 53.7 years, he could enter United Nations Model Life Tables and carry out projections as they were outlined in a preceding section.

Incidental Comment

If single years are required and the population is shown in five-year groupings, there are sets of constant multipliers that can be applied to distribute the five-year total into single-year totals. The most frequently used panels of multipliers are based on Sprague's fifth difference formula and called Sprague multipliers. They appear in standard demographic sources. (*Methods for Population Projections by Sex and Age*. United Nations, 1956, p. 68).

Behind the assumptions made about fertility and mortality rates for future years, there is generally a great deal of analysis of vital data necessary. The general models followed in making the projections are essentially the ones detailed here. The results of even the most carefully done projections provide only probabilistic guidelines for future action.

PLANNING FOR SUBNATIONAL AREAS

The planner may have to deal with subnational areas, i.e., regions, zones, states, or departments. The plan may be limited in coverage to less than an entire nation. Or, the nation may be a collection of regions or states that have very different characteristics relevant to development (rural-urban, climatic, ethnic, economic, political), which require separate analysis before they can be combined in any meaningful way into a national plan. Presumably the school organization, curriculum, teacher force, and physical facilities will be planned to accord with these differences. The ethnic difference may necessitate a different language of instruction; the rural environment may require different emphasis in curriculum content; the climatic conditions may suggest that different physical facilities are appropriate; and differences in wealth may limit the quality level of the program.

Different regions within the same country may be at entirely different stages of economic, cultural, and social development, and plans will have to take this into account. To use the Harbison typology, regions within a country may be at Level I (underdeveloped), Level II (partially developed) and even Level III (semi-advanced). Charles Myers, Jr. (1964) cites Mexico as an example of this. National aggregates—economic and educational—in which Chiapas, Coahuila, and the Distrito Federal are blended, may yield an average that has no meaning.

The schemata and models which are applied at the national level need only slight modifications to make them suitable for subnational applications. Going from the national to the regional both complicates and simplifies the planner's task. Generally, subnational surveys and censuses are easier to take and cheaper to run, and permit more depth and elaboration. But regional projections are much trickier. Nonsystematic errors are more likely to even out in the larger populations dealt with at the national levels.

The necessary past data on which assumptions about future trends may be based are generally difficult to obtain for subnational areas. Internal migration, which underlies population and work-force projections, is a fair example. The components for national projections are births, deaths, and migration. External migration is not usually very accurately registered in developing countries, but neither is it a very important component in national population change. Quite the contrary is true with respect to population changes between regions or areas within the country, and internal migration rates are important in the projection of populations for subnational areas. Substantial population shifts do occur within developing countries; in fact, the trek from rural to urban center characterizes developing countries at a certain stage of growth. Assessing this migration and incorporating it into regional projections is a demanding task. But it is a necessary one, above all in areas which are undergoing very rapid economic and social change. For a region such as the Guayana in Venezuela, a detailed study of migrants is fundamental. The application of closed population models is useless until this step has been taken. It is not so easy to make this study, short of a house-to-house canvass and census run at frequent intervals over a period of time. Sometimes employment records and job applications to the major industries in the area will give first approximation, as in the steel mill at Matanzas in Guayana to which almost all new migrants are attracted.

Rather than elaborate the methods used, the tables in Appendix D, taken from Stanbery (1960), sketch out the essentials of the method. The Stanbery formulae and schemata are run using the State of California as a subnational area of the United States. Better data are available there than would be available in the states or departments of developing countries. But the methods are essentially the same, given the existence of reasonably adequate subnational data. The essentials of the method are:

1. The basic assumptions underlying both national and subnational projections are established.
2. The population of the national area by major age groups is projected for future years.
3. The size and the rate of migration into and out of the subnational area is derived from past trends according to the formats in Appendix D.
4. Net migration (excess of in-migrants or out-migrants) is established.
5. The population of the subarea is projected, taking into account natural increase (excess of births over deaths), net migration and the survival of in-migrants.
6. Further characteristics of the population, e.g., labor force participation rates for age groups can be derived from the basic population in the subnational area and participation rates in the total country workforce. School-age populations can also be determined.

From the basic data above, all of the usual statistics and projections for education and human resource development can be established.

Failing census data for the subnational area, sample surveys can be employed and estimates derived.

For the purposes of school location planning, more specific techniques have to be applied in the local areas. The basis is usually a census of school-age and preschool-age children. Irons and Kern (1953) used a land-utilization study technique which is a variant of methods used in other studies. A short-cut system suitable for urban areas entails a survey and enumeration of existing residences. To this is added the number of probable future homes, which is based on the number of suitable vacant lots. The average number of children per dwelling is determined in the survey, and this is multiplied by the number of dwellings estimated. Estimates can be modified according to the zoning for commerical and industrial establishments. The load can be reduced according to the existing and planned enrollments in private schools. This method will not serve in the rural areas or the swarming 'temporary' neighborhoods that cluster on the outskirts of the cities in many developing countries.

EXPANDING WORK FORCE TARGETS TO THE TOTAL POPULATION

With the total population for the target year projected by age and sex, and with the human resource requirements estimated for the economically active portion of the total population, the educational requirements of the work force can be expanded to the total population. Most simply, the same percentages of educated people in the work force are set for the total population—even when this makes no sense.

The work force represents varying proportions of the total population in the countries of the world. The *1960 Yearbook of Labor Statistics* shows a range from 60 per cent in a workers' paradise like Rumania to about 21 per cent in a loafers' paradise in Pacific Oceania. The United States is near the middle of the distribution with about 40 per cent of its total population economically active. International comparisons based on such statistics are risky, because in some heavily agricultural countries there is much informal work-force participation by women and young people that may or may not be counted; there are differences in definitions of economically active, and some unemployed persons may or may not be included. Lastly, the population base may be in error in the first place.

In the simplest expansion, basic education (complete primary school or four grades) might be programmed for the total population of young males according to the participation of adult males in the work force. If 95 per cent of the males between 20–64 participate in the work force, as they do in Ghana for example, then 95 per cent of the males in school age groups might be programmed for complete primary education. However, it would be foolish to program education for only 26 per cent of the females in Argentina where this is the rate of participation of females from 20–64 years old.

In higher education, if the planner wished to program education sufficient to cover both the work force demand and the excess demand for those in the general population who do not participate, he might use the expansion:

$$\frac{n_j}{p_j} \cdot 100 \tag{8}$$

Here n_j is the number required in the work force with education level or type j, and p_j is the rate of participation of adults (ages 20–64) with this level of education. If 95 per cent participate and 4,000 are required in the work force with this level of education, then the expansion would be:

$$\frac{4,000}{95} \cdot 100 = 4210, \text{ approximately.}$$

This would mean that about 105 would be given the education for every hundred required for the work force. The planner could go through the work force, level by level and type by type, and assess the demand for education in the total population on the assumption that the manpower minima will be met and there will be a surplus to cover the so-called social demand. The planner would have to have better labor force statistics than he usually has, and he would have to assume past participation has more stability than it might have. There is no real warranty for such expansions, but they might serve to give some guidelines to the planner when he is working from labor force demand to total demand. Inasmuch as the planner can not control the demand and it will undoubtedly be subject, at higher education levels, to movement in personal income, the exercise is fairly sterile. The planner could use the work force demand as minimum and move the social demand figure up according to projected rises in personal income, but the projected rise in personal income might very well change the participation rates. In summary, there are ways to go from work force demand to total demand, but they are crude expansions at best. There is no sure basis to generalize work force educational attainment levels to the total population. A country may, for political, social, or cultural reasons, opt for any mix of educational attainment in the total population. The limits will be imposed by what the country can afford.

Knowledge of the educational attainment requirements for the work force may still enable a country to set a more reasonable over-all strategy for human resource development. The country may take the work force requirements as basic minima to be accomplished, whatever the strain on resources. A comparison of the cost of meeting these minimal goals with the resources and revenues likely to be available may reveal how much the country will have left over to meet social, political and cultural aims through education. Hence, instead of setting a target of 100 per cent primary school graduates in a given period when meeting this target may so tax resources that none are left for meeting requirements at other levels, the country might adopt a strategy for meeting requirements at all levels and in all kinds of education according to work force demand. Whatever resources are left over may be allocated to cutting into the additional primary deficits.

A country's work force requirements profile might show the need for 50 per cent completing primary and beyond, 25 per cent completing various intermediate levels and 8 per cent completing higher education. When this is costed out, there may still be sufficient resources to provide 15 per cent more primary school graduates. Allocation to this target is sometimes called meeting the social demand for education, although a government might choose to do so on political or cultural grounds. Even on economic grounds, there is no reason to think that this will not in the long run contribute to increased output and improved economic performance. The secondary and tertiary benefits of general education are still little understood.

The whole matter of earmarking so much for meeting economic and so much for social or political targets becomes something less than snug when the reality of the situation suggests that as of the time the resources are allocated there is no way of knowing in the individual or aggregate case whether the education and training will ever be turned to productive (in an economic sense) ends. In most countries, one can program only for leading the horse to water.

A second possible strategy is for a country to set fixed goals on a social or political basis. The government may decree that in 20 years all persons over 10 will have a minimal education of three, six, or nine complete grades. The cost of this can be roughly programmed. The cost of meeting economic-requirement minima can also be established with reasonable precision. If the two sets of targets are impossible under the most likely estimates of revenue, then the country can choose to cut its economic development goals in order to make its social and political obligations. It is difficult to conceive of this being done explictly, but the position is possible.

A third possibilty is to work out a compromise somewhere between the two sets of targets, and this is in fact what most often happens—although not consciously—in developing countries. It happens not because of explicit planning decisions but because of the nature of educational development, where decisions are made on the basis of projects considered in isolation from total context. Planners plump for the establishment of a vocational school, pointing out convincingly the close connection between this kind of training and job performace. That the connection can be illusory, and that there are alternative and less expensive paths through industry and educational cooperation, often escapes the executive's notice. The executive may also fail to notice, at first, that the provision of one vocational place precludes the provision of five primary school places. The project goes forward and the resources are withheld from primary schools, not deliberately, but inevitably.

Enters now the keen planning critic who at once sees the 5/1 cost ratio between vocational and primary school education and the fact that the performance of vocational school graduates has not always lived up to the billing given it by vocational education enthusiasts. The critic may then argue against it. If the argument is advanced on a project basis it may be just as unsound.

Vocational education must be planned within the context of total general education and in accord with the requirements of the economy. Though the cost of any specific program may be five times as high as general educational program costs, the need for vocationally trained graduates may, at one point in time, be worth all of this and more. Untrained teachers and supervisors, insufficient equipment, and inadequate stock may have ruined any past vocational program, but it does not prove the worthlessness of the notion of training people for specific jobs. The only way that a sensible evaluation can be made is to relate the output to work force requirements. But work force requirements cannot be the sole determinant either. The requirements of the total population for all kinds and types of education must be examined.

Total Population Requirements

The simplest approach is to set the human resource requirements in the target year for the total population. The targets must be set high enough to cover the requirements of the economically active population (as they are estimated in the schemata) as well as to meet such additional social and political goal requirements as the resources of the country will bear.

Toward a Model of the System

For those with a taste for such things, Figure III.1 is offered, with

FIGURE III.1
System-Population Relationship in Planning

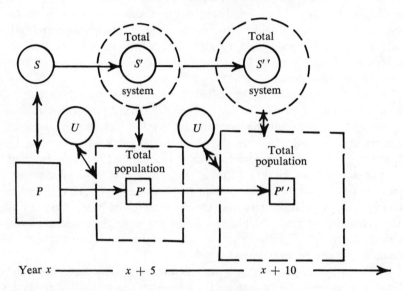

Year x ———— $x + 5$ ———— $x + 10$ ———→

P = Original population P'' = Survivors 10 years
P' = Survivors 5 years S = Original system
  from original S' = Surviving system
  population   from original

seemly diffidence. It shows the population p, and the system S as they suffer attrition and replacement over time. The Us represent outside pools of education and training that stock or deplete the population over time. The double arrows suggest that the system feeds the population trained human resource and also absorbs it in the form of teachers and administrators.

There are deficits to fill, both to replenish loss in the system and the population and to provide for a richer human resource stock over the years so that growth and development are insured.

The planner could aggregate all of the deficits to a total deficit and thus have the total requirements. He could then program satisfaction of these requirements over the years from x to n. He would then have to relate these to input requirements. But the input requirements would have to satisfy the fundamental constraint:

$$\sum_{x}^{n} I^i \geq TR \quad \text{Inputs equal or less than} \quad \text{(total resources available for the system)} \quad (9)$$

All of this may have seemed perfectly obvious from the outset. The question is not whether any general model can be made an appropriate analogue of reality. More important is the development of subroutines and schemata that will make sense of the general relationships and indicate the need for valid and reliable data which can be used in the schemata. If this is possible, a large computer can do the rest, from view haloo to the death.

The first problem is the calculation of the output requirements, which will depend on the deficits; the second general problem is relating outputs to input requirements; and the third is determining resource constraints. Leaving aside for the moment the problem of making the calculations, it is appropriate to ask: If inequality (9) could be made meaningful, in what kind of a format could it be cast to make sense to a planner? The planner's game would be to optimize outputs, given the required input relationships and the constraints on resources. Within any given time period, the planner might not have the resources available to satisfy the output requirements, but he would do the best he could under the circumstances.

The minimal requirements in schemata and data have been outlined. It is appropriate to inquire, then, whether these minimal requisites for setting a planning strategy are likely to be obtainable. No general statement can be made for all countries. Pieces of the data are available in some countries and not so readily obtainable in others. But in principle they are all obtainable. If the schemata and data are not obtainable, there is not much practical significance in discussing a model which requires them.

Minimal Data Required for a Planning Model

The essential schemata and the data required for a planning model are:

Minima for Planning Model

A. Population

1. Census or sample survey assessment of human resource stock in starting year x.
2. Projection methodology that will show absolute growth of population to year n.

3. Projection methodology that will show attrition in human resource stock between x and n.
4. Methods for establishing human resource stock in year n, qualitatively and quantitatively and in economic, social, cultural, and and political terms: human resource requirements in year n.
5. Subtraction of 3 from 1.
6. Subtraction of result (5) from (4). This sets population human resource goal.

B. Educational System: Output

1. Status assessment of the system for output and input relationships.
2. Projection methodology to show output over years, assuming present level of intensity.
3. Projection methodology that will show attrition likely in the system.
4. Reduction of (2) because of (3).
5. Simulated output of system, given 1–4, and simulated input schedules.

C. Comparison Population and System

1. Subtract B-5 from A-6 and set up outputs necessary, given system and population goals.

D. Educational System: Input

1. Set program qualitatively and quantitatively to meet C-1.
2. Estimate costs of program by input-output relationships.

E. Resources Available for Education

1. Project product, income and productivity according to growth model of population and economy.
2. Estimate likely revenues from taxation.
3. On the basis of total revenues, estimate resources available for education (D-1) and strike best balance according to C-1 and D-2.

F. Readjust and Reprogram

1. By scaling down C-1 targets, e.g., educating fewer.
2. By adjusting D-2 relationships, e.g., lowering educational quality levels.
3. By increasing revenues and resources available, e.g., increasing taxes or securing resources from outside.

Basic to selecting an educational development strategy are: A-6 which sets the human resource targets for the population in future years; E-3 which estimates the resources likely to be available, the allotment of them to education (as an alternative to some other investment), and the allocation within education to specific sizes and kinds of programs; and C-2, the input-output relationships of the system, i.e. how much resource must be allocated to produce graduates to fulfill the targets or deficits.

A general model would associate everything in one schema, and by operating with this the planner could program satisfaction of requirements within the limits of resource. With the advances in computer simulation and the machine capacity that exists, some variant of the scheme advocated by Orcutt (1961) and his associates would be required. The use of simulation would have certain advantages over the use of mathematical models which require so many simplifying assumptions that reality is assumed away. The simulation model would require a status assessment of the population human resource stock in a base year, the population and human resource stock required in the target year, and a simulated output of an educational and training system sufficient to replace the wastage in the original stock and bring it toward the target population in year *n*.

When this is set up, the program would generate the numbers that the educational system would have to spin out in the intervening year to reach the targets, given the base year stock, the wastage, and the increase necessary to reach the targets. The operating characteristics would be the survival rates of the population classified by educational levels in the base year; the survival of educational cohorts through the system to various levels and their survival after entering the population. There are data for computing these rates and, in a very large population and with sufficient machine capacity, results that bear a fairly close relation to reality could be generated. Rates could be made to vary over the course of the run. Population mortality rates would be varied, just as they are in demographic projection, by studying the likely reason for vital rates to change. Mortality in the educational system would vary, according to assumed changes and improvements in the system. Certain model systems presently existing would provide the upper limits.

In human resource planning, because of the long lag time for education and training, it is not merely sufficient to know the static requirements at the end of some period of time. It is also necessary to know the intervening year inputs and moves that must be made to insure such output. This is the subject of the next section, Chapter IV.

IV

Flow, Output, and Strategies for Education Systems

A HUMAN RESOURCE DEVELOPMENT PLAN MUST ESTABLISH NOT SO much the total investment and output over a long time span as the appropriate sequence of investments of men and money during the plan period, so that the end product will add up to the required output. The long lag time between the entrance of students in the early grades and their graduation from higher levels is an obvious feature of educational systems. Students who are to be graduated from a 20-year medical training in 1985 must already be in the system in 1965 or must be already educated up to a certain point and be qualified to be fed into the system at higher levels during the intervening years.

The longer the time span, the less likely that fixed coefficients describing the status of the system at any given time will hold. The planner has the usual dilemma. He must make his decisions as far in advance as possible, but the further in advance he makes the decision the less reliable and valid are the bases on which it is done. Yet, planning over too short a span, e.g., two or three years, is not really to plan at all, because the central notion of planning is to promote decisions when choice is still possible.

The plan must also be checked and validated with the passage of time and modified before it is again pushed forward into the future. Planning is a continuous operation. Past experience enables the planner to go forward in terms of new information.

The planner faced with the time dilemma, must borrow the techniques of the demographer and projection methodologists. Instead of shooting to a far future date in one jump, the future years might better be broken into segments or steps. The methodology outlined in Chapter III is suggested. The planner should project a limited span of years ahead, then adjust and aggregate, and project on for another period. The planner then needs some kind of picture of the system during transitional stages, i.e., views of alternative possibilities in the system between the base year and the final plan year.

A Mathematical Model Relating Target Numbers and System Output

Mathematical expressions which relate requirements target numbers to system output can be cast in elegant form. Moser and Redfern (1964) offer this one:

$$\underline{n}(0) = \Pi^{-1} \cdot \underline{n}(t) \tag{1}$$

The sense of the expression is that the numbers in various levels and processes of the system at an earlier period, symbolized by the vector $n(0)$, can be derived from the target requirements of the system at a later period, symbolized by $n(t)$, multiplied by the inverted matrix of the transitional probabilities of going from one process and state in the system to another in a time period. The expression then offers a model for deriving the enrollments necessary at an earlier period, given the output requirements at the end of a plan period and the probabilities of going from one level or state to another within the system. In terms of Figure IV.1, the output requirements expressed along the right hand margins of the rows would be represented by $n(t)$; the enrollments in the cells at each level would represent $n(0)$; and the probability of going from one cell to another (or staying in the same one) would be p. This model relates final outputs to original enrollments by working back through levels according to retention or wastage rates, as in the simpler routines at the end of this section, or by using Figure IV.1 and varying the cell frequencies according to output targets and assumptions about wastage or retention. The continued product of the probabilities is Π.

Moser and Redfern set their model up to describe the system in this way:

$n(r,t)$ = The number of people in process r at time t.

$F(r,s,t)$ = The number of people who move from process r at time t to process s at time $t + 1$. This is the flow from process r to process s and the unit at time t is taken as one year.

$F(r,r,t)$ = The number who stay in process r during the period t to $t + 1$.

FIGURE IV.1
Flow Model for System Output Strategy

	x	$x+1$	$x+2$	$x+3$	$x+4$	$x+5$	$x+6$	$x+7$	$x+8$	$x+9$	$x+10$	$x+11$	$x+12$	$x+13$	$x+14$	$x+15$	$x+16$	$x+17$	$x+18$	$x+19$	
1	$1-x$	$1-x+1$	$1-x+2$	$1-x+3$	$1-x+4$	$1-x+5$	•	•	•	•	•	•	•	•	•	•	•	•	•	•	Σ_1
2	$2-x$	$1-x$	$1-x+1$	$1-x+2$	$1-x+3$	$1-x+4$	$1-x+5$	•	•	•	•	•	•	•	•	•	•	•	•	•	Σ_2
I 3	$3-x$	$2-x$	$1-x$	$1-x+1$	$1-x+2$	$1-x+3$	$1-x+4$	$1-x+5$	•	•	•	•	•	•	•	•	•	•	•	•	Σ_3 p_s
4	$4-x$	$3-x$	$2-x$	$1-x$	$1-x+1$	$1-x+2$	$1-x+3$	$1-x+4$	$1-x+5$	•	•	•	•	•	•	•	•	•	•	•	Σ_4
5	$5-x$	$4-x$	$3-x$	$2-x$	$1-x$	$1-x+1$	$1-x+2$	$1-x+3$	$1-x+4$	$1-x+5$	•	•	•	•	•	•	•	•	•	•	Σ_5
																					p_s
1	$6-x$	$5-x$	$4-x$	$3-x$	$2-x$	$1-x$	$1-x+1$	$1-x+2$	$1-x+3$	$1-x+4$	$1-x+5$	•	•	•	•	•	•	•	•	•	Σ_6
2	$7-x$	$6-x$	$5-x$	$4-x$	$3-x$	$2-x$	$1-x$	$1-x+1$	$1-x+2$	$1-x+3$	$1-x+4$	$1-x+5$	•	•	•	•	•	•	•	•	Σ_7
II 3	$8-x$	$7-x$	$6-x$	$5-x$	$4-x$	$3-x$	$2-x$	$1-x$	$1-x+1$	$1-x+2$	$1-x+3$	$1-x+4$	$1-x+5$	•	•	•	•	•	•	•	Σ_8
4	$9-x$	$8-x$	$7-x$	$6-x$	$5-x$	$4-x$	$3-x$	$2-x$	$1-x$	$1-x+1$	$1-x+2$	$1-x+3$	$1-x+4$	$1-x+5$	•	•	•	•	•	•	Σ_9
5	$10-x$	$9-x$	$8-x$	$7-x$	$6-x$	$5-x$	$4-x$	$3-x$	$2-x$	$1-x$	$1-x+1$	$1-x+2$	$1-x+3$	$1-x+4$	$1-x+5$	•	•	•	•	•	Σ_{10}
																					p_s
1	$11-x$	$10-x$	$9-x$	$8-x$	$7-x$	$6-x$	$5-x$	$4-x$	$3-x$	$2-x$	$1-x$	$1-x+1$	$1-x+2$	$1-x+3$	$1-x+4$	$1-x+5$	•	•	•	•	Σ_{11}
2	$12-x$	$11-x$	$10-x$	$9-x$	$8-x$	$7-x$	$6-x$	$5-x$	$4-x$	$3-x$	$2-x$	$1-x$	$1-x+1$	$1-x+2$	$1-x+3$	$1-x+4$	$1-x+5$	•	•	•	Σ_{12}
III 3	$13-x$	$12-x$	$11-x$	$10-x$	$9-x$	$8-x$	$7-x$	$6-x$	$5-x$	$4-x$	$3-x$	$2-x$	$1-x$	$1-x+1$	$1-x+2$	$1-x+3$	$1-x+4$	$1-x+5$		•	Σ_{13}
4	$14-x$	$13-x$	$12-x$	$11-x$	$10-x$	$9-x$	$8-x$	$7-x$	$6-x$	$5-x$	$4-x$	$3-x$	$2-x$	$1-x$	$1-x+1$	$1-x+2$	$1-x+3$	$1-x+4$	$1-x+5$	•	Σ_{14}
5	$15-x$	$14-x$	$13-x$	$12-x$	$11-x$	$10-x$	$9-x$	$8-x$	$7-x$	$6-x$	$5-x$	$4-x$	$3-x$	$2-x$	$1-x$	$1-x+1$	$1-x+2$	$1-x+3$	$1-x+4$	$1-x+5$	Σ_{15}
	Σ_x	Σ_{x+1}	Σ_{x+2}	Σ_{x+3}	Σ_{x+4}	Σ_{x+5}	Σ_{x+6}	Σ_{x+7}	Σ_{x+8}	Σ_{x+9}	Σ_{x+10}	Σ_{x+11}	Σ_{x+12}	Σ_{x+13}	$x+14$	Σ_{x+15}	Σ_{x+16}	Σ_{x+17}	Σ_{x+18}	Σ_{x+19}	Σ_{16}
						p_s					p_s										

The system can then be described by the numbers in the system and the flows from one process to another at different times, $t = 0, 1, 2, \ldots$. To bound the system within a closed population model, the authors consider processes which include people not in education. They must also take into account people who have died or emigrated and those who, by birth and immigration, will enter the population. Within the closed system are the recurrence relationships:

$$n(r,t) = \sum_s f(r,s,t) \qquad (2)$$

From the sum of the flows into any following process, one can obtain the original numbers in the previous process r.

$$n(s, t+1) = \sum_r f(r,s,t) \qquad (2a)$$

From the sum of the flows out of r, one can obtain the numbers in the following processes.

$$p(r,s,t) = f(r,s,t) / n(r,t) \qquad (3)$$

The ps are transitional proportions, i.e., the proportion of the number in one process who go on to another.

$$\sum_s p(r,s,t) = 1 \qquad (4)$$

The sum of the proportions equals 1, algebraically from (1) and (3).

$$n(s, t+1) = \sum_r p(r,s,t)\, n(r,t) \qquad (5)$$

The number in another process at a later time is equal to the sum of the product of each transition proportion by each number in a previous process at a previous time.

With the transition proportions (ps) for all values of r and s and t, and given the values of n for each r, and $t = 0$, the output of the system could be forecast. This is precisely what is done in the simpler models using rough measures of retention or wastage applied to entering enrollments.

The authors then rewrite equation (5) with matrix notation.

$\underline{n}(t)$ is the vector whose r^{th} element is $n(r,t)$, e.g., a column of enrollments.

$P(t)$ is the square matrix whose element in the rth row and s^{th} column is $p(r,s,t)$, i.e., a table of transition probabilities of going from one process to another.

$P(t)$ can be transposed to $p'(t)$ and:

$$\underline{n}(t+1) = p'(t) \cdot \underline{n}(t) \qquad (6)$$

A set of enrollments at a later time can be derived from the product of each transitional probability and the enrollments of an earlier time. Hence, in general terms:

$$\underline{n}(t) = P'(t-1) \cdot P'(t-2) \cdot P'(t-3) \ldots P'(0) \cdot \underline{n}(0) \qquad (7)$$
$$= \Pi \cdot \underline{n}(0)$$

The Π is the product of the matrices of transitional probabilities $P'(t-1) \ldots P'(0)$. If values of these probabilities can be calculated it is possible to solve for the original column of enrollments by inverting the matrix:

$$\underline{n}(0) = \Pi^{-1} \cdot \underline{n}(t) \qquad (8)$$

The solution will give the numbers that must be in the different processes at time $t = 0$ to meet the output targets specified by $n(t)$.

The problem is how precisely to reflect the characteristics of the population to which the model will be applied. This covers the processes within (e.g., sixth-grade student, 12th-grade teacher) and outside the educational system and the characteristics of the people found there which will influence their progress from one process to another. The authors are working on a model which considers 80 processes, two sexes, 61 ages from 4 to 64, 22 educational qualifications, and previous experience as a teacher. The number of cells formed by this cross-classification of process by characteristics is 429,440 ($80 \times 2 \times 61 \times 22 \times 2$). There will be, of course, many zero cells, e.g., four-year-olds with a university degree. The preliminary estimate is that the number of cells (values of n for each value of t) will reduce to 25,000. But for each of the 25,000 cells there are about 20 possibilities (of going from some r to some s) and, hence, a matrix of transitional proportions that could reach a half million.

If the authors' classification scheme were used, this would put the model out of practical range for present planning operations. Even if the computer capacity were available to handle such a problem, the system characteristics would change before the transition proportions could be calculated and imputed to the model. But a much cruder classification system, such as Figure IV.1, could be used and the number of cells reduced. Again the question arises as to how well this crude model would reflect reality; but that is a problem with any model and would exist even if one worked with a half a million cells.

A second, more serious problem is that the Moser-Redfern model has no feedback over time. A solution, no matter how laboriously derived (no matter how carefully transitions are estimated), would be based on the population and system at one time. If it were applied to the future—and this would be the sense of it—the flows would change, because educational systems evolve and develop over time. But how could these changes be worked into the model? In developing countries, the whole notion of planning is the building of a system which will change transition proportions. New levels and kinds of programs would be introduced during the plan period, for which no historical calculation base is possible. The proportions would have to be modified in the future, according to hypotheses about qualitative improvements in the system that will cause changes in the flows; but how would these be built into the model?

The model might be confined to subpopulations and to fewer levels and kinds of education. But closure would be affected.

Stone (1965) offers a flow equation for the system that seems to be more compact and less detailed and adaptable to computation than the Moser Redfern work. If the Stone model were applied it would have all of the difficulties cited. The same would be true of the simple manpower requirements flow model in the previous chapter, and the models in Chapter V. None of them offer the possibility of feeding back changes in technology that will influence flow in the system. This can be done in rough and analogous ways over the periods of the plan; but there is no way to formulate this for an analytic solution.

At present, in planning, one is driven to something even simpler, such as Figure IV.1.

An alternate possibility is shown in Figure IV.2, a preliminary flow chart developed by Cooke to study the flow-through in vocational education within a state school system. When enrollment numbers are placed in along the paths, the volume of student flow through the system can be assessed for future years; duplication of services can be revealed and the bottlenecks and dead-ends identified. The flow along the paths multiplied by the unit costs of following the paths can be assessed and alternative costings and output schedules drawn.

Figure IV.1 reveals in all its starkness the sequential nature of the decisions which the planner faces. The linear programming formulations in Chapter V serve to reveal the relationship between present and future targets and resources. Running the models in Chapter V will give the planner a long-range estimate of the feasibility of meeting human resource development goals, given the resources and costs. But if the goals are not feasible, *the only policy suggested is one of despair—that the goals cannot be met in the time period with the resources estimated.* And if the goals are feasible, the planner still must resort to a device like Figure IV.1 in order to time his decisions appropriately over the span of years.

FIGURE IV.2

Flow Chart to Facilitate Measurement in Manpower and Vocational Training
(proposal to the Commonwealth of Massachusetts)

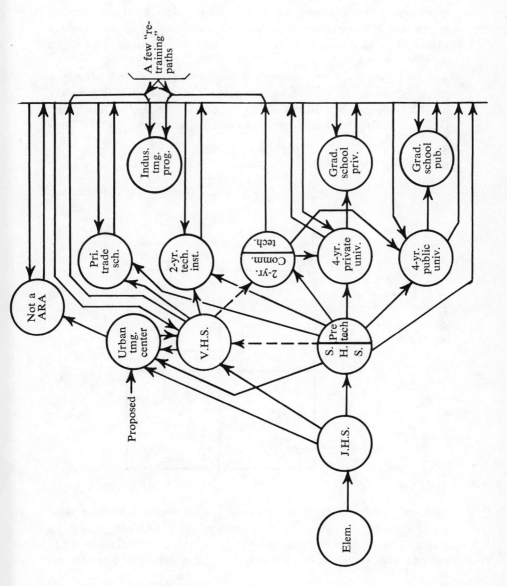

In Figure IV.1 the output requirements can be shown in the summation signs from 1 to 15 along the right-hand margin of the rows. There are, over the course of the years, several hundred ways in which the output can fail to meet the requirements, but only a few ways in which it can be made to meet them. For simplicity, the system has three levels, *Primary, Secondary,* and *Higher.* There are five grades within each level. There may be many other kinds of systems, public and private, and many more levels and kinds of educational and training programs which a planner must take into account, but for the moment Figure IV.1 is a model of the central core of a system. This offers complications enough.

In Figure IV.1 the number-letter combinations merely identify a group by its original year and grade at the start of the planning period. In order not to overload the chart, the flows were not put in; Figure IV.3, an enlargement of four grade-year cells, shows how the flows

FIGURE IV.3
Flows

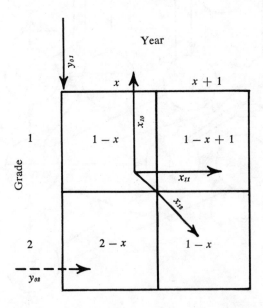

could be sketched. The group in grade 1, year x, can flow along three possible paths, x_{12} (promoted to second grade in following year), x_{11} (repeat first grade in following year), x_{10} (out of system through dropout into work force, death, or migration to other system or work force).

There are also flows into the system, initial enrollments, y_{01} (entrants into first grade) being the most common; but it is also possible that students will come in at higher grades y_{02}. . . . This is what opens up most closed models of the system and makes them unreal, except when one deals with a national system, public and private, with no external migration.

The planner starts in year x and forecasts twenty years to year $x + 19$. The output requirements along the right-hand margins of the rows can be set, as earlier discussion suggested, by incorporating economic, social, political and cultural goals into simulated forecasts. The educational planner's main problem is to schedule the system output to meet the targets. In the cells of Figure IV.1 the planner can enter the numbers who will complete each grade of the system during each year of the plan. The planner can also enter various flow possibilities. The planner may set up many different sets of numbers and flows in dummy replicas of Figure IV.1, and thereby schedule alternative possibilities of meeting requirements, given varying transitional possibilities in the system.

The planner may set Σ_1 and Σ_2 both at 0. This setting does not mean that no students are to complete these grades, but rather than terminal output at these low levels is meaningless. We assume here that a measurement of achievement in a school system indicates that students who do not reach the third-grade level do not cross the threshhold of functional literacy. As a terminal target, then, graduates of these two levels, and no higher, should be set at zero, and resources that are put into educating such students are in the general case wasted.

This may at once suggest a policy to educational administrators in developing countries: *the provision of first- and second-grade places in a situation where there is little possibility of opening continuing grades, e.g., in isolated rural areas, may have no beneficial effect and merely waste resources.* This situation is so common in developing areas and its consequences so patent that the planner may at least offer this suggested strategy: *All school units of less than three complete grades and where circumstances indicate little likelihood of addition of higher grades, might better be closed down or, at the very least, never opened.* This is an appropriate strategy, but for political and social reasons it may never be accepted because it is closely tied to the strategy so often adopted in developing areas of building from the first grade up, and hoping. More of this later.

The planner may not necessarily have to take into account all the terminal requirements from Σ_3 through Σ_{15} but select only significant terminal levels:

1. according to some measure of achievement, e.g., literacy at completion of grade 3,
2. or significant junctures between levels, e.g. grade 5 (graduation tion from primary),
3. grade 10 (graduation from secondary), and
4. grade 15 (graduation from higher level).

Two ratios may be of use to the planner in analyzing necessary balance within the system and in selecting strategies. These are $p_2 = \dfrac{5}{10}$ the ratio of fifth-grade graduates (primary school) to 10th-grade graduates (secondary), and $p_3 = \dfrac{10}{15}$ the ratio of secondary graduates to university graduates. These ratios can be used as guidelines to show whether the system is balanced according to final demand. Other ratios of equal importance are graduates of primary to enrollments in the first year of secondary (grade 6) and graduates of secondary to enrollments in the first year of university (grade 11). On the assumption that enrollments in the first year of secondary and higher reflect the number of places in that level, then these ratios are important for determining admission and expansion policy at the upper levels of the system. The opening of places in secondary and higher education can be regulated accordingly. It is highly unlikely that the system conforms to ideal proportions early in a plan period, especially to p_3. The planner must start operating on the p_3 ratio early because after 10 years in a 20-year plan period, the time has passed when the system output can be adjusted for this high level.

At the foot of each column are summations which indicate the enrollment totals for any given year. These are useful for indicating where adjustments must be made in the system and whether or not the system is falling behind any set schedule. Within Figure IV.1 any diagonal of grade-year combinations can be pushed forward to test for the feasibility of future moves. For example, if graduates of the third level are necessary as teachers in the second, the planner, if he knows the available supply of these graduates up to any date, can move forward and test the feasibility of opening new places at the second level in some future year during the course of the plan.

Figure IV.1 does reveal at once the appalling fact that, barring additions of students and resources from outside the system, the planner has only five years (from x to $x + 5$) in which to make the moves that will insure meeting the full requirements at grade 15, within a 20-year span. Even then these moves must be good.

If the planner is going to satisfy the requirement for grade 15 graduates before year $x + 19$, i.e., within 20 years from the start of the plan, he must face the fact that output at this level will largely consist of:

1. Students already in grades 2 to 15 with retention maximized.
2. Entrants into grade 1 during the year x up to $x + 5$, with retention maximized.

Beyond that the system is closed. For example, if the planner elects to open places at grade 6 in year $x + 5$, he will be limited by the number of first graders he took in in year x. If he elects to open 11th-grade places in year $x + 5$, he will be limited by the number of sixth-graders he took in in year x. Figure IV.1 shows how little freedom the planner has in meeting upper grade level quotas. Freedom starts to be cut down the minute the first plan year opens. After year $x + 5$ begins, the output of the system has already been set by cohorts entered in the earlier grades and retention.

The matter of retention is often ignored in educational planning. Flat or increasing rates are assumed at the outset, with no accounting for the fact that retention will bring increased cost, just as surely as the creating of new places, inasmuch as it generally involves improving the quality of the education (more favorable teacher pupil ratios and larger book and equipment allocations). In the upper levels it may entail the provision of scholarship and student aid. Working out the relationship between retention and inputs and costs is the heart of educational planning and is discussed in Chapter VI. Resource allocation for creation of new places may not be as significant as allocations for maximizing retention; and this will be shown. Progress of pupil cohorts through the system depends on promotion policy and retention. Later strategies will demonstrate that retention should be maximized in the higher grades of each level.

If the planner can fill numbers into the cells of Figure IV.1 so that the output requirements are met in future years within resource limitations, then the problem is solved in general terms.

At first glance it might appear that there are 300 actions (15×20) which the planner, beginning at the start of the year x, could contemplate taking, and that these actions could be combined into clusters of strategies. However, 109 of these are such that the planner has no control unless he can improve retention within the system. For example all the output to the left of the diagonal formed by $2—X$ is limited by the number who have completed more than one grade and are available to enter the system at some high grade or level.

Further along in this section, the projection models and methods for estimating the enrollments to fill the cells of Figure IV.1 will be offered. On the basis of alternate enrollment and graduates forecast, strategies may be devised.

One strategy has already been mentioned, that of despair: The planner can simply say that the system cannot meet the requirements in any foreseeable fashion. This is not purely useless information, however, and it may be sensible to accept it and plan for meeting the requirements at some future date. Or, requirements can be scaled down.

A second strategy is to accelerate progress through the system. This entails adjusting the program so that the same performance level can be equalled in a shorter time—otherwise it is like cheating at solitaire. It will also entail increased cost and a level of skill and sophistication greater than most developing countries possess. It implies selection procedures to identify those who can do the accelerated program and a degree of flexibility not very likely in the chaos or highly formalistic settings of primitive educational development.

Almost the same kind of strategy is involved in reducing the number of years required within the levels. It can certainly be done and is in fact done as an alternative, but in education the Hebrew aphorism 'nothing for nothing' is overwhelmingly true. Medical assistants and midwives and practical nurses can be trained in far less time than doctors and graduate nurses. In fact, for certain tasks in a country they may be perfectly adequate. But they are, in the last analysis, exactly what they are and no more, and the day may come when they are outmoded. They may be outmoded by customer preference. Patients may insist on having their wonder drugs prescribed by a man whose competence is attested by a Latin text inscribed on the well fleeced hide of a sheep.

Technicians rapidly become technologically outmoded. This is particularly true in industry, where short technical courses are given, rather than full academic, related, and shop training. Other things being equal, the graduates are not as readily retrainable as graduates with a sound general educational background. This is usually not a decision which the educational planner makes, but the implications of it should be clear to him. It is fundamentally important that resource requirements be expressed in such a form that flexible and retrainable graduates are produced. Spurious precision in manpower forecasts and training programs that hew too closely to what these forecasts seem to imply can promote dangerously short-sighted education policy. Educational systems should be arranged for maximum flexibility and corrigibility, with transfer possible at the maximum number of junctures. Currently, estimates are that engineers become obsolete, without retraining, within ten years.

This is the basis of the vast programs of continuing education run by large U.S. corporations and universities. No school system can completely forfend against technological obsolescence in its graduates, but developing countries can hold it to a minimum by avoiding shallow occupational specialization. Courses must offer a knowledge of basics such as skill in communication, mathematics, and the methods of the sciences, as well as trade training.

The strategy which most underdeveloped countries tend to follow, when, indeed, they are following a coherent one, consists of increasing grade 1 entrants and hoping for the rest. The planner faced with Figure IV.1 would put enough entrants in the first grade during the years x to $x+5$ to assure output requirements at each grade level before the end of $x + 19$. The essential moves are:

(1.) Given enrollments at the beginning of year x in grades 2 to 15, outputs of these grades are estimated up to year $x+14$, with some retention ratio calculated or assumed.

(2.) Sufficient places are created in grade 1 in the years from x *to* $x+5$ so that with assumed or calculated retention, the outputs, along with those estimated in (1), will equal requirements.

This strategy has some reason for being chosen. The opening of places in grade 1 requires the least knowledge of educational stocks within the population. It also requires, at the outset, the smallest inputs of trained manpower (teachers are presumed to require the least (!) training at the primary level) and minimal provision of books, equipment and facilities. There is even an assumption that pupil/teacher ratios can be far larger at these levels, although such experimental evidence as exists in developed countries does not support this any more than it indicates primary teachers can be less well trained.

The result of this strategy in developing countries, as even a cursory glance at educational statistics shows, is a pile-up of enrollments at grade 1 and sometimes grade 2. Teacher inputs are so skimpy in quantity (ratios) and quality (training levels) and the rest of the facilities and equipment so inadequate that first-graders enter, learn nothing, repeat, again learn nothing, and drop out of the system without attaining literacy. Inputs, thin as they are, appear to be wasted. One of the first moves for developing countries would be to clear the first-grade log jam.

The strategy of unlimited openings in first grade ignores a necessary corollary. That paths must be open to all of the higher levels of the system, and that the program must be of sufficient quality so that pupils are passed on to the higher levels to fill them.

97

Another strategy is to open places in first grade, but at the same time provide for new places at the entering grades in higher levels, e.g., at sixth and 11th grade in this model system. The ratios p_2 and p_3 are useful for suggesting when this strategy is desirable, but they do not tell the planner when it is feasible. There are two fundamental constraints on the creation of places at grade 6:

(1.) Previous graduates of grade 5 available to enter and fill any new places that might be created for year x.

(2.) Graduates of grade 15, or whatever criterion is selected for determining teacher preparation, who can and would teach in the sixth grade.

The planner can get an estimate of (1) by cumulating graduates of grade 5 for the past four years,[1] and subtracting entrants to six for the same period. The resulting figure represents a pool of potential entrants. If the number is large—and it almost never will be in an underdeveloped country—a proportion of it can be selected by multiplying by an appropriate p_2 ratio. This is in summary:

$$p_2 \left(\sum_{x-5}^{x-1} \text{Graduates } 5 - \sum_{x-4}^{x-1} \text{Entrants } 6 \right) \qquad (9)$$

Constraint (2) is much more severe. It will depend on the existing stock of qualified teachers and the output of grade 15 in previous years who could be brought in and trained as teachers. Over time, teachers who die or retire would have to be replaced. The number of graduates of grade 15 who could be brought in and trained as teachers will depend on the professional and fiscal attractions of this post in comparison to other posts in the work force which demand equal preparation. The adjustment of incentives is usually out of the hands of the educational planner. A common practice in developing countries is to reduce the qualifications of the teacher force or to hire people who earn the main portion of their income from other work. Both of these have harmful consequences, and the result may merely be the piling up of enrollments at the early grades of the higher levels (secondary or higher), as students enter, fail, repeat, and never graduate.

For the country that cannot import teachers from abroad but must stay within the limits of the output of its own system, a *perfectly obvious strategy is that a high proportion of graduates of the upper levels must*

---

[1] Selection of four is purely arbitrary but it appears to be the modal limit in which students stay out of school and then return with profit in developing countries.

be committed to teaching at the earliest possible point. This policy is almost always indicated but rarely followed.

In practice, the planner will maintain two subcharts which are very much like Figure IV.1. These are shown in Figure IV.4 and IV.5.

FIGURE IV.4
Secondary Level Program for Primary
Teachers (Year x)

$1x$	$1-x+1$	$1-x+2$	$1-x+3$	$1-x+4$
$2x$	$1x$	$1-x+1$	$1-x+2$	$1-x+3$
$3x$	$2x$	$1x$	$1-x+1$	$1-x+2$
$4x$	$3x$	$2x$	$1x$	$1-x+1$
$5x$	$4x$	$3x$	$2x$	$1x$

FIGURE IV.5
Higher Education Program for
Secondary Teachers

$1x$	$1-x+1$	$1-x+2$	$1-x+3$	$1-x+4$
$2x$	$1x$	$1-x+1$	$1-x+2$	$1-x+3$
$3x$	$2x$	$1x$	$1-x+1$	$1-x+2$
$4x$	$3x$	$2x$	$1x$	$1-x+1$
$5x$	$4x$	$3x$	$2x$	$1x$

Assuming that quality levels are to be maintained by the use of trained teachers and barring the existence of a pool of trained teachers in the population who are working at something else, the outputs of Figures IV.4 and IV.5 will control the creation of places in the system. Further, only a portion of the graduates are actually to be available. Many will not enter teaching. Because graduates can not be assigned to teaching, incentives must be created, and this is beyond the power of the educational planner.

When faced with a limited supply of teachers, developing countries open first-grade places with untrained teachers. There is a hope that these place-holders for teachers can be given special short courses and trained in-service. But there is usually no thought of who will offer the courses and in-service training. Ultimately the problem comes back to the outputs in Figure IV.5, and the strategy that the country should maximize the output of higher level teachers. If this is done by creation of places in the first year x, the country must still wait five years before places can be materially increased in Primary Teacher training institutions. It may be 10 years before primary school output rises.

Rather than create places at the beginning grade of levels, it is better strategy to maximize retention of students who are already somewhere along within the level. On practical grounds, it can be argued that the further along a student is, the greater investment he represents and the smaller his future cost. The statistics of developing countries also indicate that the higher the grade attained within the level, the smaller the probability of dropout or noncompletion. Further, the costs of education in the various grades within the same level are about equal.

No very sophisticated decision model is necessary to show the advantage of working from the highest grade down. In Table IV.1 and Table IV.2 cost, probability of passing grades and expectations are computed, based on a secondary level program in Central America.

Table IV.1 assumes that what is laid out annually to educate a

TABLE IV.1
Utility
(Based on costs and cumulated costs)

	Grade 2	Grade 3	Grade 4	Grade 5
Pass Grade:	210	430	680	940
Fail Grade:	210	220	250	260

student at grades 2 through 5 is lost if the grade is failed. The gain is the cumulation of the costs, in that a student who graduates from the fifth and last level represents an investment cumulated through all the others. A better measure of gain or return might be the net income differences of graduates as opposed to dropouts of the level. They would show an even greater advantage for the graduate.

Probabilities of passing or failing are shown in Table IV.2.

TABLE IV.2
Expectation of Gain (Utility Probability of Pass-Fail)

	Grade 2	Grade 3	Grade 4	Grade 5
Pass	.84	.88	.90	.95
Fail	.16	.12	.10	.05

expectations of gains are:

$$e_5 = .95 (940) - .05 (260) = \$763.00$$
$$e_4 = .90 (680) - .10 (250) = \$587.00$$
$$e_3 = .88 (430) - .12 (220) = \$352.00$$
$$e_2 = .84 (210) - .16 (210) = \$142.80$$

The situation can be incorporated into a full decision model, but the result will be the same. The strategy—expand in the highest grade—will dominate. The planner should keep in mind that expansion of enrollments at the higher grades means not so much the creation of new places as the improvement of the quality of education so that retention and number of graduates are maximized. This entails providing more highly trained teachers, better laboratories and libraries, books and supplies and, perhaps, boarding facilities and scholarships. If resources are sufficient to expand in the highest grade and still increase places further down, an examination of other actions is possible. It will still show that the next grade below should be expanded to the utmost, and so on.

Statistically, the strategy that entails enhancing and expanding at the uppermost grades within any level will always dominate but, because of practical constraints, it may not always be possible. Constraints which may prevail are these:

1. Teachers most necessary at higher grades (e.g., science teachers) may not be available.
2. Equipment and supplies may not be available. It is slightly more expensive to provide them in the higher levels.
3. There may be more plant space available at lower levels and, hence, the marginal cost of creating places at higher grades may be greater than the data used for illustration suggest.
4. Students who have completed their schooling up to that level will limit the number of new places.
5. Larger scholarships may be necessary at higher grades.

This strategy does not imply that it is always better to begin with the highest level in the system. Restrictions that have been mentioned in connection with other strategies, e.g., shortage of trained teachers, may prevent the opening of places at the higher levels and limit the operation to the first level. Within the level, however, it does suggest that places should be opened from the top, with the proviso that there is sufficient supply of students who have completed grades up to that level. This may be an acute restriction within a developing country.

In rural areas where student populations at the upper-grade levels are thin, the cost of providing upper-level places for very limited numbers may be very high. A concomitant of this strategy may then be creation of central boarding facilities, especially at secondary and higher levels, provision of scholarships which will enable rural youngsters to attend urban schools, or provision of transportation to central or nuclear schools. All of these alternatives may turn out to be very costly in a developing country. The provision of one fifth- or sixth-grade place in a boarding facility may equal the cost of providing three places in the first grade of an incomplete rural primary school. But the three places in the first grade may provide no meaningful output whatsoever, and it is on this basis—and not enrollments—that the measurement must be made.

One of the first places the planner should apply the strategy is in increasing the teacher places shown in Figures IV.4 and IV.5. The provision of places here, though costly on a per-student basis, may be a critical first step in long-range planning.

The strategy of maximizing retention at the upper levels may suggest two practices which are common in developing countries:

1. Sending students who have completed a substantial portion of their studies out of their home areas, and perhaps even out of their countries, for study. This practice demands sound testing, selection, and fair administration of awards. The student may have problems—social, political and work-adjustment—on his return, and the indirect benefits of having a teaching and research institute in the country may be sacrificed; but the solution may be the only possible one in the case of educating for critical professions with very high training costs.
2. Importing teachers for the upper levels. The importation of competent teachers will also tend to raise unit costs but it may be the only sensible practice.

The use of Peace Corps teachers in secondary schools and colleges has freed countries from the serious restriction on opening secondary-level places. While the cost of volunteer Peace Corps teachers is often higher than local paid teachers, the burden falls on another country, presumably more able to afford it. Missionaries have long provided the same advantage, but they should move ahead of the country's development, working at the higher levels rather than elementary, as the country progresses. A strategy for mission groups who want to stay, is to operate at the very highest levels of education and in the costliest and most critical branches, e.g., sciences and engineering. This will produce more graduates than converts and cost more than elementary school programs, but the organization is more likely to survive.

A model which shows how the system functions in the country as a whole is no substitute for the careful analysis of specific schools and places in all sections of the country to see where staff ratios and room use are lightest, so that places can be created and students admitted at the smallest marginal costs. For this, a distribution analysis of teaching staff and facilities in the three upper grades of each level is necessary.

In summary, the strategy for the planner between the years x to $x + 4$ could be outlined in Table IV.3.

The essentials of the strategy are to maximize teacher outputs and to maximize retention in the highest grades within levels. The cost per student enrolled will come out much higher but the cost per graduate may even go down. This is a strategy for developing countries that have expanded enrollments very rapidly at the cost of quality and real output

TABLE IV.3
Priority Table (Based on Strategy of Maximizing at Higher Grades)

Year	Priority 1	Priority 2	Priority 3	Priority 4	Priority 5
x	Max 1B $(5x)$	Max 1 $(10x, 15x)$	Max 1A $(5x)$	Max 1 $(5x)$	Max 1 $(9x, 14x)$
$x+1$	Max 1B $(4x)$	Max 1 $(\ 9x, 14x)$	Max 1A $(4x)$	Max 1 $(4x)$	Max 1 $(8x, 13x)$
$x+2$	Max 1B $(3x)$	Max 1 $(\ 8x, 13x)$	Max 1A $(3x)$	Max 1 $(3x)$	Max 1 $(7x, 12x)$
$x+3$	Max 1B $(2x)$	Max 1 $(\ 7x, 12x)$	Max 1A $(2x)$	Max 1 $(2x)$	Open 1B $(1-x+4)$ Places

Max 1-Maximize student places Figure IV.1
Max 1A-Maximize primary teacher training, Figure IV.4
Max 1B-Maximize secondary teacher training, Figure IV.5

in the system. For those few countries that have maintained program quality at the cost of holding down enrollments, a different strategy would be appropriate. There are few developing countries in this situation. For countries with resources sufficient to expand in both quality and quantity there is no major problem of a strategy: *The more the better.*

Measures of Flow and Output in the System

Before any strategy can be devised, the planner must analyze the rates of flow through the system. The analysis provides measures to evaluate the present and past efficiency of the system, as well as the means for projecting future output. Flow rates are necessary inputs to the Moser-Redfern model, to the Stone equations, to the manpower-educational flow model of Chapter II, and for work with data in Figure IV.1.

The flow of a cohort of students through an educational system is determined by retardation and dropout and, to a lesser extent, by death and migration. A rough measure of the output of a system is the number of graduates. The efficiency of a system may be measured by the number of graduates that survive from enrollments in previous years.

COHORT ANALYSIS. Cohort analysis, in which a group of students is followed through the system from entrance to final status (dropout, graduate, death, migrant), is the only certain way to determine flow, output, and efficiency in the system. Cohort analysis in a six-grade primary school system of a developing country may show that to produce 15 graduates (from every 100 entrants) almost 300 pupil-years of education have to be offered, rather than the 90 (6 × 15) that would be expected under ideal conditions. Hence, the actual number of years of instruction that must be offered in the system to produce a graduate is 20 (300/15), almost four times what the legal number of years in the level suggests. Not all of the years offered to the 85 who did not graduate are wasted, however. Those who attain more than third grade may become functionally literate, although the likelihood of this achievement —the real yield of the system—has to be measured in each country and often in different kinds of schools in the country.

Cohort analysis is neither easy nor inexpensive. Longitudinal studies never are. Following students along the tortuous paths of the schools of developing countries is incredibly difficult, given the record systems and pupil accounting that prevail. Hence, the few cohort analyses that have been done have often based on a very inadequate sample of the children who can be followed. One would suspect that the studies lead to overestimates of retention and graduation because the children who are easiest to follow are the ones most likely to complete the level. The rest disappear in a great fen of poverty and illiteracy where record keepers can not follow. Other rougher measures of the productivity of a system are used in place of cohort analysis.

MULTI-YEAR ENROLLMENTS WITH REPEATERS AND NEW ENTRANTS SEPARATED. If there are enrollments for a period of years equal to the legal number of years in the level, and if the initial enrollments are classified by repeaters and new entrants, then a fair approximation of a cohort analysis can be made. This approximation is shown in Table IV.4 in which uncorrected data from the Costa Rican national schools are used.

The numbers in parenthesis are those in enrollment in that year who are repeating the grade. The number of repeaters is the key element in the schema. One assumes that the enrollments beginning in the year 1959 represent the number promoted from the previous grade the year before plus the number kept back in the same grade from the year befor. The difference between the sum of these two numbers and the enrollments the year before represents the dropouts. Strictly speaking, this is not true because we are not dealing with the same cohort, but in a large system a fair approximation is possible. Three components are involved: students promoted, students retarded one year, and students who drop out between the years.

1. For those promoted from grade 1 in the first year to grade 2 in the second year, subtract the repeaters in the second grade in the second year:

$$40,283 - 8276 = 32,007$$

2. For those kept in the first grade between the first and second year use the repeaters in the first grade of the second year, i.e., 16,114.

TABLE IV.4

Approximation of a Cohort Analysis (Data from Costa Rica uncorrected)

Grades	Drop-Outs Enrollment 1958	Enrollment 1959	Enrollment 1960	Enrollment 1961	Enrollment 1962	Enrollment 1963	(1963) Final Yr. Pass
		2,104	*4,586*	*4,466*	*3,575*	*2,000*	*409*
1	50,225	55,210 (*16,114*)	59,875 (17,012)	59,811 (18,104)	66,010 (18,487)	67,363	44,871
2	37,125	40,283 (8,276)	42,582 (*8,305*)	43,394 (8,877)	47,008 (9,258)	51,794	38,202
3	28,383	30,975 (5,719)	33,091 (5,699)	35,712 (*6,576*)	38,662 (6,485)	41,806	31,273
4	20,611	22,621 (3,268)	24,038 (3,265)	25,761 (3,712)	29,028 (*3,579*)	32,531	25,036
5	13,867	15,598 (1,444)	16,986 (1,595)	18,321 (1,818)	20,352 (1,745)	23,643 (*1,631*)	18,831
6	9,886	11,328 (394)	12,355 (328)	13,451 (385)	14,938 (374)	17,062 (341) (*630*)	16,023
	32,007	27,392	22,049	18,607	16,721		

3. For dropouts, add promoted and repeaters and subtract from the original first-grade enrollment: $50,225 - (32,007 + 16,114) = 2,104$. The dropouts are entered in the top line.
4. Repeat the procedure with repeaters in grade 3 in the third year and get those promoted between grades 2 and 3.
5. The numbers on the diagonals are an approximate estimate of the cohort going through from first to sixth grade and graduation at the end of 1963. (The number 648 in the last cell represents those who did not get sufficient credit to graduate in the final exam. Apparently, about half, 257, repeat the examination to graduate.)

Conversion to Years of Education to Produce a Graduate

Table IV.4 yields the basis for computing approximate number of years of education which must be offered to produce a graduate.

Graduates	*Repeaters* (assume 1 year)	*Dropouts* (cumulated)
$6 \times 16,023 = 96,138$	16,114	$2104 \times 1 = 2,104$
	8,276	$4586 \times 2 = 9,172$
	5,699	$4466 \times 3 = 13,398$
	3,712	$3575 \times 4 = 14,300$
	1,745	$2000 \times 5 = 10,000$
	341	$409 \times 6 = 2,454$
(Total$=183,453$)	35,887	51,428

Dividing by 16,023 gives $\dfrac{183,453}{16,023} = 11.45$ years, approximately.

SIX YEARS' DATA BUT NO DISTINCTION BETWEEN REPEATERS IN THE GRADES. If the educational data do not provide six years of enrollments classified by new students and repeaters, (and many school systems in developing countries are only now gathering such data), a somewhat less accurate calculation can be used by following Figure IV.6. If the Costa Rican data were used this would mean taking the differences between grades and years down the main diagonal, i.e., $50,225 - 40,283 = 9942$; $40,283 - 33,091 = 7192$. . . . Summing these and dividing by 16,023 would give 11.4 years, approximately. The results are close enough to be useful.

This method requires initial enrollments in grades 1–6 over a six-year period and the number of graduates at the end of that sixth year. It is not as accurate as cohort analysis, nor as informative. A few students are double-counted, a few are missed, and some students are credited

FIGURE IV.6

Average Years to Produce a Graduate

(for year x)

1 Year	2 Grade	3 Enrollments	4 Differnce	5 Cumulative Years	6 4×5
$x-5$	1	n_1	n_1-n_2	1	$1\,(n_1-n_2)$
$x-4$	2	n_2	n_2-n_3	2	$2\,(n_2-n_3)$
$x-3$	3	n_3	n_3-n_4	3	$3\,(n_3-n_4)$
$x-2$	4	n_4	n_4-n_5	4	$4\,(n_4-n_5)$
$x-1$	5	n_5	n_5-n_6	5	$5\,(n_5-n_6)$
x	6	n_6	n_6-Grads	6	$6\,(n_6-$Grads$)$
x	Grads$_6$*	Grads$_6$	Grads		
					Total

* There are losses between enrollment in grade six and graduation.

An estimate of the number of years to produce a graduate is: $\dfrac{\text{Total}}{\text{Grads}}$

with an entire year of education when they drop out before this whereas other students are credited with a single year of education when they may have received more. With large enrollments, it averages out. In the developing countries, where students drop out, repeat, return, and sometimes graduate, there should be no illusions that the graduates at the end of six grades necessarily represent a surviving portion of the cohort in grade 1, six years before. However, the estimate is useful and simple to compute when data are scanty.

Failing six years of data, a fair approximation can be obtained with enrollments from one year as in Table IV.5. The use of single-year enrollments yields a less stable estimate than multiple years. But it may

TABLE IV.5

Approximate Method for Computing Average Number of Years to Produce a Graduate

1 Year	2 Grade	3 Initial Enrollments	4 Difference	5 Cumulative	6 4×5
	1	26,867	11,672	1	11,672
All	2	15,195	2,383	2	4,766
in	3	12,812	2,634	3	7,902
Year x	4	10,178	3,067	4	12,268
	5	7,111	1,624	5	8,120
	6	5,487	510	6	3,060
	Grads	4,977	Grads = 4,977	6	29,862
					77,650

$$\text{Estimated Years} = \frac{77{,}650}{4{,}977} = 15.6$$

be all that can be done with the data that are available or obtainable at reasonable cost in a developing country.

THE ENROLLMENT MODEL OF THE SYSTEM

In Table IV.6, enrollments for six grades are built up from ratios computed along the diagonals of Table IV.4. The enrollment ratio be-

TABLE IV.6
Enrollment to Graduates Ratios
(Based on Diagonal Enrollments of Table IV.4)

Grades	Enrollments	Ratios	Reconstructed Enrollments Target Year on the basis of 20,000 graduates
1	50,225		62,685 D_6
		$1/2 = 1.2468$	
2	40,283		50,277 D_5
		$2/3 = 1.2173$	
3	33,091		41,302 D_4
		$3/4 = 1.2845$	
4	25,761		32,154 D_3
		$4/5 = 1.2658$	
5	20,352		25,402 D_2
		$5/6 = 1.1928$	
6	17,062		21,296 D_1
		$6/\text{grads} = 1.0648$	
Grads	16,023		20,000

tween grade 1 and grade 2 is $\frac{50,225}{40,283} = 1.2468$. The enrollment ratios of each successive grade pair (down to sixth grade enrollment to graduate, $\frac{17,062}{16,023} = 1.0648$), are computed and entered in the third column of Table IV.6. With the number of graduates given as a requirement target from an application of the manpower schemata, the enrollment for all grades in the system can be simply constructed. For example, the enrollment necessary in the sixth grade, given a requirement target of 20,000 graduates and assuming the same flow in the system as the one observed (a dubious assumption for a planner), would be: $20,000 \times 1.0648 = 21,296$.

Changing Flow Ratios in the System

The object of planning is to stimulate changes in educational programs that will effectively change flow rates in the system. If the strategy of maximizing retention in the upper grades is adopted, the plan must provide for the assignment of more and better teachers; curricula must be strengthened and materials and facilities provided. The costing of these changes is the essence of planning. The changes will lower the ratios $D_1, D_2 \ldots$ shown in Table IV.6.

Planners have searched outside the educational system for parameters that will govern, or at least reflect, the way rates and ratios move. Enrollments are projected according to assumed or projected increases in product, income, population, and work force. These methods provide a certain amount of aesthetic satisfaction but they do not reflect the way governments and educational systems operate.

The flow of students through an educational system will quicken when the government adopts a policy, conceives a strategy, and takes steps to implement it. These antecedents, rather than movements in income and population, will stimulate increased enrollments and graduates in future years. Policy, strategy, and implementation will not conflict with political, demographic, and economic developments, but the relationships among them cannot be readily described with aggregate statistics and simple functions. The effects of policy, strategy, and implementation appear lumpy in the system and do not follow smooth statistical paths.

Table IV.7 shows the possible evolution of enrollments and graduates in the national primary schools of a small country. Behind this table are policies, strategies, and actions.

POLICY. In the country, it has been government policy for over 40 years to offer a complete primary education to all children between the ages of six and 14. The current primary day program has six grades. The country has not been able to provide universal, primary education, but it has moved steadily toward this policy goal. Currently, about 89 per cent of all children reaching school-entrance age are being accomodated in the first grades of national and private schools. Despite fairly heavy retardation and dropout in the system (somewhat better than that of Costa Rica shown in Table IV.4), the government has, over the past ten years, moved most over-age children out of the regular primary day-school system. Currently, children three years over the legal age for the grade—the age for grade one is 6–7; for grade two, 7–8—are removed from day primary and taught in afternoon and night courses where such facilities can be provided.

STRATEGY. The strategy adopted is to maximize retention and graduates in the day primary system. The target for graduates at the end of the sixth plan year is forty thousand. This number will meet the requirements for terminal and continuing primary graduates. In the country, completion of the fourth year of primary is equivalent to attain-

TABLE IV.7
Strategy One: Evolution of Enrollments and Graduates over a Six-Year Period (thousands)

	Year 0 (Existing)	Year 1	Year 2	Year 3	Year 4	Year 5	Year 6
Pop. 6–7		64.9	69.7	70.0	74.1	76.5	79.7
Admitted Nat. School 6–7		49.7	53.4	54.3	57.3	59.2	61.7
Admitted 7–9		5.5	5.9	6.0	5.7	5.9	6.1
Grade I	67.4						
T =		70.0	71.6	72.3	74.0	75.8	77.4
N =		55.2	59.3	60.3	63.0	65.1	67.8
R =		14.8	12.3	12.0	11.0	10.7	9.6
D.O. =	8.0	5.0	5.0	6.0	8.0	7.2	
Grade II	52.0						
T =		54.4	61.0	64.6	65.0	66.3	67.9
N =		44.6	52.7	54.6	55.3	56.9	59.0
R =		9.4	8.3	10.0	9.7	9.4	8.9
D.O. =	4.1	4.4	3.2	5.6	5.4	5.7	
Grade III	42.0						
T =		43.4	45.0	50.8	53.8	54.2	55.3
N =		38.5	41.7	47.8	49.3	50.2	51.7
R =		4.8	3.3	3.0	4.5	4.0	3.6
D.O. =	2.0	2.9	2.5	2.0	1.8	.5	
Grade IV	32.5						
T =		36.7	39.4	40.9	46.2	48.9	52.0
N =		35.2	37.1	39.5	44.3	48.0	50.1
R =		1.5	2.3	1.4	1.9	.9	1.9
D.O. =	1.0	1.4	1.1	1.2	2.2	.3	
Grade V	23.6						
T =		31	35.0	37.5	38.9	44.0	47.6
N =		30	34.3	36.9	37.8	43.1	46.7
R =		1	0.7	0.6	1.1	0.9	0.9
D.O. =	.7	.6	.8	.5	.7	.8	
Grade VI	17.1						
T =		22	30.5	33.8	36.4	37.9	42.9
N =		21.9	29.7	33.6	35.9	37.3	42.3
R =		0.1	0.8	0.2	0.5	0.6	0.6
D.O. =	.1	.1	.2	.2	.3	.4	.3
Graduates	16.9	21.1	30.1	33.1	35.5	36.7	42.2

T = Total   N = New   R = Repeaters   D.O. = Drop Out

ment of functional literacy. The objective is to produce at least fifty thousand students who complete the fourth grade by the sixth year of the plan.

The strategy chosen and the limitations of country resources imply only a gradual move toward admission of all children reaching the legal entrance age of six years. About 15 per cent of children reaching the school age are admitted to private schools. Over 95 per cent of these schools are run by the Church. Church policy and strategy are to continue absorbing 15 per cent in future years, expanding only enough to maintain the same percentage of the increasing population. The admission of six-year-olds is programmed along the top lines of Table IV.7. The top line is based on a population projection of children reaching admission age during the coming six years. Private schools will admit approximately 15 per cent of this population. The national schools, following a strategy of maximizing retention in the upper grades, will take 90 per cent of the remainder during the first three plan years, and 91 per cent during the last three years. The final target will not be 100 per cent in any case, as about 5 per cent of the age group cannot be served in regular day school programs because of inaccessibility or marked physical or mental handicaps. The country is obligated to serve this group, but cannot within the present period because of resource limitations.

IMPLEMENTATION. Action to implement the strategy begins some time in the middle of school year 0. Graduation from sixth grade is made virtually automatic (99 per cent), and teachers, material inputs, guidance, and student aid are provided to insure that this is accomplished with some semblance of standards maintained. The planning and costing of quality programs is covered in Chapter VI.

The flow ratios prior to year 0 are shown in the first column of Table IV.8. These ratios are computed from one grade to the next higher

TABLE IV.8
Flow Ratios of Enrollments from Table IV.4

Year −1 to 0	Year 0–1	Year 3–4	Year 5–6
1.274	1.248	1.112	1.116
1.124	1.200	1.200	1.198
1.227	1.144	1.099	1.042
1.192	1.048	1.051	1.027
1.151	1.072	1.030	1.025
1.064[1]	1.042[1]	1.025[1]	1.016[1]

[1] The ratio of sixth grade enrollments to graduates is within the same school year.

in the following year. The strategy entails taking actions that will affect mainly the last three ratios: fourth/fifth, fifth/sixth and sixth/graduate. To reach the flows mapped out in the other columns of Table IV.7, the schools must institute the promotions shown in Table IV.8. This requires the closing or expansion of grades in many rural two-grade schools that have dead-ended enrollments over a period of years. Even though the government moves toward this over the six-year period, political pressures will hold many such schools open and fairly large numbers of children will be lost at the end of the second grade throughout the period. Though the number of dropouts here is increasing over the years the percentages remain about the same; and, in general, the lack of success in this effort illustrates the fact that all ills cannot be cured at the same time. The paths toward improvement are quite irregular over the plan years, but the major strategy targets are achieved. The problem of rural dead-end schools is not solved in this plan period but, with the upper grade promotions at present levels, this may be an appropriate target of planners in the next period.

Estimation of System Output by Application of Survival Rates

Grade-specific survival and wastage rates can be calculated and used to estimate future output of the system. Estimation of system output is not a straightforward task. Progress through the grades is most irregular because of retardation and dropout. Few developing countries have adequate pupil accounting, and it is difficult to recommend large outlays for mechanical tabulating equipment when books, teachers, and plant are already woefully undersubscribed.

Minimally, the statistics section of the Ministry of Education should report initial enrollments (taken as soon as conditions stabilize after the opening of the school year) and terminal enrollments. Initial enrollments should be classified into Repeaters (those kept in grade from the year before) and New (those promoted into the grade from the previous year and grade). Terminal enrollments should show those who *passed* the grade and those who *failed*.

Hence:

Initial Enrollments (I)	Terminal Enrollments (T)
New (N) Repeaters (R)	Passed (P) Failed (F)

The enrollments should appear in an age-grade matrix, and be reported and published at the end of each school year. The collection, tabulation, and reporting of the data are not beyond the capacity of any school system in any developing country. Masses of other interesting, but not very useful, data are put out in such countries. With the minimal data, wastage rates (retardation and drop-out) and retention rates (survivors) can be calculated; future output of the system can be projected, sound promotion policy established, and qualitative improvement of the system planned.

For any year i and any grade j drop-out and survival rates can be calculated as averages of several years' data. There is a loss between the initial enrollment and the terminal enrollment which may be called a Within-Year Dropout and symbolized:

Within Year Dropout $= \dfrac{I_{ij} - T_{ij}}{I_{ij}} = 1 - \dfrac{T_{ij}}{I_{ij}}$ Survival is: $\dfrac{T_{ij}}{I_{ij}}$ (10)

Between year dropout has two components:

Between-Year Dropout (Passed)

This equals: $\dfrac{P_{ij} - N_{i+1, j+1}}{P_{ij}} = 1 - \dfrac{N_{i+1, j+1}}{P_{ij}}$ Survival is: $\dfrac{N_{i+1, j+1}}{P_{ij}}$ (11)

Between-Year Dropout (Failed)

This is: $\dfrac{F_{i, j+1} - R_{i+1, j+1}}{F_{i, j+1}} = 1 - \dfrac{R_{i+1, j+1}}{F_{i, j+1}}$ Survival is: $\dfrac{R_{i+1, j+1}}{F_{i, j+1}}$ (12)

To project enrollments for the first year beyond existing data:

First Grade

The enrollment in the first grade will be made up of the percentage of children reaching entrance age· which the country plans to take into its schools, plus the survivors from those who failed the grade the year before. This survival rate, calculated on the basis of past data for the first grade, would be

$$\frac{R_{i+1, j}}{F_{ij}}.$$ (13)

It would be multiplied by the Fails of the first grade, taken from the existing data.

For each subsequent grade, the enrollment would be made up of:
1. the survivors of the passed from the grade before in the year before.

$$\frac{N_{i+1, j+1}}{P_{ij}} \cdot \text{Number passed (existing data)}[1]$$ (14)

2. The survivors of the failed from the same grade the year before.

$$\frac{R_{i+1, j+1}}{F_{i, j+1}} \cdot \text{Number failed}$$ (15)

The enrollment can be pushed through, using the rates computed on past data and taking into account the percentage of children reaching entrance age who will, or can, be admitted to first grade. The formula will give slightly distorted results because of students who drop out for more than one year and then return. The advantage of breaking down the failure and survival rates into within- and between-year rates is that

[1] The existing data are the data on actual enrollments in the last year taken over before the plan period. The survival rates are based on averages computed on data several years prior to this year.

specific action can be taken to remedy the problem of the between-year dropout of students who passed. This problem should be remedied in any sensible planning strategy because it represents the loss of students who have met system standards. To secure the flows of Table IV.7, the unreal standards applied in the schools of developing countries would have to be relaxed. The standards serve no purpose except to pile up over-age children in the early grades. With a relaxation of the 'standards' and a rise in the quality of inputs, the children could be moved on through the system.

AGE-GRADE MODELS IN AN OPEN SYSTEM

The weakness of all flow models and rates which are not based on individual pupil accounting and cohort analysis is that planners assume a regular flow through the system and a closed school-age population; and this is not true of school systems in developing countries or school systems in subnational areas in developed ones. The whole purpose of planning may be to derive estimates for these open situations.

For example, when dropouts (and deaths) are calculated as in Table IV.4:

Enrollment grade$_j$ year$_i$ — (repeaters, grade$_j$ year$_{i+1}$ + new, grade$_{j+1}$, year$_{i+1}$)

The difference may represent dropouts and deaths and also pupils who have transferred to another school. The difference may also be influenced by retardees from some previous year who have been out of the system or transfers entering from another system. When enrollments are handled in the round, one cannot know if he is comparing the same populations in the two different years. When dealing with the national system migration may be a slight problem, although attendance rolls may be so inaccurately maintained that substantial errors are possible.

It is also commonly assumed that to project future enrollments and graduates one need only know the number of new entrants to grade 1 and the rates of flow through the rest of the grades. Actually, in a subnational area, particularly in the capital city, students may come in at any given grade. Hence, to project school populations for future years, it is necessary to know more than the number of children who will reach school entrance age (6 or 7 or whatever the legal age may be).

In developed countries, where progress through the grades is regular, and there is high correlation between age and grade, there is no major problem in estimating future enrollments for all primary schools.

In the basic population, the children are classified by single years of age. The children reaching school entrance age are entered, and this cohort is progressed through the grades.

In countries where there is not so regular a relationship, a different method may be necessary. The planner determines the percentage distribution of age-groups by grades and then multiplies the percentages by the numbers estimated in single age-groups for future years. In developing countries, however, age-grade distributions may be changing rapidly, and one has to take as a model distribution the percentages expected in future years. The usual practice is to take a stable urban school population as the model and move the situation toward it. In projections for Santo Tomé de Guayana in Venezuela, where there will be heavy in-migration of overage children from country schools during the next 15 years, the Caracas urban distribution in the present year was used as the model for the future year, and Guayana distributions were moved toward this.

The grade distribution of seven-year-old children in the Federal District in 1962 showed:

		Grades					
Age	0[a]	1	2	3	4	5	6
7	7	61	28	4			
8							
.							
.							
.							

[a] Estimated as residual from total population age 7 in Federal District.

The total number of 7-year-old children estimated for Santo Tomé de Guayana in 1975 was 12,850. These children were distributed in the grades:

TABLE IV.9
Grade Enrollments, 1975

Age	*0*	*1*	*2*	*3*	*4*	*5*	*6*
7	(897)	7839	3598	514			
8							

The same was done for ages 8 to 14, and the enrollments were totaled for each grade.

Derivation of Flow Rates through Least-Squares Analysis

Working with the Venezuelan enrollment data in Table IV.10, Durstine applied a least-squares analysis to derive flow rates through the

TABLE IV.10
Enrollments in Venezuelan Primary Schools (1957–8 through 1963–4)

| | *229,955* | *125,838* | *102,586* | *75,209* | *55,373* | *40,394* |
| | *242,203* | *133,325* | *111,314* | *83,882* | *61,751* | *44,691* |
	1	*2*	*3*	*4*	*5*	*6*
1957–58						
Total	262,072	143,962	119,029	93,196	68,576	48,276
Repeaters	75,200	24,374	20,980	17,213	10,933	4,770
New	186,872	119,588	98,049	75,983	57,643	43,506
Terminal = (260,981)						
1958–59						
Total	371,062	163,367	132,540	102,383	76,706	54,155
Repeaters	86,474	25,239	19,781	14,986	8,456	2,593
New	284,588	138,128	112,759	87,397	68,250	51,562
T = (366,094)						
1959–60						
Total	431,907	215,352	156,472	119,175	87,635	63,693
Repeaters	116,918	26,483	23,192	18,875	10,949	3,738
New	314,989	188,869	133,280	100,300	76,686	59,955
T = (428,763)						
1960–61						
Total	463,711	259,467	192,869	136,316	99,294	71,321
Repeaters	137,844	32,534	26,364	20,963	12,420	4,599
New	325,867	226,933	166,505	115,353	86,874	66,722
T = (463,063)						
1961–62						
Total	422,593	270,840	226,974	161,911	113,725	80,979
Repeaters	134,177	38,033	30,082	22,470	13,588	5,276
New	288,416	232,807	196,892	139,441	100,137	75,703
T = (424,877)						
1962–63						
Total	409,535	259,768	241,716	183,249	132,099	91,420
Repeaters	123,496	40,822	37,459	27,281	15,510	5,700
New	286,039	218,946	204,257	155,968	116,589	85,720
T = (409,249)						
1963–64						
Total	400,350	262,041	237,262	196,854	147,493	105,119
Repeaters	114,269	37,878	38,481	29,164	16,673	5,938
New	286,081	224,163	198,781	167,690	130,820	99,181

system. The basic data were seven years of Venezuelan enrollments, classified into Initial and Terminal. Initial enrollments were divided by New and Repeaters, so that a diagonal analysis was carried out, as in Table IV.4.

RATES FOR CONTINUING STUDENTS. Let:

$N_k(t)$ be the number of new students in grade k in year t
$T_k(t)$ be total number of students in grade k in year t
$R_k(t)$ be number of repeaters in grade k in year t

Then approximations for passing students would be:

$$N'_{k+1}(t+1) = aT_k(t)$$

In which enrollment of New students is given as a function of enrollments of Total students in the previous year. (16)

$$N''_{k+1}(t+2) = bT_k(t+1) + cT_k(t)$$

In which enrollments of New students is given as a function of Total students in the two previous years (the effect of retardation and exit and reentry over a two-year period are built in). (17)

$$N'''_{k+1}(t+3) = dT_k(t+2) + eT_k(t+1) + fT_k(t)$$

In which enrollments of New students is a function of total students in three previous years. (18)

The approach through least-squares is the usual one.[1] For rates based on two previous years the function is differentiated with respect to b and c, set equal to zero and the resulting two equations solved simultaneously. In the symbols used here, b and c are:

$$b = \frac{\left[\Sigma N_{k+1}(t+2)T_k(t+1)\right]\left[\Sigma T_k^2(t)\right] - \left[\Sigma N_{k+1}(t+2)T_k(t)\right]\left[\Sigma T_k(t+1)T_k(t)\right]}{\left[\Sigma T_k^2(t+1)\right]\left[\Sigma T_k^2(t)\right] - \left[\Sigma T_k(t+1)T_k(t)\right]^2} \quad (19)$$

$$c = \frac{\left[\Sigma T_k^2(t+1)\right]\left[\Sigma N_{t+1}(t+2)T_k(t)\right] - \left[\Sigma T_k(t+1)T_k(t)\right]\left[\Sigma N_{k+1}(t+2)T_k(t+1)\right]}{\left[\Sigma T_k^2(t+1)\right]\left[\Sigma T_k^2(t)\right] - \left[\Sigma T_k(t+1)T_k(t)\right]^2} \quad (20)$$

The rates for continuers between grade 1 and grade 2 have been computed in Table IV.11. The rates for continuers between grade 2 and 3 are computed in Table IV.12. The same methods can be used to get transition rates through all the grades of the system.

1. Taking the one year estimate for continuers, the objective is to minimize the sum of the squared differences between new students predicted and actual:

$$\min \Sigma(N' - N)^2$$

$$\frac{\partial e}{\partial a} = 2\Sigma[aT_{k-1(t-1)} - N_k] T_{k-1(t-1)} = 0$$

$$a\Sigma T_{k-1(t-1)}^2 = \Sigma N_k, {}_tT_{k-1}(t-1)$$

$$a = \frac{\Sigma N_{k(t)}T_{k-1(t-1)}}{\Sigma T_{k-1(t-1)}^2}$$

TABLE IV.11
Grade I Continuers[a]

Year	$N_2(t)$	$T_1(t)$	$T_1(t+1)$	$N_2(t+2)$	
56–7		242203	262072	138128	
57–8	119588	262072	371062	188869	
58–9	138128	371062	431907	226933	
59–60	188869	431907	463711	232807	
60–61	226933	463711	422593	218946	
61–2	232807	422593	409535	224163	
62–3	218946	409535	400350		
63–4	224163	400350			
	$\Sigma T_1^2(t)$	$\Sigma T_1^2(t+1)$	$\Sigma T_1(t)T_1(t+1)$	$\Sigma N_2 T_1(t)$	$\Sigma N_2 T_1(t+1)$
	$10^8 \times$ 8451.874	9542.940	8902.915	4639.669	4965.783

[a] rate of those continuing from grade 1 to grade 2

$$b = \frac{663593}{1389605} = .4775$$

$$c = \frac{63819}{1389605} = .0459$$

TABLE IV.12
Grade II Continuers

Year	$N_3(t)$	$T_2(t)$	$T_2(t+1)$	$N_3(t+2)$	
56–7		133325	143962	112759	
57–8	98049	143962	163367	133280	
58–9	112759	163367	215352	166505	
59–60	133280	215352	259467	196892	
60–1	166505	259467	270840	204257	
61–2	196892	270840	259768	198781	
62–3	204257	259768	262041		
63–4	198781	262041			
	$\Sigma T_2^2(t)$	$\Sigma T_2^2(t+1)$	$\Sigma T_2(t)T_2(t+1)$	$\Sigma N_3 T_2(t)$	$\Sigma N_3 T_2(t+1)$
	$10^8 \times$ 2522.433	3019.472	2744.001	2106.592	2369.086

$$b = \frac{69248}{186874} = .7971$$

$$c = \frac{2779}{186874} = .0320$$

Comment on the Method

Parameters for estimating both continuer and noncontinuer rates for the system can be derived. The data are based on only seven years of enrollment. These data are useful for diagnosing how the system performed during those past seven years. When the past performance is used for estimating future performance, i.e., when the rates are used to project flows in future years, the method has all the weaknesses of any estimation routine. The assumption is that the seven years are representative of all years and that the rate will hold in the future. In the rapidly evolving educational systems of developing countries this is a dubious assumption. Brown (1960) has shown that such estimation procedures work out fairly well in the more stable systems of developed countries, although there are anomalous years that cause instability. Brown used least-squares to derive entrance and flow rates for university students on the basis of past high school enrollments and certain national events (the draft).

The continuer rate is easy to apply to estimate enrollments for future years. It is applied somewhat as the survival rate in life table projections. Given the enrollments for Grade 1:

	Year -1	Year 0	Year 1
Grade 1	90,000	100,000	

Applying the continuer rate from Table IV.11, the new enrollment in Grade 2 for year 1 would be:

$$.4775 \times 100,000 = 47,750$$
$$.0459 \times 90,000 = 4,131$$

$$\overline{51,881} \text{ new enrollees}$$
$$\text{grade 2, year 1}$$

Total enrollment for grade 2 can be obtained by estimating repeaters as a proportion of new enrollment and adding repeaters and new to get total. Rates can be built up for each of the higher grades, and the planner merely has to estimate the new enrollments that will come into the first grade in future years, add in repeaters (as a proportion of new), calculate the total enrollment for the first grade, and pass it through the other grades with the use of the grade-specific continuer rates.

THE COMPUTATION OF FLOW RATES AND PROJECTIONS BASED ON EDUCATIONAL DATA

All of the methods for using flow rates to project educational enrollments have holes in them. Difficulties come from two main causes:

1. Rates based on past performance of school systems in developing countries are not reliable guides for the future. Nor should they be. The whole point of the planning exercise is improvements in the rates. The improvement cannot merely be set as some hopeless target; it must be accomplished and paid for.
2. Without individual pupil accounting and system-wide coverage the data on which rates are based do not permit the planner to close the system and determine the origins and destinations of all pupils in the system at any given time.

Correa (1965) has made an attempt to plug some of the holes by elaborating an enrollment structure built around a pivotal year.

FIGURE IV.7
Enrollment Structure (Correa)

		−5	−4	−3	−2	−1	Pivotal Year 0	1	2	3	4	5
I.	Total	T	T	T	T	T						
	New	N	N	N	N	N						
	Repeat	R	R	R	R	R						
II.			T	T	T	T	T	T				
			N	N	N	N	N	N				
			R	R	R	R	R	R				
III.				T	T	T	T	T	T			
				N	N	N	N	N	N			
				R	R	R	R	R	R			
IV.					T	T	T	T	T	T		
					N	N	N	N	N	N		
					R	R	R	R	R	R		
V.						T	T	T	T	T	T	
						N	N	N	N	N	N	
						R	R	R	R	R	R	
VI.							T	T	T	T	T	T
							N	N	N	N	N	N
							R	R	R	R	R	R

The enrollment structure is made up of those grade-year combinations that will influence or be influenced by enrollments in the pivotal year. If there are six grades in the level (cf. Figure IV.7), then enrollments in the first grade five years before (-5) will come in to the pivotal year (0) as sixth graders. Enrollments in the second grade four years before will also come in. Any grade-year combination on and above the main diagonal will feed into the pivotal year. The same is so after the pivotal year. Grade-years on and below the diagonal will be influenced by enrollments in the pivotal year. For example, first-grade enrollments in the pivotal year will be sixth-grade enrollments five years later.

The notion is that the enrollments in the pivotal year can be expressed in terms of the origin of the enrollments prior to the pivotal year and the destination of the enrollments subsequent to it.

Hence the enrollments in the pivotal year S_t could be described by two equations:

1. Where the students came from in the system
2. Where the students go

Students come from new enrollments in the pivotal year and previous grade-year combinations in the structure. Students also repeat in grade-year combinations that will carry them into the pivotal year. The total of these is reduced by the number who drop out and die before the pivotal year.

Students go out as graduates during and after the pivotal year; as dropouts, during and after the pivotal year; as repeaters who will go into the next structure, and as deaths during and after the pivotal year. Correa writes the equations:

$$
\underset{\text{(new enrol)}}{n_t} \quad \underset{\text{(repeats)}}{+r_t} \quad \underset{\text{(dropouts)}}{-b_t} \quad \underset{\text{(deaths)}}{-d_t} \ =
$$

Origin

(21)

Pivotal
Year   Destination
Enrol. g_t $+a_t$ $+r_{t+k}$ $+d_t^2$
$S_t =$ (grads) (dropouts) (repeats) (deaths)

Correa then constructs indices and flow rates to project future year enrollments and outputs in the system. Various indices are computed:

$$\frac{\text{Dropouts before pivotal year}}{\text{New enrollments + repeaters}}, \quad \frac{\text{Deaths, during and after pivotal year}}{\text{Enrollment, pivotal year}},$$

$$\frac{\text{Repeaters, before pivotal}}{\text{Enrollments + repeaters}}, \text{ etc. Once new enrollments are determined as}$$
a proportion of school age population in future years, the structures for future years can be built up by applying the flow rates reflected in the indices.

Despite the elaboration and the fact that the approach avoids some of the pitfalls in the enrollment analysis methods previously described, the model has limitations. There is no basis for assuming that the indices will hold into any future time period, but this is a problem common to any projection methodology. More interesting is the fact that despite heroic efforts the structure is not closed, except in very unusual circumstances. The circumstances would be found only in a country where there is no external migration and no other parallel system (e.g., private schools) and only at the primary-school level where all programs are of the same length. Otherwise the structure will be open. Correa shows dropouts calculated by the diagonal method, as in Table IV.4.

$$\text{Dropouts} = T_{ij} - (N_i +_{1,j+1} + R_{i,j+1}) \quad j = \text{year}, \ i = \text{grade} \quad (22)$$

This will not equal dropouts except in a closed, unitary national system where all programs within level have the same duration. Otherwise, the difference will be influenced by migrants, in and out, from some parallel system. The only way this can be ascertained is by pupil accounting, and if the country can afford this it does not need such an elaborate analysis. It can merely run cohorts of individuals through the computer. There is also of course the problem of dropouts who remain out more than one year and who may re-enter at the same, higher or lower levels.

For individual schools or groups of schools within a country, the method does not work at all because the structure can open to any other school, and the only way to distinguish between a dropout and a transfer is by pupil accounting. Insofar as the rates are used to measure the efficiency of the system, there is a vast difference between a dropout and a transfer. When planners project enrollments in a subnational school system, entrance and promotion rates can only be used as Whitla (1954) used them in the Chelsea study where a regular pattern of transfer had been built up between the parochial and public schools.

Measurement of System Output: Tests, Norm Tables, and Sampling Applications

Measurement of what an educational or training program produces is a formidable task. Planners use enrollments to describe the educational effort of a country. The number of graduates can be a measure of output, and retention rates a measure of efficiency. Retention and wastage rates are also used to project the output of the system in future years. Data on enrollments and graduates are gross criteria, indeed, for measuring the output of an educational system or program. A large pile-up of enrollments in the early grades may swell the rolls without making any improvement in human resources. Even the number of graduates at various levels is an indifferent indicator. Students may be crammed through the system without learning anything. To assess meaningful output in a system, some measure of pupil achievement is required. This measurement need not be made at every grade level in the system but it should be available at critical juncture points:

1. At third or fourth grade when the presumption is that the students who have completed this level have attained literacy.
2. At the end of primary school.
3. At the end of secondary school.
4. At the end of tertiary programs.

Pupil achievement may not be the only relevant measurement. Planners and administrators may be interested in assessing aptitudes, interest, teacher performance, or any of a number of variates that may be taken to reflect the performance of the system. Even if all of these could be readily measured and used to characterize the system as a whole, the assessment of the system is still being done indirectly. The criterion for measuring system output directly would be the performance of graduates in the significant tasks that they will take on after finishing their education and training. But this would be enormously difficult to do for an entire educational system and a country as a whole. Furthermore, the difference in initial aptitude (intelligence) would have to be pre-assessed and taken out by some such technique as analysis of co-variance, if the difference in later performance is to be attributed to schooling. But then, a whole host of social and intellectual characteristics, on which the school brought little influence to bear, might account for performance differences. Various indirect indicators could be found in the economic, social, and political behavior of the citizens who had passed through the system, but it would be difficult to attribute this performance to the schools. When faced with these facts, the planner is driven to rather sketchy measurements and no more than probabilistic evidence of what an educational system produces.

The performance of the school system as a whole is not readily measurable by direct means. Student achievement is taken as one indicator of the skills and knowledge which the school generates. In the assessment of achievement by a test, the classic problems of measurement must be faced.

First, the validity and reliability of the test are at issue. To be valid the test must measure what it purports to measure, i.e., performance on the test must be relevant to performance in the criterion situation. The true criterion performance is the economic, social, and political behavior of graduates. The test is at least two removes from this. First, the curriculum of the school is only a pale reflection of the life and work tasks of the graduates. Second, the achievement test is only some sampling of curriculum. The test-maker is forced to use indirect means when assessing validity. Independent judgments of performance of the criterion tasks are made and correlated with test performance. If there is fairly high agreement, then the test is valid to some extent.

To be reliable the test must, whatever it measures, measure consistently. Evidence from repeated applications of the test can be used as an assessment of reliability.

Probability theory and sampling models lie beneath the problem of reliability and validity in testing. The elements of the curriculum are assumed to be a representative sample of the universe of life and work behavior of the graduate. The elements of the test are assumed to be a representative sample of the curriculum. The criterion performance measure used to validate the test is again assumed to be a representative sample of relevant behavior. The results yielded on any one application of the test are assumed to represent the results of a universe of possible applications.

NORMS FOR MEASURING ACHIEVEMENT AND SYSTEM OUTPUT. The results of a reliable and valid test can be used to establish norms for the assessment of achievement of individuals and groups within a school system.

The norm table is a compilation of past performances of students who make up a representative sample of some larger population. The footnote to Table IV.13 states that the performances compiled into this

TABLE IV.13
Percentile ranks: SAT, *all seniors*[a]

| | Boys | | Girls | |
Score	Verbal	Mathematical	Verbal	Mathematical
800	99+	99+	99+	99+
750	99+	99+	99+	99+
700	99+	99	99	99+
650	99	95	98	98
600	97	89	94	96
550	91	80	90	91
500	85	69	84	84
450	76	57	76	75
400	65	41	64	62
350	50	25	49	43
300	32	9	31	20
250	12	1	12	3
200	3	1−	2	1−
Average score	372	438	376	385

[a] Based on a sample representative of all secondary school seniors.

table are based on a representative sample of all secondary school seniors. Presumably, these norms can be applied to an assessment of the scholastic aptitude of all secondary school seniors in the United States. On the basis of the tabled verbal scores, the expectation would be that 50 per cent of the boy secondary school seniors would score above 350; and 50 per cent below. If a group of secondary school seniors scored markedly higher than this, the inference would be that it was superior to the average.

If the norm table were based on an achievement test in mathematics, the same inference would be possible, i.e., that the group that performed higher was superior to the average. If that group came from a certain school within the system, the inference might even be drawn that this school produced a superior product. If another school scored markedly lower, it would be classed as below average. The first school could be compared to the second on the basis of performance of the students as well as being compared with a national average (which is presumably what the norm tables reflect). Holding constant intelligence and other characteristics that might be presumed to influence the result, schools could be compared for differences in curriculum, teaching, staff and program and some estimate made of the influence of these inputs on achievement. This is the subject of educational research and experimentation which annually generates a volume of results too large for any one person to cover.

It would be another matter, however, if the norm table were used for assessing the scholastic aptitude of secondary school seniors in another country and another school system. This could be justified only if the second country believed that its students were or should be like the U.S. students. This is quite a different and unwarranted extention of the use of norms, somewhat like the former practice of using external examinations concocted in the home country to measure the achievement of students in the colonies.

The more sensible procedure would be for the second country to construct its own test, demonstrate that it was valid and reliable for the setting and the task at hand, and administer it to a representative sample of its own students. The results would then be compiled into a norm table that held for that country. These norms could be used to measure the output of different schools within the system, or even to compare the achievement of the system as a whole in different years. While a school system has no external norms to apply to itself unless it is willing to make an assumption about the similarity or identity of its students with those of another country, it can profitably confect tables of norms for self-measurement. Norm tables may be compiled and expressed in a variety of metrics. A common form is that of percentile norms as in Table IV.13. A simple approach to the construction of percentile norms would cover these steps:

1. Selection of a sample representing the relevant group for which norms are to be used, e.g., a sample of all fourth-grade students.
2. Application of the test.
3. The number, or frequency, of students getting each score is tallied and tabled.
4. Frequencies are cumulated, usually from the bottom up.
5. The cumulated frequencies are converted to cumulative percentages by dividing by the number of cases in the sample.
6. Cumulative percentages are plotted against raw scores. (Usually it is easier to read high and low scores if the plot is on arithmetical probability paper.)

7. A smooth curve is drawn through the plotted points.
8. The percentile equivalent of a raw score (unmodified score taken directly from the test) can be read off.

Tests can be constructed and administered and norms built up for age groups or grade groups. Modal age-group norms far each grade might be useful in countries where there are wide differences in ages among children in any given grade. The modal age for a grade is determined by the heaviest concentration of children from that grade falling in a twelve-month age band. This grouping frees the grade norms from the influence of retardation and acceleration endemic in schools of developing countries. Norms need not always be expressed in percentiles. Sometimes, probability of success for each raw score is tabled. Raw scores may also be transformed in various ways (by subtracting and multiplying constants) to give them a comparable basis for system-wide comparison. Standard texts on educational tests and measurement detail the methods.

Sampling Applications for Educational Surveys and School Districting

Planners must often assess system-wide characteristics of schools through special surveys which provide data to supplement continuing statistics and censuses. The survey generally covers some sample of the school districts, schools, or students in the total system. The same models, error formulas, and sampling applications schemes that are used for surveys in any other field are used in educational planning surveys. Hansen and Hurwitz (1953), and Cochran (1953) provide comprehensive coverage of the theory and methods of sampling. From almost all countries, developed and developing, come useful descriptions of sampling applications that can be applied to education surveys. Indian sources are particularly good and a large series has been issued on the design, methods, and results of the Indian National-Sample Survey. Technical Paper No. 70 (1962) on sample design is most useful.

Sampling as a general problem cannot be covered here. Only features unique to educational surveys require comment, brief comment at that. An educational system does have certain characteristics which affect the kind of sampling plan that must be developed. First, in the construction of the sampling frame and selection of sampling units. In most educational surveys, the basic element to be sampled and observed would be a student. At the national level, however, it is not usual to construct a frame—list of all the elements in the population—using students as the one and only sampling unit. Pupil-accounting is at too rudimentary a stage in developing countries to provide a complete list of students, and even if one were possible it would not be the most efficient or cheapest basis for a sampling plan.

Students are, in the nature of things, found already grouped into classes and grades which in turn are organized into schools, school districts and even larger units. Most sampling plans take advantage of this structure and employ multi-stage plans or subsampling. Districts may be the primary sampling unit in the first stage, schools in the second, students in a third. In ministries of education there are usually complete lists of districts, within the district there are complete listings of schools, and within the schools there are rosters of students that provide the basis for the final random selection.

In countries where there is great heterogeneity among schools (rural-urban differences, ethnic differences, geographical differences, public-private and economic differences) all of which might measurably relate to the variate (e.g. achievement) to be measured, variations on simple random sampling models are usually in order. Since students are grouped into schools and in some cases this grouping is systematic and in other cases fortuitous, cluster and stratified sampling prove more efficient and less costly than random sampling of the individual students. Intact groups may have to be used, with later controls imposed through analysis of covariance. Sample size may have to be increased to reach the same level of precision.

Existing political, geographic and school district boundaries may affect the plan. Political subdivisions seem to be obvious bases for strata classifications, but they may not be relevant either as a basis for organizing the school system or surveying it. One of the great weaknesses of school organization in developing countries is the absence of studies and research on districting. School areas are usually made coterminous with political and geographical subdivisions, states, departments, and districts. This may make administration and supervision difficult. In countries with centralized systems, the communications between school and ministry are often fatally flawed. Ministry hierarchies are shuffled again and again and organizational charts proliferate, but the organization comes from the top down and rarely centers on the meaningful entity, the operating school and its attendance district. This is the major problem for administering and surveying such systems. Elaborate samples applications schemes are not needed. The Ministry merely needs to know where its schools are and why they are where they are.

Systems should be carrying out continuing studies of district organization patterns, and for such studies land-use maps are fundamental. Ministry planning offices should have maps showing population density, the location of residential housing (present and planned, according to zoning restrictions), utility extensions, traffic patterns, and natural barriers. On the basis of residential, school enrollment, and land-use maps, school attendance areas and district bounds and service areas can be planned. The districts become the basis of stratification for surveys. (Cf., Appendix K).

The Indian National Sample Survey attempted to develop a national multi-purpose sampling plan that could be used for everything from assessing agricultural production to surveying social and demographic change. Tehsils (subdistricts) were grouped into strata on the basis of contiguity, population density, altitude, and food crops. Large strata were later divided into investigation zones. If the educational planner can make use of a multi-purpose sampling plan so much the better; but the groupings might not always be the most efficient ones for an educational survey. So, too, educational surveys, carried out by teacher volunteers can often be used to yield data useful to economists, public health authorities, and public works and housing officials. The educational planner, who usually operates with a low budget for data-gathering, must be ready to run questions of interest to him on multi-purpose surveys that are designed originally for quite different ends. In turn, he may have to reciprocate by including questions in his own surveys that interest the economist or demographer.

It is impossible to provide a general plan for all school sampling applications. The appropriate one will depend on the characteristic or variate to be measured, its estimated value in the population, its distribution and accessibility to observation and the resources of the observers and the degree of precision required in the result.

Stratification and then random sampling within strata can, up to a point, provide more precise data than simple random sampling. But it is difficult to make a prescription for the most useful all-purpose stratification bases. For one country, the following model might hold for a survey of some characteristic of the primary schools:

	Public		*Private*	
	Rural	Urban	Rural	Urban
School Size (enrollment)				
Class 1	h_1	h_2	h_7	h_8
Class 2	h_3	h_4	h_9	h_{10}
Class 3	h_5	h_6	h_{11}	h_{12}

In most countries there would be sufficiently precise data to make up the 12 strata and determine the proportionate sample to be drawn from each. Within the schools there would be rosters that provide a ready frame for a random sampling from the relevant groups. However, it is often difficult to get data from private schools. Differences might

TABLE IV.14
Sampling Plan for School Survey

Enrollment Classes	No. of Schools	Enrollments	Sampling Rate Schools	No. Schools in Sample	Student Sample Rate	Student Sample	Rate[1] (Final)
1. 600 or greater	50	50,000	1:1	50	1:39	1300	1:39
2. 400–599	150	72,000	1:3	50	1:13	1800	1:40
3. 300–399	255	90,000	1:3	85	1:13	2250	1:40
4. 1–299	600	60,000	1:5	120	1:8	1500	1:40

[1] Combined probability of selection. For a variety of reasons the final rate did not come out exactly equal. Further, the plan had to be modified by introducing a later classification by school grades, but the essentials of the plan were as listed in Table IV.14. As with the norm tables the planner should move early to work up multipurpose sampling schemes and models.

not even be sufficient to make it worth using the Public-Private break-down. Rural-Urban in many countries, especially Latin American, might also be a difficult distinction to make, at least if official statistics were used as the basis. The school-size classes might take care of this any-way. Ethnic background might be more important. Hence a second plan might be more useful with nine strata:

	Ethnic Group 1	Ethnic Group 2	Ethnic Group 3
Class 1	h_1	h_4	h_7
Class 2	h_2	h_5	h_8
Class 3	h_3	h_6	h_9

Ethnic groups might be intermixed in the population in such a way as to make this a difficult basis to use. Ultimately, the plan may come down to a simple system in which only school size strata are used. The size of the school unit will almost always be a meaningful basis for stratification, being related to urban-rural, quality level, retention and student achievement.

A sampling plan used for a questionnaire on primary school students was a most simple four-strata plan in which schools were grouped by sizes of enrollments reported in the previous year:

Strata

Class 1	h_1	(p_1)	Class 3	h_3	(p_3)
Class 2	h_2	(p_2)	Class 4	h_4	(p_4)

Mass testing for the purpose of establishing country norm tables can be carried out according to the sampling plans that have been out-lined. Measurement of system-wide productivity, based on achievement, would still be a most difficult task. It would seem necessary to control at least for intelligence and motivation. The measurement of 'intelligence' has difficulties which are amply documented in other sources; the measurement of achievement need or motivation is by a projective test and a clinical interpretation. Controlling the influence of these variates by analysis of covariance presents no special problems, but the measurement of them does. As Guilford (1952) and others have shown, the common measures of intelligence may not be sensitive enough to assess potential creativity, and it may be these very traits that are most significant for future development. With achievement so difficult to measure on a mass basis, most planners assess output in mere numbers of graduates.

OUTPUT OF THE SYSTEM IN NUMBERS OF GRADUATES

The educational attainment targets set by the schemata in Chapter II express requirements in the form of numbers completing some given level and kind of education and training program. Number of graduates is the usual expression. Costs are usually reckoned on an annual basis for students enrolled, or students in average daily attendance or live membership. Converting from enrollments to graduates is not always a straightforward routine in developing countries where waste, inefficiency and dead-end educational programs (e.g. incomplete elementary schools) may bring high enrollments and small yield in graduates. Yet, graduates, or numbers completing some significant portion of education, represent one good approximation of system yield; and the huge numbers endlessly turning over in the first few grades without ever reaching the threshold of literacy may be only so much political or social camouflage—a cruel hoax in which politicians may deceive themselves as much as their constituents.

Discounting Nonproducing Units

The planner, working in terms of national requirements and public expenditures, may choose to leave no-yield schools out of his reckoning entirely, just as future public burdens may be reduced by the numbers that will be turned out in the private schools. The private schools reduce the burden by supplying a certain number of graduates. The requirements targets may be reduced by this number and, in the optimal case, public expenditure is saved. The education does not come without cost to someone but the costs need not enter into direct calculations. In the case of the no-yield public facilities, the burden remains and only the yield is missing.

The planner may separate the system into productive and nonproductive units. The output of the productive units may be fitted to the requirements and the costs calculated. The nonproductive units may be left aside as a social or political burden unconnected with human resource development. Many rural schools of one, two, and three grades produce nothing. There is no possible way for students to continue, and the three years of education usually do not lift the students into literacy.

In his analysis the planner should separate the productive from the nonproductive schools and calculate the costs and benefits separately. In the case of the nonproductive schools there are no clear human resource development benefits and this should be clearly shown. Sometimes this stimulates officials to extend and improve incomplete schools and to close and consolidate nonproductive units.

In the usual case nothing is done. So-called 'side benefits' are cited as a justification for dead-end schools. These side benefits are largely political rather than economic or social, i.e., some local chieftain is hailed for providing a school, even when it does not produce. Something is better than nothing. But the advantage of singling out the nonproductive is that it makes it clear that the provision is not without cost. Even such pitiable outlays as are made could produce more somewhere else. Some countries, Mexico for one, face their inability to provide primary education in isolated and sparsely populated rural areas and reduce their plan targets accordingly. Other countries close and consolidate, sometimes providing transportation or central boarding facilities. This raises cost but it also raises output to some meaningful level. An alternative is to select highly trained teachers who can handle more than one grade. A pair of skilled teachers can handle all six elementary grades between them. This was an expedient used in U.S. rural areas until recently. It may not even be out of tune with developments in team teaching. But the ungraded school teachers must be highly trained and experienced and few of this breed are found in rural areas of developing countries.

Nevertheless, the model for discounting nonproducing units is simple. The planner simply holds them apart, projecting no meaningful output from them. The costs are charged to political or social ends.

Transfer within the System

Figure IV.8 shows a systems model for the simplest educational situation. Appendix H, the educational system in Peru in 1961, suggests the vast varieties of programs that may be offered, even at the secondary level. The planner must have such a schema; and once his general secondary and higher educational outputs are set, a subsidiary round of decisions must be made. Here, the use of manpower requirement forecasts can be helpful, in specifying the kinds of educated and trained people required. But the estimates can also beget decisions which will bring a certain amount of inflexibility and irreversibility into a system. Once a student is forced too far down one track or stream in the educational system, it may be difficult to turn him toward another higher goal for which he may subsequently acquire new confidence based on hitherto undreamed of aptitudes and possibilities.

In developing countries a common and basic preparation should be offered, at least up through the eighth or ninth year of education. After that, there should be provision for transfer of able individuals from one track or program to another. The comprehensive high school (preparatory, commercial, technical-vocational tracks) offers more flexibility than specialized secondary schools, if only because internal transfers may be easier than transfers from one school to another. Space does not permit a treatise on balancing specialization and flexibility in

FIGURE IV.8
Model of the Educational System by Levels (Simplified)

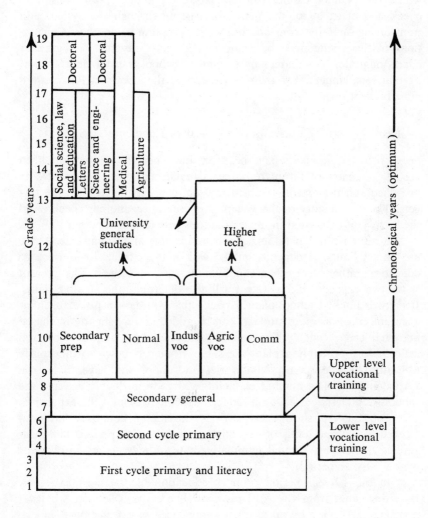

secondary and higher education. The working out of this depends on a great many individual decisions by teachers, administrators and pupils, which the planner cannot foresee. However, a plan must constantly check and chart all of the paths for passing through the system and transferring laterally from one branch or program to another. Calculations of this traffic must be made in the same way the demographer charts migration in subareas of a country. School transfer data are important for planners. The paths suggested by the arrows in Figure IV.8 must be kept open.

LIMITS ON THE EXPANSION OF OUTPUT IN EDUCATIONAL SYSTEMS

When requirements have been set and when this output has been costed, estimates of future resources (human and fiscal) will serve as one check on the extent which the system can expand to meet the targets. The past history of the system itself serves as another check. And the history of expansion in other countries provides yet another.

A nation can expand its schools at any rate and to any size. There are no set limits. It depends on the will of the citizens to sacrifice to education rather than other equally necessary objectives. The present status and capacity of the system will also determine the possible limits. If there is unfilled school plant capacity this will have a powerful influence, inasmuch as more students can be added at very slightly increased marginal cost. Roughly this can be estimated by classroom to pupil ratios. More probably a plant-use survey that gets down to the hourly utilization of classrooms, laboratories and shops will have to be run (Appendix P). The number of facilities already in double use and the schools and classes already on reduced sessions will limit the expansion.

Table IV.15 shows how various developing countries have expanded their three levels of education over a 10-year period. The measure is the average annual cumulative rate of increase in enrollments over a 10-year period.

In the 10-year period primary education has been expanded by rates that range from 4.4 to 12 per cent. The entire collection, whatever it means, expanded by an average annual rate of 8.9 per cent, in primary. In secondary the range was from 5.3 to 20 per cent, with a conglomerate average of 16 per cent. At the higher level the fluctuation was very wide, ranging from 3.2 to 27 with a general average of 16 per cent.

A country could use these rates, as rough outside limits, but some important cautions are in order. The measure used is, of course, dependent on the size of the base from which expansion began. The coun-

TABLE IV.15
Growth in Various Developing Country Systems During Assorted Ten-Year Spans

Country	Primary Enrollments		Cum. Annual Increase	Secondary Enrollments		Cum. Annual Increase	Higher Enrollments		Cum. Annual Increase
	Period t	Period t+10	r	Period t	Period t+10	r	Period t	Period t+10	r
Algeria 1950–1960	362,336	738,391	8.1%	30,318	81,230	10.4%	4,563	7,769	5.5%
Cambodia 1950–1960	173,269	533,892	11.9%	3,548	21,862	20.0%	81	886	27.0%
Costa Rica 1951–1961	129,422	207,653	4.9%	6,562	29,226	16.1%	1,416	4,203	11.5%
Iran 1950–1960	756,683	1,431,626	6.6%	49,553	279,741	18.9%	5,624	19,815	13.4%
Nigeria 1949–1959	933,333	2,775,938	11.5%	23,358	111,868	16.9%	293	1,978	21.0%
Paraguay 1950–1960	195,607	301,711	4.4%	8,000	13,427	5.3%	1,651	3,329	7.3%
Saudi-Arabia 1949–1959	27,712	85,847	12.0%	1,116	5,726	17.8%	25	206	24.0%
Sierra Leone 1951–1961	37,297	91,895	9.5%	2,709	8,753	12.5%	246	348	3.5%
Uganda 1950–1960	299,119	532,918	6.0%	6,453	31,285[1]	17.1%	231	913	14.7%
Tunisia 1951–1961	168,563	483,837	11.1%	12,942	55,537	15.7%	1,595	2,200	3.2%
TOTALS:	3,083,341	7,233,708	8.9%	144,559	638,705	16 %	15,725	41,647	10.0%

[1] These enrollments may be inflated by inclusion of certain two year post-primary schools that would not normally be classed as secondary.

try that went from 81 enrolled in third-level education to 886, shows the highest rate, even though this expansion could represent the establishment of one less than full-scale institution.

A country, to use this kind of a measure, should study countries which have an initial enrollments about equal to its own. All the other factors that influence expansion would have to be considered. Only then might there be some normative significance. But the weakness of measuring system output by mere enrollments has been explored. Even if these international data were accurate, and they often aren't, numerical increase could mean very little. The quality of the product is the all-important criterion.

V

MODELS FOR HUMAN RESOURCE
DEVELOPMENT PLANNING

VARIOUS POINTS OF DEPARTURE ARE POSSIBLE IN HUMAN RESOURCE development. The election of a point of departure will influence the choice of a model. Selection of a point of departure will depend on the viewpoint of the planner, the political, social, and economic goals of the country, and, for mean but practical reasons, the data available when planning commences. Three general kinds of models are discussed here to exemplify but by no means exhaust the possibilities:

1. Departure from a set of political, cultural, or social goals which state that some specified portion of the population has a right to some specified amount of education and training;
2. Departure from estimates of the resources (human and fiscal) available for assignment to education and training so that returns are maximized.
3. Departure from a set of human resource requirements or targets in the work force. The objective is to equal or exceed the targets with allocations minimized.

Planning might better be approached from all three bases simultaneously, i.e., the number entitled to demand education, the number that must be educated and trained in the work force, and the resources available for allocation to education and training. At the moment there is no model for handling all of these factors simultaneously. Educational administrators have been criticized for handling planning on a partial and project related basis. In view of the limitations on existing models and the fact that the administrators are directing schools that are open and running, it is *mirabile dictu* that educational programs are planned and run as well as they are. The intuition of educational practitioners should never be sacrificed to the tuition of a tight model. The model can clarify creative programming; it can not substitute for it.

MODELS BASED ON POLITICAL AND SOCIAL GOALS

A statement of political and social goals, in which some portion of the population is said to have the right to a specified amount of education and training, may serve as the basis for a human resource development model. These models serve to give an estimate of the gap to be filled, i.e., the number of people in various age groups that must be given education if the promissory statement is to be fulfilled in the country.

The statement that all children within certain specified ages are to be given a primary education illustrates the basis for this kind of planning model. Inasmuch as the calculations and projections of the gap will be based on populations, the first requisites are:

1. Calculation of the population and projection of it between years *x* and *n* of the plan:

$$P_x \longrightarrow P_n$$

2. Calculation and projection of the population in the relevant age group. In this case the plan is universal primary education and the relevant age group is that specified for primary education, e.g., 6–13 or 7–14, or however it is fixed by law. A projection of the relevant age-group then is calculated, based on the general population:

$$P'_x \longrightarrow P'_n \quad P' = \text{population 6-13}$$

The gap is symbolized:

$$G = (P' - P'_c) - (E - L) - 0 \tag{1}$$

where:

P' = population in primary age group

P'_c = population in primary age group who have already completed primary

E = primary school enrollments

L = enrollments in primary school, over-age (e.g., 13+)

O = children in school age attending other than public primary schools, e.g., private

An example of this relationship with Costa Rican data (in thousands):

TABLE V.1
Enrollment Deficit in Costa Rican Schools

P'	P'_c	$P' - P'_c$	E	L	$E - L$	O	G
267.7	10.0	257.7	221.0	11.2	209.8	8.9	39.0

	d_1		d_2			

YEARS

Grades	x_c	x_1	x_2	x_3	x_4	x_5
I	Q_0 66.6	Q_1	Q_2	Q_3	Q_4	Q_5
II	R_0 47.7	Q_0	Q_1	Q_2	Q_3	Q_4
III	S_0 39.4	R_0	Q_0	Q_1	Q_2	Q_3
IV	T_0 30.0	S_0	R_0	Q_0	Q_1	Q_2
V	U_0 21.3	T_0	S_0	R_0	Q_0	Q_1
VI	V_0 16.0	U_0	T_0	S_0	R_0	Q_0
L_0	11.2	L_1	L_2	L_3	L_4	L_5
$.e_0$	209.8	e_1	e_2	e_3	e_4	e_5

Using the format of Table V.1, the planner could project enrollments for the next five years, i.e., x_1 through x_5.

The vector of enrollments, e (from year x_1 to year x_5), based on a policy of giving all children in school age primary education can be symbolized:

$$\underline{e} = A_1 \cdot \underline{Q} + \underline{S} - \underline{L} \qquad (2)$$

Here, A_1 is a matrix of transitional probabilities between years and grades. Assume that all transitional probabilities would be 1, i.e., there would be no wastage within the system. Q is a vector of first grade enrollments. Assume that all children reaching the legal entering age (six) would be admitted to first grade. S would be a vector of enrollments shown along and below the diagonal, after year 0, in Correa's enrollment structure discussed in Chapter IV. The S vector would be:

$$
\begin{bmatrix} S_5 \\ S_4 \\ S_3 \\ S_2 \\ S_1 \end{bmatrix}
\qquad
\begin{aligned}
S_5 &= Q_0 \\
S_4 &= Q_0 + R_0 \\
S_3 &= Q_0 + R_0 + S_0 \\
S_2 &= Q_0 + R_0 + S_0 + T_0 \\
S_1 &= Q_0 + R_0 + S_0 + T_0 + U_0
\end{aligned}
\qquad (3)
$$

S would be known from the base year, (c.f., Table V.1) and the assumption is that there is no loss during the five years. The vector L would be the over-age children in each year, x_1 through x_5. CEPAL planners show the situation in a form similar to this:

$$
I \quad
\begin{bmatrix} e_5 \\ e_4 \\ e_3 \\ e_2 \\ e_1 \end{bmatrix}
=
\overset{A_1}{\begin{bmatrix}
1 & 1 & 1 & 1 & 1 \\
0 & 1 & 1 & 1 & 1 \\
0 & 0 & 1 & 1 & 1 \\
0 & 0 & 0 & 1 & 1 \\
0 & 0 & 0 & 0 & 1
\end{bmatrix}}
\cdot
\overset{Q}{\begin{bmatrix} Q_5 \\ Q_4 \\ Q_3 \\ Q_2 \\ Q_1 \end{bmatrix}}
+
\overset{S}{\begin{bmatrix} S_5 \\ S_4 \\ S_3 \\ S_2 \\ S_1 \end{bmatrix}}
-
\overset{L}{\begin{bmatrix} L_5 \\ L_4 \\ L_3 \\ L_2 \\ L_1 \end{bmatrix}}
$$

Even on the unreal assumption that there was no wastage (all 1s in the matrix) and that the vector Q of entrants could either be solved for by inverting the matrix or set so that all children coming to the age of six would be admitted, this model is not easy to work. First the O in the original formula (school-age children enrolled in private schools) would have to be known and another vector added to the left of L prefixed by a minus sign:

$$
-\begin{bmatrix} O_5 \\ O_4 \\ O_3 \\ O_2 \\ O_1 \end{bmatrix}
$$

Or, the children in both public and private school systems could be combined and one enrollment forecast made for both, irrespective of private or public status. In that case, O could go out of the original formula (1).

This implies that not only would enrollments have to be projected in nonpublic schools, but that the enrollments that represent school-age, rather than over-age children, would have to be determined. This task is more difficult than projecting the public school provisional enrollments in the first place.

A second major difficulty is in the L (over-age enrollments in public schools by years). The L could be determined if:

1. A policy was adopted that no more over-age children would be admitted to the system.
2. The planners would construct an age-grade matrix for the system so that L could be calculated from:

$$\begin{bmatrix} L_5 \\ L_4 \\ L_3 \\ L_2 \\ L_1 \end{bmatrix} = \begin{bmatrix} L_4 - L_{c_5} + L'_5 \\ L_3 - L_{c_4} + L'_4 \\ L_2 - L_{c_3} + L'_3 \\ L_1 - L_{c_2} + L'_2 \\ L_0 - L_{c_1} + L'_1 \end{bmatrix} \qquad (4)$$

L_0 = number over-age known in base year

$L_{c_{j+1}}$ = number over-age completing school before year $j+1$

L'_{j+1} = number coming into over-age status before year $j+1$

This is clearly not an easy estimation to make.

The provisional enrollments e calculated in I can be used to project the enrollment gap for future years.

From:

$$\text{I} \qquad \begin{bmatrix} e_5 \\ e_4 \\ e_3 \\ e_2 \\ e_1 \end{bmatrix} = \overset{A_1}{\begin{bmatrix} 1 & 1 & 1 & 1 & 1 \\ 0 & 1 & 1 & 1 & 1 \\ 0 & 0 & 1 & 1 & 1 \\ 0 & 0 & 0 & 1 & 1 \\ 0 & 0 & 0 & 0 & 1 \end{bmatrix}} \cdot \begin{bmatrix} Q_5 \\ Q_4 \\ Q_3 \\ Q_2 \\ Q_1 \end{bmatrix} + \begin{bmatrix} S_5 \\ S_4 \\ S_3 \\ S_2 \\ S_1 \end{bmatrix} - \begin{bmatrix} L_5 \\ L_4 \\ L_3 \\ L_2 \\ L_1 \end{bmatrix}$$

Subtract:

$$\text{II} \qquad \begin{bmatrix} E_5 \\ E_4 \\ E_3 \\ E_2 \\ E_1 \end{bmatrix} = \overset{A_2}{\begin{bmatrix} 1 & a_{25} & a_{35} & a_{45} & a_{55} \\ 0 & 1 & a_{24} & a_{34} & a_{44} \\ 0 & 0 & 1 & a_{23} & a_{33} \\ 0 & 0 & 0 & 1 & a_{22} \\ 0 & 0 & 0 & 0 & 1 \end{bmatrix}} \cdot \begin{bmatrix} Q_5 \\ Q_4 \\ Q_3 \\ Q_2 \\ Q_1 \end{bmatrix} + \begin{bmatrix} S'_5 \\ S'_4 \\ S'_3 \\ S'_2 \\ S'_1 \end{bmatrix} - \begin{bmatrix} N_5 \\ N_4 \\ N_3 \\ N_2 \\ N_1 \end{bmatrix} - \begin{bmatrix} L_5 \\ L_4 \\ L_3 \\ L_2 \\ L_1 \end{bmatrix}$$

In II, the original enrollment vector Q is multiplied by survival rates, the as. In the survival rates, the first subscript stands for the grade and the second, the year. Thus a_{25} is the survival to the second grade in the fifth year, a_{55} is the survival (first to fifth grade) to the fifth grade in the fifth year. This is not the conventional way of calculating survival. The rate is subtracted from 1 to get the complement, i.e., drop-out rates. Survival rates are calculated here on that portion of the original cohort (Q) that survives to the year indicated by the final subscript.

If the first grade enrollment were 50,000, and four years later the enrollment in fifth grade were 40,000, then $a_{55} = \dfrac{40{,}000}{50{,}000} = .80$. This would, of course, be only an approximation because of retardation in the system and instability in the size of entering cohorts over the years.

In II the vector S' is the same as the vector S in I, with a modification for survival through the system. Thus:

$$\begin{aligned}
S_5' &= Q_0\,a_{65} && \text{i.e., the first grade enrollment year} \\
S_4' &= Q_0\,a_{54} + R_0\,a_{64} && \text{zero survived to sixth grade in year 5} \\
S_3' &= Q_0\,a_{43} + R_0\,a_{53} + S_0\,a_{63} && \hspace{2cm}(5) \\
S_2' &= Q_0\,a_{32} + R_0\,a_{42} + S_0\,a_{52} + T_0\,a_{62} \\
S_1' &= Q_0\,a_{21} + R_0\,a_{31} + S_0\,a_{41} + T_0\,a_{51} + U_0\,a_{61}
\end{aligned}$$

In II the vector N is not easy to calculate for future years. It is the vector of nonattenders and actually represents:

$$
\begin{bmatrix} N_5 \\ N_4 \\ N_3 \\ N_2 \\ N_1 \end{bmatrix}
=
\begin{bmatrix}
p_5' - p_{c_5}' - e_5 \\
p_4' - p_{c_4}' - e_4 \\
p_3' - p_{c_3}' - e_3 \\
p_2' - p_{c_2}' - e_2 \\
p_1' - p_{c_1}' - e_1
\end{bmatrix}
\qquad
\begin{aligned}
& p' = \text{estimated school-} \\
& \quad\;\; \text{age population} \\[4pt]
& p_c' = \text{estimated school-} \\
& \quad\;\; \text{age population that} \qquad (6) \\
& \quad\;\; \text{has completed primary} \\[4pt]
& e = \text{provisional enroll-} \\
& \quad\;\; \text{ment estimated in I}
\end{aligned}
$$

First the school-age population for each year from x_1 through x_5 is estimated. Then the school-age population that will have completed school in each of those years is estimated and subtracted. From this result, subtract the provisional enrollment estimated in I. The difficulty of accomplishing this is glossed over in the CEPAL material, but the calculation of the school-age population that has already completed primary is difficult. Usually, only the roughest sort of estimates can be made.

When II is subtracted from I the L's go out and the result is the gap vector in years x_1 to x_5:

$$
\begin{bmatrix} G_5 \\ G_4 \\ G_3 \\ G_2 \\ G_1 \end{bmatrix}
=
\overset{\displaystyle A_3}{
\begin{bmatrix}
0 & (1-a_{25}) & (1-a_{35}) & (1-a_{45}) & (1-a_{55}) \\
0 & 0 & (1-a_{24}) & (1-a_{34}) & (1-a_{44}) \\
0 & 0 & 0 & (1-a_{23}) & (1-a_{33}) \\
0 & 0 & 0 & 0 & (1-a_{22}) \\
0 & 0 & 0 & 0 & 0
\end{bmatrix}}
\cdot
\begin{bmatrix} Q_5 \\ Q_4 \\ Q_3 \\ Q_2 \\ Q_1 \end{bmatrix}
+
\begin{bmatrix} S_5\text{-}S_5' \\ S_4\text{-}S_4' \\ S_3\text{-}S_3' \\ S_2\text{-}S_2' \\ S_1\text{-}S_1' \end{bmatrix}
+
\begin{bmatrix} N_5 \\ N_4 \\ N_3 \\ N_2 \\ N_1 \end{bmatrix}
\qquad (7)
$$

By inverting A_3 planners can solve for the original vector of first grade re-enrollments necessary to cover the gap, assuming wastage rates as set forth by the matrix A_3 and a vector of nonattenders N.

$$
Q = A_3^{-1} \cdot
\begin{vmatrix}
G_5 & - & S_5 & + & S_5' & - & N_5 \\
G_4 & - & S_4 & + & S_4' & - & N_4 \\
G_3 & - & S_3 & + & S_3' & - & N_3 \\
G_2 & - & S_2 & + & S_2' & - & N_2 \\
G_1 & - & S_1 & + & S_1' & - & N_1
\end{vmatrix}
\qquad (8)
$$

Future Costs and Investment Necessary to Fill Gap

The gap vector for the five years ahead can be multiplied by a per-student unit cost vector or scalar to give investment and outlay necessary in those years:

$$
\begin{vmatrix} G_5 \\ G_4 \\ G_3 \\ G_2 \\ G_1 \end{vmatrix} \cdot C_1\,C_2\,C_3\,C_4\,C_5
\quad
\begin{aligned}
C_1 &= \text{Capital cost per student (buildings)} \\
C_2 &= \text{Instructional cost per student (teaching)} \\
C_3 &= \text{Materials cost per student (books, etc.)} \\
C_4 &= \text{Other costs per student (supplies, etc.)} \\
C_5 &= \text{Cost per student administration-supervision}
\end{aligned}
\quad (9)
$$

Or simply:

$$
C \cdot \begin{vmatrix} G_5 \\ G_4 \\ G_3 \\ G_2 \\ G_1 \end{vmatrix}
\qquad C = \text{Cost per student} \qquad (10)
$$

A simple numerical example based on the Costa Rican data but not necessarily reflecting the reality of the Costa Rican future will illustrate use of the enrollment gap model. In this exercise, enrollments in the private schools are pooled with public school enrollments and the gap is calculated for both based on the total age group.

The basic data are:

Year	p' Population in Age Group	p' Age Group Completed Schooling	L Over-Age Enrolled[1]	Q Entrants, First Grade
5	498	18	7	75.8
4	451	17	7	74.0
3	408	16	8	72.3
2	365	14	11	71.6
1	310	13	12	70.0

[1] The difficulties of computing this column for private and public schools have been assumed away for purposes of this exercise.

$$
\begin{array}{ll}
O - Year & A_2 \\
Q_o = 66.6 & 1 \quad a_{25}(.98)\ a_{35}(.87)\ a_{45}(.80)\ a_{55}(.78) \\
R_o = 42.7 & \quad 1 \quad a_{24}(.97)\ a_{34}(.86)\ a_{44}(.79) \\
S_o = 39.4 & \quad 1 \quad a_{23}(.96)\ a_{33}(.85) \\
T_o = 30.0 & \quad 1 \quad a_{22}(.96) \\
U_o = 21.3 & \quad 1 \\
(V_o = 16.0) &
\end{array}
$$

A_2 shows the survival rates that prevail in the system, i.e., a_{55} being the proportion of the (11) original entrants that survive to the fifth grade in the fifth year.

To compute the provisional enrollment vector $\bar{e}$ the survival matrix A_1 is used. This shows no wastage in the system:

$$A_1$$

$$\begin{vmatrix} 1 & 1 & 1 & 1 & 1 \\ 0 & 1 & 1 & 1 & 1 \\ 0 & 0 & 1 & 1 & 1 \\ 0 & 0 & 0 & 1 & 1 \\ 0 & 0 & 0 & 0 & 1 \end{vmatrix}$$

The vector of provisional enrollments, i.e. the enrollments that there would be if present enrollments in the base year and new entrants all survived to graduate, would be:

$$
\begin{matrix} e_5 \\ e_4 \\ e_3 = \\ e_2 \\ e_1 \end{matrix}
\begin{vmatrix} A_1 \\ 1\,1\,1\,1\,1 \\ 0\,1\,1\,1\,1 \\ 0\,0\,1\,1\,1 \\ 0\,0\,0\,1\,1 \\ 0\,0\,0\,0\,1 \end{vmatrix} \cdot
\begin{vmatrix} Q \\ 75.8 \\ 74.0 \\ 72.3 \\ 71.6 \\ 70.0 \end{vmatrix} +
\begin{vmatrix} S \\ 66.6 \\ 42.7+66.6 \\ 39.4+42.7+66.6 \\ 30.0+39.4+42.7+66.6 \\ 21.3+30.0+39.4+42.7+66.6 \end{vmatrix} -
\begin{vmatrix} L \\ 7 \\ 7 \\ 8 \\ 11 \\ 12 \end{vmatrix} \quad (12)
$$

$$
\begin{matrix} e_5 \\ e_4 \\ e_3 = \\ e_2 \\ e_1 \end{matrix}
\begin{vmatrix} A_1Q \\ 363.7 \\ 287.9 \\ 213.9 \\ 141.6 \\ 70.0 \end{vmatrix} +
\begin{vmatrix} S \\ 66.6 \\ 109.3 \\ 148.7 \\ 178.7 \\ 200.0 \end{vmatrix} -
\begin{vmatrix} L \\ 7 \\ 7 \\ 8 \\ 11 \\ 12 \end{vmatrix} =
\begin{vmatrix} 423.3 \\ 390.2 \\ 354.6 \\ 309.3 \\ 258.0 \end{vmatrix} \quad (13)
$$

For those who have not looked at rudimentary matrix algebra for a while, A_1Q comes from multiplying each row of the matrix A_1 by the column vector Q. The top line 363.7 comes from: $1 \times 75.8 + 1 \times 74.0 + 1 \times 72.3 + 1 \times 71.6 + 1 \times 70.0 = 363.7$. The next row 287.9 comes from: $0 \times 75.8 + 74.0 + 72.3 + 71.6 + 70.0 = 287.9$. The other rows follow.

The vector of provisional enrollments for the five following years can now be used to estimate the nonattenders. From the population in the age group (p') projected for the five following years, subtract the population estimated as having completed school (p'_c) and the provisional enrollments (e). The problems of making these calculations are discussed in the text.

$$
\begin{matrix} N_5 \\ N_4 \\ N_3 = \\ N_2 \\ N_1 \end{matrix}
\begin{matrix} p' \\ 498 \\ 451 \\ 408 \\ 365 \\ 310 \end{matrix}
\begin{matrix} \\ - \\ - \\ - \\ - \\ - \end{matrix}
\begin{matrix} p'_c \\ 18 \\ 17 \\ 16 \\ 14 \\ 13 \end{matrix}
\begin{matrix} \\ - \\ - \\ - \\ - \\ - \end{matrix}
\begin{matrix} e \\ 423.3 \\ 390.2 \\ 354.6 \\ 309.3 \\ 258 \end{matrix} =
\begin{matrix} N \\ 56.7 \\ 43.8 \\ 37.4 \\ 41.7 \\ 39.0 \end{matrix} \quad (14)
$$

Note that nonattenders are increasing as population grows and entrants (Q) have only a modest increase.

The future year gap will be calculated from:

$$
\begin{vmatrix} G_5 \\ G_4 \\ G_3 \\ G_2 \\ G_1 \end{vmatrix} = \begin{vmatrix} 0 & 1\text{-}a_{25} & 1\text{-}a_{35} & 1\text{-}a_{45} & 1\text{-}a_{55} \\ 0 & 0 & 1\text{-}a_{24} & 1\text{-}a_{34} & 1\text{-}a_{44} \\ 0 & 0 & 0 & 1\text{-}a_{23} & 1\text{-}a_{33} \\ 0 & 0 & 0 & 0 & 1\text{-}a_{22} \\ 0 & 0 & 0 & 0 & 0 \end{vmatrix} \cdot \begin{vmatrix} Q_5 \\ Q_4 \\ Q_3 \\ Q_2 \\ Q_1 \end{vmatrix} + \begin{vmatrix} S_5\text{-}S_5' \\ S_4\text{-}S_4' \\ S_3\text{-}S_3' \\ S_2\text{-}S_2' \\ S_1\text{-}S_1' \end{vmatrix} + \begin{vmatrix} N_5 \\ N_4 \\ N_3 \\ N_2 \\ N_1 \end{vmatrix} \quad (15)
$$

The a represents survival proportions, i.e., a_{25} is the proportion surviving to the second grade in the fifth year. In the subscript the first number is the grade and the second the year. This is a crude and unstable way of calculating survival and wastage.

Only S' (S modified for wastage) remains to be evaluated. It is:

S'

$$
S_5' = \begin{vmatrix} a_{65} \\ 66.6(.78) \end{vmatrix} = 52.0
$$

$$
S_4' = \begin{vmatrix} a_{64} & a_{54} \\ 42.7(.77) + 66.6(.78) \end{vmatrix} = 84.8
$$

$$
S_3' = \begin{vmatrix} a_{63} & a_{53} & a_{43} \\ 39.4(.76) + 42.7(.77) + 66.6(.79) \end{vmatrix} = 115.4 \quad (16)
$$

$$
S_2' = \begin{vmatrix} a_{62} & a_{52} & a_{42} & a_{32} \\ 30.0(.75) + 39.4(.76) + 42.7(.78) + 66.6(.84) \end{vmatrix} = 141.7
$$

$$
S_1' = \begin{vmatrix} a_{61} & a_{51} & a_{41} & a_{31} & a_{21} \\ 21.3(.74) + 30.0(.76) + 39.4(.77) + 42.7(.88) + 66.6(.95) \end{vmatrix} = 169.8
$$

The gap can now be calculated as:

$$
\begin{array}{c} \\ G_5 \\ G_4 \\ G_3 \\ G_2 \\ G_1 \end{array} = \begin{array}{c} A_3 \\ \begin{vmatrix} 0 & .02 & .13 & .20 & .22 \\ 0 & 0 & .03 & .14 & .21 \\ 0 & 0 & 0 & .04 & .15 \\ 0 & 0 & 0 & 0 & .04 \\ 0 & 0 & 0 & 0 & 0 \end{vmatrix} \end{array} \cdot \begin{array}{c} Q \\ \begin{vmatrix} 75.8 \\ 74.0 \\ 72.3 \\ 71.6 \\ 70.0 \end{vmatrix} \end{array} + \begin{array}{c} S - S' \\ \begin{vmatrix} 66.6 - 52.0 \\ 109.3 - 84.8 \\ 148.7 - 115.4 \\ 178.7 - 141.7 \\ 200.0 - 169.8 \end{vmatrix} \end{array} + \begin{array}{c} N \\ \begin{vmatrix} 56.7 \\ 43.8 \\ 37.4 \\ 41.7 \\ 39.0 \end{vmatrix} \end{array} \quad (17)
$$

$$
\begin{array}{c} \\ G_5 \\ G_4 \\ G_3 \\ G_2 \\ G_1 \end{array} = \begin{array}{c} A_3Q \\ \begin{vmatrix} 40.6 \\ 26.9 \\ 13.4 \\ 2.8 \\ 0.0 \end{vmatrix} \end{array} + \begin{array}{c} S - S' \\ \begin{vmatrix} 14.6 \\ 24.5 \\ 33.3 \\ 37.0 \\ 30.2 \end{vmatrix} \end{array} + \begin{array}{c} N \\ \begin{vmatrix} 56.7 \\ 43.8 \\ 37.4 \\ 41.7 \\ 39.0 \end{vmatrix} \end{array} = \begin{vmatrix} 111.9 \\ 95.2 \\ 84.1 \\ 81.5 \\ 69.2 \end{vmatrix} \quad (18)
$$

The difficulties of making actual calculations with this format have been discussed. It is worth noting that by these results the gap is growing in absolute terms over the next five years. This is because the school population is increasing at a rapid rate and the authorities, although improving wastage and retention in the system, are not taking substantially more new entrants into first grade over the years. Nonattenders are increasing over the period. The gap is a lamentable problem for the country to face; but if resources are limited and a strategy of improving retention in the upper grades is chosen, first grade entrants may have to be held down, even in the face of rapidly increasing school-age populations.

The weakness of numerical examples is that they suggest that the model is more practical and workable than it is in reality. The problems of securing the data for this simple format are formidable ones.

When these models are used, either to plan on the basis of covering the gap or deficit based on a policy of universal primary education, or to calculate original numbers of entrants, there are certain problems.

a. The vector N of nonattenders is not easy to calculate and demands the projections and estimates noted.
b. To close the system, a vector, O, children attending other schools outside the public system, must be incorporated. The planner would have to know not only enrollments in other schools, but also the age-grade breakdowns. If private school enrollments are not built into the model it will open up, just as in the structure proposed by Correa, as students in various age and grade combinations shuttle in and out of the parallel system.
c. The survival and wastage rates are difficult to calculate, and it is even more difficult to assume that they will hold into the future years of the plan.
d. Retardation and re-entry into the system will throw off the calculations.

Presumably the model could be used iteratively, as with the life-table projections in Chapter III, i.e., one could project ahead five years and use this as a new base. If taken beyond one stage the flow rates become very unstable.

The determination of flow rates from the usual kind of data is difficult in itself. A series of approximations are discussed in Chapter IV. Least squares can also be used; but, no matter what the method, there are problems in assuming that rates will remain stable in the future.

Educational Targets Derived from Production Functions

In the schemata in Chapter II, educational attainment targets are derived from product, productivity, employment and the occupational structure of the work force. The Correa, Tinbergen, Bos models also derive educational attainment targets from product. The stroke is bolder here, however, and the relationships between volume of production and educational attainment in the work force are directly stated in two of a set of six linear difference equations:

$$n_t^2 = a^2 v_t \tag{19}$$

$$\cdot$$
$$\cdot$$
$$\cdot$$

$$n_t^3 = a^3 v_t + \pi^2 e^2 + \pi^3 n e_t^3 \tag{24}$$

The sense of the first equation is that the labor force with secondary education n_t^2 is directly proportional to volume of production v_t and can be expressed by the coefficient a^2 ($a^2 = n_t^2/v_t$). Equation (24) states that work force with third level education n_t^3 is proportional to volume of production; and it also accounts for those teaching at secondary and tertiary levels, i.e. the πs represent teacher/pupil ratios of tertiary graduates teaching at secondary and tertiary levels respectively. The other four equations in the first basic set relate work force members having specified educational attainment to new entrants in the work force and then back to school enrollments in previous time periods.

$$n_t^2 = (1 - \lambda^2)n_{t-1}^2 + m_t^2$$ This states that the number in the work force with second-level education at time t is equal to the number in the work force with second-level education in the previous periods reduced by the proportion who die or leave the work force λ and augmented by the number who join the work force in the period (m_t^2). (20)

$$m_t^2 = e_{t-1}^2 - e_t^3$$ The number with second-level education who join the work force in the period equal the number enrolled in second level education in the previous time period less the number who went on to third level education and are now in it in this period. (21)

$$m_t^3 = e_{t-1}^3$$ The number joining the work force with third-level education in the period equal the number enrolled in third-level education in the previous period. (22)

$$n_t^3 = (1 - \lambda^3)n_{t-1}^3 + m_t^3$$ The number in the work force with third-level education equal the number in the work force with third-level education in a previous period reduced by the proportion who die or retire and augmented by those who join the work force with third-level education in the period. (23)

Given the pattern of growth for a country, expressed as percentage increase in volume of production, and the coefficient relating this to work force members with specified educational attainment in equations

(19) and (24) and calculating or assuming teacher/pupil ratios and work force wastage rates, the equations can be solved to yield the numbers that must be educated at various levels in the school system over various time and development paths. The illustrative calculations which the authors show need not be repeated here. The first and simplest version of the model appeared in Kyklos. A number of applications to different countries appear in planning literature, and an expanded and elaborated set of equations appear in Tinbergen and Bos (1965).

The most basic objection to the model is provoked by equations (19) and (24) above, in which proportionality between numbers of educated people in the work force and volume of production is directly asserted. It is quite obvious that the relationship might be a mere artifact in any given time period or country, and hence no basis for projecting a straight linear trend into the future. To take one possible example, the demand for secondary level trained people might fall markedly as product and productivity increase. Tinbergen and Bos (1965) have attempted to account for this by introducing a per-capita income factor and changing the form of the function to an exponential. This doesn't meet the basic objection but gives further tools for analysis of the problem.

A second criticism of the model is addressed to the aggregative nature of the production side of equations (19) and (24). Even the crudest country plans project differential growth rates by sectors of the economy, rather than one aggregated national growth rate. Demand for educated people will be very different by sectors and within sectors. Superficially, at any rate, one would expect to gain more precision, perhaps spurious, in the schemata which proceeds sector-by-sector and occupation-by-occupation within sectors and industries. Tinbergen and Bos have elaborated the model to take into account various groupings of sectors in the economy. Instead of a single equation (19), Tinbergen divides the economy into two sectors:

$$\text{Sector One:} \quad {}^1n_t^2 = {}^1a^2\, v_t^1 \tag{25}$$

$$\text{Sector Two:} \quad {}^2n^2 = {}^2a^2\, v_t^2 \tag{26}$$

This modification yields two sets of 10 equations in 10 unknowns; and if one worked with as much sectoral and industrial detail as one generally tries to handle in the schemata, there would be many equations to solve. There has been as yet no attempt to take advantage of occupational information in the model.

Tinbergen and Bos introduced other modifications to take wastage into account. Equation (21) stated that the number joining the work force with second level education in time $t({}_m{}_t^2)$ are equal to the number in secondary education in the previous period (e^2_{t-1}) reduced by the number who entered tertiary level (e^3_t).

Persons familiar with wastage and retardation in the schools of developing countries have pointed out that this relationship is by no means as exact as the equation states. The authors recognize this by introducing a drop-out coefficient into equation (21).

u^{21} = fraction from secondary school joining work force
u^{22} = fraction tertiary students not completing that level.
Hence (21) was modified to:

$$m^2_t = u^{21}e^2_t + u^{22}e^3_{t-1} - e^3_t \qquad (27)$$

Equation (20) states that· the number in the work force with second-level education (n^2_t) in time period t is equal to the number with secondary level education in the previous time period (n^2_{t-1}) wasted by a proportion $(1-\lambda^2)$ who have died or retired and augmented by a number (m^2_t) with secondary education who have joined the work force during the period. This of course is a very simple way to handle work force wastage rates.

The authors attempt to take age structure into account in a more elaborate version of the equation. m^2_{t-T} represents the number who entered the work force T time units earlier where T stands for some estimate of the productive life of an individual.

Hence equation (20) was modified to:

$$n^2_t = n^2_{t-1} - m^2_{t-T} + m^2_t \qquad (28)$$

The model has also been criticized on a variety of other points. The use of levels of education, rather than kinds of preparation within level, is an obvious oversimplification. The assumption is that absolute level of educational attainment has some connection with production, without respect to the quality and kind of education offered. Reality suggests otherwise. Countries could turn out large numbers of secondary and tertiary graduates who might contribute nothing to production, or even hamper it. The authors suggest that refinements can be built in to resolve this problem. Perhaps they can, but there would be a second round of modifications that would also have to be incorporated, e.g., differing teacher/pupil ratios for different programs, and the format would soon become unbearably cumbersome.

Some applications of the models to planning in developing countries have produced unconvincing results. For want of local coefficients, borrowed ones (often from the U.S.) have been used, gross growth rates have been assumed, and numbers have been spun out. Misuse of the model is not the fault of the authors of it.

The Tinbergen model, as well as the manpower schemata discussed in Chapter II, can be used to generate the vector of requirements for persons with different levels and kinds of education that will serve as a basis for planning in the models of the next set.

MODELS BASED ON LINEAR PROGRAMMING TECHNIQUES

The next set of models were studied in order to exploit techniques in mathematical programming. The underlying structure of Models V.1 and V.II is the same. Model V.I is for a single period, although by putting the coefficients in terms of inputs to graduates the model may cover several years. Model V.II is the same thing moved over various time periods. Model V.III starts from a different sort of information base than V.I or V.II. In Model V.I, resources are known, and the objective is to maximize output or optimize on the basis of return. In Model V.III and its further development in V.IV, the objective is to meet a vector of final demand in the workforce over time. To work this model, the demand must be known or estimated beforehand.

The models are not worked through with sample data in order to avoid the spurious suggestion of simplicity and usefulness that such exercises suggest. Here the intention is to explain the structure of the models and the problems that still remain to be worked out when they are used for actual calculations. Bowles (1965) has developed a model similar to Model V.I and applied it to a planning situation in Nigeria. The Bowles work should be consulted both to show the model in a more advanced form of development and also to demonstrate the kind of questions that it can answer from an economist's point of view. Adelman (1965) has made an even more ambitious attempt to link investment in education with the total performance of the economy, using data from Argentina. Such algebraic frolics may some day be useful.

In the outline of the linear models that follow the intent is only to sketch out the basic structure of the approach in its simplest form, and not to suggest a format for computation in an actual planning situation. The description of educational levels is overly simplified and the description of inputs is too incomplete for practical purposes. Casting the relationships in linear form is perhaps the most serious of all simplifications because it does not reflect the way the technology of education works, nor does it express the relationship between educational attainment and output. The sole advantage of the formulation is that it does give a simple and idealized vision of how education and the economy might work and might be planned.

Models Based on Resources Available: Allocations Models

The activity analysis format of a linear programming model will serve to illustrate the kind of model that can be used to allocate resources to education in order to maximize return. For simplicity we suppose that the planner has the problem of allocating to one or all levels of the five-level school system schematized in Figure V.1.

The planner programs his allocations of the basis of the scheme in Model V.I.

In Model V.I the planner seeks to optimize allocations of resources to the various levels and kinds of education. Constrained by the limits of resources available, the planner must maximize the number of graduates at the various levels in accord with the return expected from them.

Symbolically, the situation in Model V.I is:

$x_j = x_1 \ldots x_n$	Number completing various educational programs or levels.
$C_j = C_1 \ldots C_n$	Some magnitude reflecting the utility, income, or rate of return to those educated to this level.
$a_{ij} = a_{11} \ldots a_{mn}$	Amount of resource i necessary to produce a graduate of level j under assumptions about minimal standards (teacher-pupil ratios, textbooks, physical plant. . .).
$b_i = b_1 \ldots b_m$	Resources available for education (money available for capital outlay for plant, trained teachers, equipment, books. . .).

In linear program format the analysis is:

To optimize $C_1x_1 + C_2x_2 + C_3x_3 + C_4x_4 + \ldots C_nx_n$

Given $\quad x_1 \geqslant 0,\ x_2 \geqslant 0,\ x_3 \geqslant 0,\ x_4 \geqslant 0,\ x_n \geqslant 0$ (Can't produce negative numbers of graduates)

And
$$a_{11}x_1 + a_{12}x_2 + \ldots + a_{1n}x_n \leqslant b_1$$
$$a_{21}x_1 + a_{22}x_2 + \ldots + a_{2n}x_n \leqslant b_2$$

$$\vdots$$

$$a_{m1}x_1 + a_{m2}x_2 + \ldots + a_{mn}x_n \leqslant b_m$$

(29)

This is the standard activity analysis format for linear programming, with n variables and m constraint equations with the condition that there can be no negative outputs (minus graduates). Some names for educational activities (levels and kinds of programs) and resources have been entered to suggest the sense of the model. A more detailed breakdown of these categories is given in the next chapter.

The mathematics of the model and the mechanics of the simplex computational routines which produce answers from it need no com-

FIGURE V.1
Idealized Five-Stage Educational System

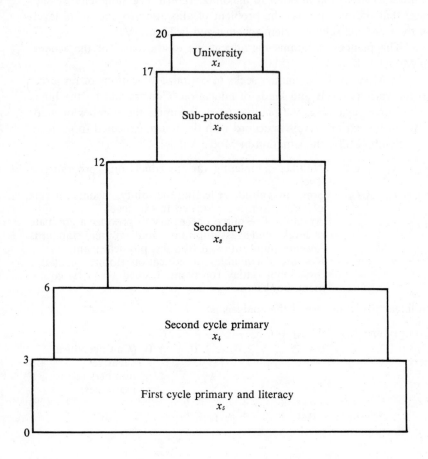

MODEL V.I

	C_1x_1 University Graduate	C_2x_2 Sub-Professional	C_3x_3 Secondary	C_4x_4 Primary Complete	$C_5x_5 + \ldots + C_nx_n$ Three Years & Literacy	Available Resources
Capital Outlay (Bldgs. & Equipment including debt service)	$a_{11}x_1$ +	$a_{12}x_2$ +	$a_{13}x_3$ +	$a_{14}x_4$ +	$a_{15}x_5$ + $\ldots$ + $a_{1n}x_n$ $\leq$	b_1
Current Expenses (Instruct. Admin.)	$a_{21}x_1$ +	$a_{22}x_2$ +	$a_{23}x_3$ +	$a_{24}x_4$ +	$a_{25}x_5$ + $\ldots$ + $a_{2n}x_n$ $\leq$	b_2
Current Other (Books, Supplies)	$a_{31}x_1$ +	$a_{32}x_2$ +	$a_{33}x_3$ +	$a_{34}x_4$ +	$a_{35}x_5$ + $\ldots$ + $a_{3n}x_n$ $\leq$	b_3
Teachers A (Secondary-Trained)	$a_{41}x_1$ +	$a_{42}x_2$ +	$a_{43}x_3$ +	$a_{44}x_4$ +	$a_{45}x_5$ + $\ldots$ + $a_{4n}x_n$ $\leq$	b_4
	. . . .	. . . .	. . . .	. . . .	. . . .	. . .
Teachers B (University-Col.)	$a_{m1}x_1$ +	$a_{m2}x_2$ +	$a_{m3}x_3$ +	$a_{m4}x_4$ +	$a_{m5}x_5$ + $\ldots$ + $a_{mn}x_n$ $\leq$	b_m

ment here. Straightforward expositions are given in standard texts by Baumol (1961), Gass (1958) or Dorfman (1958). The model will produce feasible solutions, which means here that no more resources are allocated to produce graduates at the various levels than are available. An optimal solution is also possible, i.e., the result will indicate the number of graduates (the xs) to be produced at the various levels in order to maximize return.

There are certain aspects of the model that do require detailed consideration. From the outset it is apparent that the model cannot be worked through unless the planner has accurate and precise estimates of:

1. a_{ij}, the coefficient which reflects the amount of resources that must be put in to produce a unit of output. In this situation the unit of output could represent a person completing a given level or kind of education or training.
2. b_i, the amount of different kinds of resources (teachers or money available for capital outlay on physical plant) available for allocation to education, rather than to some other activity.
3. The C coefficient which represents some estimate of the utility, advantage, or return from producing a person who completes one level and kind of education rather than another.

Unless all of these statistics are available for the base year there is little possibility of using the model for determining future year allocations, which would be the only sensible use of it for planning.

The use of a fixed input coefficient, a_{ij}, presents certain logical and statistical problems in the educational planning situation. One can see that when the model is used to allocate chemical ingredients to the manufacture of certain compounds, fairly rigorous sets of input proportions can be specified. In the educational situation, however, no such rigid input-output relationships can be readily determined. To take an obvious example, consider teacher/pupil ratios. There is a relationship between teacher inputs and graduates, but it is a fairly loose one. Does one set the ratio at 1/20, 1/40, 1/80? It is difficult to specify exactly. The same with other expenditures. What is the optimum book expenditure per graduate? Furthermore, there will be interactions and substitutability among the inputs, e.g. a good teacher can overcome a short allocation for plant or equipment. One can only say that some roughly normative coefficients can be established and used. The setting of these quality input norms is the subject of Chapter VI of this book.

The a_{ij} input coefficients can be handled in several ways. First, the coefficients can be fixed against the output of graduates within the level. The coefficients are fixed this way in Chapter VI of this book. The a_{ij} for teacher input is:

$$a_{ij} = \frac{W}{P/T}$$

$W =$ Average number of years required to produce a graduate within the level
$P/T =$ Pupil-teacher ratio $(T = 1)$

By using the average number of years, rather than the legal number of years to complete the level, the teachers needed to handle wastage and retardation are counted into the formula.

An alternative is to fix a teacher/pupil input for one year of education in the level. Here, $a_{ij} = P/T$. To account for wastage and drop-out, the pay-off in the objective function would have to be reduced by some wastage rate:

$$C_1 x_1 (W_1) + C_2 x_2 (W_2) + \ldots C_n x_n (W_n) \tag{31}$$

This seems to imply that resources allocated to educate those who do not complete the level are wasted, which is not the case.

The use of the first method of computing the coefficient seems better, but neither system gets around the basic problem of change in wastage rates and the resulting instability when the model is used to plan for a distant future. Wastage rates will—must—change, for that is the point of the planning; and hence one is forced to average coefficients over a period of time, with all the mess this implies for the calculations.

The b_i represents a column vector of resources available for allocation to education. If the model is to be used for planning over some lengthy horizon, some fair estimates of money and manpower available for education in future years must be available. This is the subject of Chapter VII of this book. Estimates of resources can come from the solution of a more general allocations problem in which the requirements and pay-off on education are determined. The problems of these large-scale social welfare analyses are obvious. A cost-benefits analysis of something so general as *health* or *education* would be almost meaningless.

But the most severe problems come with the C coefficient which must reflect the differences in earnings attributable to education over the work life of those who complete various educational programs.

In Chapter II, the use of rate-of-return and present-value calculations applied to differences in earnings was discussed. Internal rates of return could be calculated for successive levels of education and training and the objective function could be weighted accordingly. The formulas are given in Chapter II and need not be repeated. If the rate of return for college over secondary was 37 per cent; for secondary over primary 24 per cent; and primary over less than primary 16 per cent; the objective function $C_1x_1 + C_2x_2 + C_3x_3 + \ldots$ could be weighted $37x_1 + 24x_2 + 16x_3 + \ldots.$ This would give crude results in the program model and scramble the concept of shadow price.

The C coefficient could be expressed in money returns by discounting to present value the difference between income streams at successive levels of education:

$$\sum_{t=1}^{L} \frac{(x^1 - x^0)}{(1 + r)^t} \tag{32}$$

x^1 = Earnings minus direct and indirect costs of persons with educational level 1

x^0 = Earnings minus direct and indirect costs of persons with educational level immediately below 1

$(1+r)^t$ = discounts to present value over t years

L = Work life of groups

The problems of using discounted net earning streams have been covered in Chapter II. Educational attainment when measured by level may have little to do with earnings. Type of program may have more significance. And level and type of formal education may have little to do directly with increasing output and general returns. A technical library might provide a larger increment to worker productivity than a technical school. Measurement of income differentials counts in contributions that formal education doesn't make, but fails to count in benefits that it does provide.

Furthermore, there are the obvious problems of measurement. Theoretical economists may paint over these with high gloss but the measurement problems plague planners. Second, there are, as Danière points out, inherent problems in using rate-of-return criteria for long-term planning decisions. In a developing country there may be no relevant experience on which to estimate over a time horizon the changes in incomes and returns that large additions to the stock of educated people will bring. In fact, experience tends to indicate that additions of large numbers of educated people will markedly affect the earning differentials.

It is also apparent that in any objective function in which the earning differentials are used to weight the levels, allowance must be made for those who will not enter the workforce, despite receipt of education and training. Only rough participation rates for differing educational levels are available, and this further increases the instability of the function. Further, these rates may change over time and not just because of conditions of unemployment. Significant portions of educated women, for example, may work or not work at some future date.

With the data available for the C weightings, the a_{ij} coefficients, and a b vector of resources available as inputs, Model I would yield the optimal numbers to be produced at the various levels of education.

x_1 = Optimal number of university graduates
x_2 = Optimal number of subprofessional level graduates
.
.
x_5 = Optimal numbers of graduates of three full years (literacy)

Several examples, using only a few educational levels and resources, have been worked, but they will not be included here because they suggest a spurious utility for the kind of model that can be handled on a desk calculator. Without a great deal of specificity and detail in the constraints and the educational levels, the model yields useless if not misleading results. Bowles (1965) has made an ambitious attempt to apply the model in a setting with some semblance of reality, i.e., in the Northern Region of Nigeria. For a simple version of the simplex method of calculation applied to the activity analysis format, with exemplar data, one of the standard texts on linear programming can be consulted. The dual solution would yield the shadow prices of resources that must be allocated to education.

There are techniques for varying the parameters in the model and observing the effect of this on the result produced by the model. The parameters that could be varied are the coefficients in the objective function, the constraints and the a_{ij} coefficients. For the planner variation of the input coefficients would be the most interesting, but not very much work has been done on this form of parametric programming. Bowles (1965) used parametric programming to vary the objective function and the constraints.

Dynamic Extension of the Linear Program Model

Some of the statistical difficulties of the a_{ij} coefficient in Model I can be minimized by running the program over various time periods. This is illustrated in Model V.II. In this form the model might be referred to as dynamic, although it is dynamic in a highly restricted use of that term. Model V.II does permit the varying of input coefficients over time periods. Model V.II offers some advantage over Model V.I because the assumption of one technology holding over a long period is no longer necessary. In Model V.II a new set of input coefficients is devised for each successive time period. There is still the problem of estimating these coefficients on the basis of the proposed enrichment of the inputs to education that will be necessary to improve the efficiency of the system over time. The component cost analysis of Chapter VI

MODEL V.II

Structuring of Model I Over Time Periods (Three Activities, Three Time Periods, Three Resources)

	Period One			Period Two			Period Three			
	x_1^1	x_2^1	x_3^1	x_1^2	x_2^2	x_3^2	x_1^3	x_2^3	x_3^3	
	a_{11}^1	a_{12}^1	a_{13}^1							$\leqslant b_1^1$
	a_{21}^1	a_{22}^1	a_{23}^1							$\leqslant b_2^1$
	a_{31}^1	a_{32}^1	a_{33}^1							$\leqslant b_3^1$
				a_{11}^2	a_{12}^2	a_{13}^2				$\leqslant b_1^2$
				a_{21}^2	a_{22}^2	a_{23}^2				$\leqslant b_2^2$
				a_{31}^2	a_{32}^2	a_{33}^2				$\leqslant b_3^2$
							a_{11}^3	a_{12}^3	a_{13}^3	$\leqslant b_1^3$
							a_{21}^3	a_{22}^3	a_{23}^3	$\leqslant b_2^3$
							a_{31}^3	a_{32}^3	a_{33}^3	$\leqslant b_3^3$

will provide the planner with methods for relating improvements in quality to increased costs of inputs.

In Model V.II the constraints may also change over time, and this is again in accord with reality in a developing country. Presumably the country will have greater resources over time as its product increases, income increases, and revenue measures yield more resources that may be allocated to education and training. The time periods can be broken into yearly increments or made to correspond to the average duration of education levels. Resource constraints and coefficients will be modified accordingly. The a_{ij} coefficient can be the amount of resource i necessary to give one year of education or to produce a graduate in level j, taking into account wastage and retardation. The model can be run and output optimized over several periods. The use of many time periods will increase the number of variables and equations in the problem; and when all is said and done there is still no dynamic linkage in the format.

Model V.II is actually a series of smaller linear program problems. The planner could be better served by a model that would set input coefficients over successive time periods according to the coefficients of a preceding period and according to the gain in available resources forecast between the periods:

$$a_{ij}^1 = F\left(\frac{a_{ij}^0 b_i^1}{b_i^0}\right) \tag{33}$$

The coefficients of a subsequent period should be some function of the coefficients of a previous period and the ratio of estimated resources between the two periods. How such a model is to be worked out is beyond the range of this text and the ken of this writer. There are ways of simulating the coefficients over time and then working them back into the model. The program could be worked through with trial coefficients. But manipulation of the ratio alone can not guide the planner. He must take into account the possible variations in technology that will have even a more direct influence on inputs. In other words, the planner must work with the quality and cost factors that are introduced in the next chapter.

MODELS BASED ON HUMAN RESOURCE REQUIREMENTS TARGETS

This model has already been discussed briefly in Chapter II. There, Equation 5, reflecting the flow between work force and education system, was shown as:

$$(I - A) X = L \tag{34}$$

Here Y is a vector of manpower requirements; X is a vector of educational enrollments and A is a matrix of input or flow coefficients. The original enrollments necessary to produce the manpower requirements represented in L, given the flow shown in the matrix, can be obtained by inverting the matrix:

$$X = (I - A)^{-1}L \tag{35}$$

When presented in a system of equalities with the system output meeting the requirements, the model presents no basis for optimizing because the matrix is square and there is a deterministic solution. In linear programming terms, the only feasible solution (given the fixed coefficients) is the optimal one and there is no objective function to optimize.

If Model V.III is set up to run over several time periods, as it should be to reflect some semblance of reality, the fixed transition coefficients give the same kind of results. The basic feasible solution is the optimal one.

However, in reality, the problem need not be treated in deterministic form only. Gass (1958) and Wagner (1954) show how the model can be developed to yield problems amenable to linear programming both in static and dynamic situations.

Let:

$X_t = (x_{t1}, x_{t2} \ldots x_{tn})$ = the output vector of education and training activities

$Y_t = (y_{t1}, y_{t2} \ldots y_{tn})$ = the final demand vector of output of educational activities in the work force

$s_t = (s_{t1}, s_{t2} \ldots s_{tn})$ = vector of educated and trained people produced in time t but not used in education system or work force. Available in $t + 1$.

$U_t = (u_{t1}, u_{t2} \ldots v_{tn})$ = unused capacity in the educational activities of the system

$C = (1_1, 1_2 \ldots 1_m)$ = capacity level vector of the educational activities

$B = \begin{matrix} b_{11}, b_{12} \ldots b_{1m} \\ b_{21}, b_{22} \ldots b_{2m} \\ \cdot \\ \cdot \\ b_{n1}, b_{n2} \ldots b_{nm} \end{matrix}$ = a matrix showing the input from each educational activity necessary to build an additional unit of capacity in each educational activity (no negative)

$l_t = (v_{t1}, v_{t2} \ldots v_{tn})$ = capacity expansion vector for each activity of the system

$Bl_t = (b_{i1}l_{t1}, b_{i2}l_{t2} \ldots b_{im}l_{tm})$ = amount of the ith activity output used to build additional capacity in period t for all other activities

$X_t, Y_t, s_t, C_t, U_t, l_t \geqq 0$

MODEL V.III
Dynamic Structuring of Flow Model

x_1^1	x_2^1	x_3^1	x_1^2	x_2^2	x_3^2	x_1^3	x_2^3	x_3^3	
$+1$									$= x_1^0$
	$+1$								$= x_2^0$
		$+1$							$= x_3^0$
a_{11}	a_{21}	a_{31}	-1						$= y_1^1$
a_{12}	a_{22}	a_{32}		-1					$= y_2^1$
a_{13}	a_{23}	a_{33}			-1				$= y_3^1$
			a_{11}	a_{21}	a_{31}	-1			$= y_1^2$
			a_{12}	a_{22}	a_{32}		-1		$= y_2^2$
			a_{13}	a_{23}	a_{33}			-1	$= y_3^2$
						a_{11}	a_{21}	a_{31}	$= y_1^k$
						a_{12}	a_{22}	a_{32}	$= y_2^k$
						a_{13}	a_{23}	a_{33}	$= y_3^k$

Table 1. Dynamic Structuring of a Single Transition Matrix. x_1^0 is the number of persons enrolled in class level i during the initial period. y_i^0 the needed *additions* to labor force from class i at the beginning of period j, $j = 1, 2, \ldots, k$; and x_i^j the enrollment in class i at the beginning of period j. The a's are the transition matrix. The example is for three class levels.

For any time period the conditions are summarized:

$$(I - A) X_t + s_{t-1} = Y_t + Bl_t + s_t \tag{36}$$

$$X_t + U_t = C_t + \sum_{q=1}^{t-1} lq \tag{37}$$

Equation (36) states that for any time period t, the total output plus the previous stock s is equal to the final demand and capacity expansion requirements plus the current period's unused stocks. Equation (37) states that the total used and unused output equal output capacity and the previous additional increases in production capacity.

The system can be set up in tableau form. Given an appropriate objective function, e.g., optimizing output, the system can be set up in block triangular format and solved by a standard simplex procedure.

TABLE V.2
Schematic Outline of Model V.IV

	Period 1	Period 2	Period n
	x_1 l_1 s_1 u_1	x_2 l_2 s_2 $u_2.\,.\,.$	x_n l_n s_n u_n
Y_1-s_1	$(I-A)-B-I$		
C_1	$\qquad$ I		
Y_2	I	$(I-A)-B-I$	
C_2	$-I$	$I \qquad I$	
.			
.			
Y_n			$(I-A)-B-I$
C_n	$-I$	$-I$	$I \qquad I$

There are difficulties with the model. In the first place, it seems to be stretching the matter to fit education and work force into the inter-industry format. This may be said of any general model, but it seems a particularly obvious distortion in this case. There are practical problems when the model is put into computational shape. For the basic model in T time periods there are two mT equations and four mT activities. Even when only a few time periods and educational activities are considered, the number of equations and variables becomes very large.

To cut the number of equations and variables down to a manageable size, various simplifications are recommended. Wagner (1954) suggests that stock (s), capacity (C), the matrix A, and the matrix I should be held invariant from the first time period. This will simplify the matter, but it brings the planner back to the original problem of working with models that become too inflexible to be real. The need is for a model that has some pale semblance to reality. The planner requires a model in which A changes because this is the nature of reality. In

Table V.2, A is held invariant but C is changed through time. The capacity vector C takes into account all of the other inputs to the educational system that influence output capacity (expenditures for books, materials, buildings, equipment). This must change through time, or there is no reality in the model. The model has been run with trial sets of data, but the results do not seem useful enough to justify the effort. There is some question whether deterministic models of this sort have very much usefulness for educational planning, but perhaps some more ingenious model builder will introduce the flexibility needed and still keep the rigor.

Other Models from Operations Research

Other models and methods from operations research offer techniques for handling significant problems in human resource development planning. The routing of school transportation, school services, and the scheduling of school supervision and inspections might be more optimally arranged through applications of the techniques classified under the rubric Traveling Salesmen Problem. Here the objective is to minimize the distance or the costs of traveling from one point to another in the system. When the number of points on the travel route are few the problem is easy to visualize. As an example we have the problem of traveling from point 1 to 4 and back to 1 again, assuming symmetrical costs (costs the same from 1 to 2 as 2 to 1).

Routes		*Distance or Cost*			
			1	2	3	4

	1	2	3	4
1	0	7	12	9
2	7	0	6	14
3	12	6	0	8
4	9	14	8	0

The possible routes, without passing through the same point twice, are $\dfrac{(4-1)!}{2} = \dfrac{3 \times 2}{2} = 3$. The objective is to select the route that minimizes the distances or total costs if there is a cost-per-distance unit.

$$MIN \quad \Sigma x_{ij}$$
$$i = 1, i_2, i_3 \ldots i_n \tag{38}$$
$$j = i_2, i_3 \ldots i_n, 1$$

If the number of points are few, all the different route distances can be listed and their costs can be evaluated:

Route $A = 1, 2, 3, 4, 1 = 7 + 6 + 8 + 9 = 30$ (minimum route)
Route $B = 1, 2, 4, 3, 1 = 7 + 14 + 8 + 12 = 41$
Route $C = 1, 4, 2, 3, 1 = 9 + 14 + 6 + 12 = 41$

When the number of points grows into some approximation of reality the method becomes laborious and there is no general analytical solution. If there were eight points on the route and symmetrical costs, there would be slightly more than 2,500 permutations to examine. High-speed computers could examine this number readily enough, but it is obvious that the number of examinations grows as the method is applied to any semblance of a real situation, e.g., school inspection rounds, school service rounds. However, in the hierarchial arrangement of supervisory and administrative nets the problem can be worked out for districts and provinces, and then nationally. The use of PERT charting of paths is illustrated by Cooke in Appendix B.

MODELS AND HUMAN RESOURCE PLANNING

In human resource planning, one often ends up wondering if it is worthwhile fussing with models at all. But this question is gratuitous because from the simplest table format and algebraic expression, one is operating with some form of model. The question should turn on how general and ambitious a model one should strive for. At the outset, a mathematical model which covers all of human resource development planning is perhaps not the most practical objective. A simulation or analogue trial and error routine may be more useful. On the other hand, a mathematical formulation of some of the components of human resource planning is worthwhile. Here one asks:

1. Does the model require assuming away contact with reality? In which case it is hardly worth bothering with.
2. Does the model keep some contact with reality and provide heuristic advantage, i.e., reveal relationships that would not otherwise be perspicuous in comprehensive array?
3. Does the model require data that are possible to obtain so that it can be worked toward some end?

Linear program models for allocation seem to avoid the first problem and seem to have the second advantage; and the question comes with the third point. Experience with data in the model has not yet demonstrated its usefulness conclusively, but the data it has inspired have been useful for planning cost and quality at a level of specificity not heretofore possible. One of the major problems in human resource planning has been the collection of masses of descriptive data without any schemata for relating and using them, and the use of aggregates and averages that are so general that they mask the characteristics of the situation. One can be properly ashamed of the present level of development of models in this section, but it is worth offering them in the hope that they can be carried further by those who are expert in such matters.

VI

Cost Formulas and the Planning of Quality in Educational Programs

Formulas for costing educational programs must be sufficiently refined to permit the planner to estimate what will happen as the system grows better as well as bigger. The quality of inputs will be raised, and hopefully the system will become more productive . . . but at some cost. Qualitative change cannot be programmed with blunt costing instruments. Large aggregates and averages mask the essential features of the program.

Some of the cruder methods of estimating present and future costs have been examined in Chapter I. The number of new students which the system must accommodate in future years is estimated. A ratio of students to classrooms is established. (The magic numbers for primary schools are 30 when you're rich and 40 when you're poor.) The ratio of students to classroom is divided into the number of new students and the result is the number of new classrooms required. This is multiplied by a per-classroom cost and there is the capital cost for the future.

For current costs the present operating budget is raised by the ratio of future total enrollments to present total enrollments. If the present budget allocates five million dollars to a system with 150,000 students enrolled, the future budget for 300,000 children is estimated at ten million.

Capital and current costs are added and the bill is sent over to the National Planning Commission or the Minister of Finance. No further criticism of the method is profitable. It might be necessary under some circumstances, and almost all planners have had to handle the matter this way. When the present school system is inadequate, the method leads to planning an inadequate future system.

A second method consists of computing per-pupil costs for students in different levels and kinds of educational programs. Future costs are then estimated in a straightforward fashion: Per-pupil cost (raised by some factor) multiplied by the number of students estimated for future date. The improvement factor in per-pupil cost is presumed to take into account price increases and raises in the quality of inputs. But the problem is in determining exactly how much the costs should be raised. Recourse is had to the usual dodges. Increases from the past are extrapolated. But sometimes, in fact very often, in developing countries that are expanding their educational systems rapidly, there is no increase in per-pupil costs—at least in real terms. In fact, there is quite likely to have been a decline, with more students being educated for less money. If this trend is extrapolated the result, in qualitative terms, could be a disaster.

Failing a historical basis, the comparative barrel can be fished. Per-pupil costs from other countries, with model systems, can be used as a target. But this is almost wholly inappropriate, without a searching analysis of the reasons for differences in prices of all the component inputs to education. Hence, inevitably, the planner must face a detailed study of the components that go to make up the aggregated current per-pupil costs.

EXPENDITURE ESTIMATES BASED ON PER-PUPIL
CURRENT AND CAPITAL COSTS

Current expenditure for future years can be estimated from the relationship:

$$C_j^i = E_j^i \cdot \frac{S_j^i}{r_j^i p_j^i} \qquad (1)$$

E_j^i = Enrollment level i, year j
S_j^i = Average teacher's salary i, j
r_j^i = Pupil teacher ratio i, j
p_j^i = Proportion of per-pupil cost (current) represented by teachers' salaries

For example:

$$C_j^i = 150{,}000 \cdot \frac{\$2000}{30(.80)} = \$12.5 \text{ (million)}$$

The estimate is a rough one and depends on crude estimates of pupil/teacher ratios and the relationship of instructional costs to total current costs.

This formula will give poor results in developing countries where new programs have recently been launched in vocational and technical education and enrollments are still low and pupil/teacher ratios are as a result correspondingly low. For example: In the base year there are 3,000 enrolled in a secondary level vocational program, the average teacher salary is $2500, the pupil/teacher ratio (because of the newness of the program) is 8:1 and the proportion of teacher's salary to total current per-pupil cost is .90. The total current expenditure would be $1.04 million; the per-pupil current expenditure would be $347.00. On this basis, other inputs for administration, expendable supplies etc., would be $34.70. The planner then projects to some future date when the enrollment will be 7,000; average teacher salaries in constant dollars will have gone up to $3,400; pupil/teacher ratios will be 25:1, and the planners estimate that the proportion of current costs represented by teachers' salaries is 82 per cent. This gives:

$$7000 \cdot \frac{\$3,400}{25(.82)} = \text{per-pupil cost of } \$165.85, \text{ of which other costs}$$

in constant dollars now represent $29.85. It is unlikely that other costs for this kind of training will drop, even when prices are deflated to base-year dollars. Hence, for some purposes the formula will give bad estimates. It is, however, a costing formula often used by planners.

On the capital outlay side, a quick and rough estimate may be based on a per-pupil place cost. This, too, requires more effort than merely taking the capital expenditures of any past period and dividing them by the number of new student places created during that period. Nor can it be based automatically on the average costs of some other country.

The alternatives to the rougher per-pupil costing methods require analysis of the components of cost and program quality. Price-relative indexes for the components can be constructed and moved to future years. Or, the cost of the inputs of the major components can be calculated in the form of cost coefficients per student enrolled or graduated. These are not the last word in costing, but they are improvements over aggregate and average methods which make it difficult to relate cost to specific program quality changes. Because so much planning is based on per-pupil average costs, it is worth examining these approaches first.

Costing by Per-Pupil Averages

Costing by per-pupil averages consists in this:

Per-pupil costs × numbers of students estimated at future date. In some schemes a progressive rise in per-pupil costs is assumed, not only to reflect price increases, but also on the basis of an assumed improvement in quality of education. The per-pupil costs are usually based on enrollments; and if requirements are expressed in graduates, one of the methods of converting from enrollments to graduates (cf., Chapter IV) must be applied.

The usual cost ratio is:

$$\text{Per-pupil cost} = \frac{\text{Expenditure (for students in level \& kind of education)}}{\text{Total of Students (in level and kind of education)}}$$

Both numerator and denominator of this simple ratio may be made more precise. The expenditure in the numerator may be broken down into Capital, Current and Total.

The three ratios, then, are:

$$1. \quad \frac{\text{Capital Expenditure (for level and kind)}}{\text{Total of Students}}$$

$$2. \quad \frac{\text{Current Expenditures}}{\text{Total of Students}}$$

$$3. \quad \text{Total} = \frac{\text{Capital} + \text{Current Expenditures}}{\text{Total of Students}}$$

More important is the denominator. In developing countries it is common to use enrollments to compute the ratio:

$$\frac{\text{Expenditure (in level \& kind)}}{\text{Enrollment (in level \& kind)}}$$

Common practice is to use Initial Enrollments, i.e., enrollments taken shortly after the opening of the school year. In the educational systems of a developing country, this practice may produce serious errors. Simple cross-section estimates of enrollment may be highly unstable. The approach seriously overestimates the number of children who are being served in the schools, and seriously underestimates the cost of providing an education in the future. In some countries in Latin America, on any given day, only 60 per cent of the enrollments officially carried on the rolls can be found in the schools. Enrollments are mainly useful for making a country seem to be doing more than it actually is.

Increasingly, now, countries are computing Average Daily Attendance and percentage of students in Average Daily Attendance. Symbolically this is:

$$ADA = \frac{\Sigma \text{ Present}}{\text{Class Days}} \tag{2}$$

Average Daily Attendance is the sum of all the markings of 'present' (not absent) on the attendance rolls, divided by the number of official class days. The ratio can be computed for any given time period: monthly, for a semester, or for a school year. Monthly ratios can be weighted and aggregated and made into an annual ratio. The monthly ratio reveals low attendance months which are often indicators of major crop harvesting or planting seasons, periods of inclement weather, or migratory periods for nomadic families. Monthly ratios may help in adjusting school calendars to the economic, climatic and social characteristics that prevail.

If ADA is divided by enrollment, the result is a ratio, expressed as a percentage which is most useful for attendance analysis.

$$E = 100 \cdot \frac{ADA}{\text{Enrollment}} \tag{3}$$

There are months in the school calendar of Central American countries when this dips down below 50 per cent, e.g., coffee harvesting seasons in some districts. In these periods, the schools in certain areas might just as well be closed. Based on monthly estimates and flexible calendars, school supervisors and inspectors can be shifted in teams to various areas. Administrative costs can be reduced this way and scarce talent better utilized. Most administrative arrangements in developing countries are too rigid to carry out such a program, however; and poor internal communications add to the difficulties.

Administrators in the United States have found that for purposes of calculating cost, particularly for making foundation program subsidies and school assistance grants to local systems, a ratio called Average Daily Membership is more appropriate than *ADA*. This ratio of *ADM,* or *PLM* (pupils in live membership) is:

$$\text{ADM} = \frac{\Sigma \text{ Present} + \Sigma \text{ Absent}}{\text{Official school days in period}} \tag{4}$$

The notion of using *ADM,* which comes out larger than *ADA,* is that students are counted as long as they are 'live' or 'active' members of the class, whether or not they are present on any given day. Usually, a period of time, e.g. 10 or 15 days, is established, during which the student can be absent and still considered an active member. After that period, he is taken from the rolls, and must be re-entered.

The advantage of *ADM* over *ADA* is that cost estimates usually turn out more stable on this base, because the major components of education have to be supplied, whether one or a few students are absent on any given day. Teachers have to be there and be paid; the classroom is there; as are books and equipment. In the United States it has proved a stable statistic for estimating average costs of educational programs.

This does not necessarily make it a better one for developing countries, but it is far less likely to lead to underestimates of costs than the use of enrollment figures.

Dividing three different expenditures (Current, Capital, Total) by three different denominators (Enrollment, Average Daily Attendance and Average Daily Membership) yields nine different per-pupil cost ratios which can give a rough estimate of total costs for future years.

TABLE VI.1
Summary of Cost Ratios: Level One Primary (6 grades)

	Current	Capital	Total	Average Cost Grad.
Enrollment	$CU/En = R_1$	$CA/En = R_2$	$To/En = R_3$	$6 \times R_3$
ADA	$CU/ADA = R_4$	$CA/ADA = R_5$	$To/ADA = R_6$	$6 \times R_6$
ADM	$CU/ADM = R_7$	$CA/ADM = R_8$	$To/ADM = R_9$	$6 \times R_9$

Estimating Outlay for Future Years on the Basis of Per-Pupil Cost Ratios

It is a straightforward task to prepare estimates of future year outlay based on per-pupil cost ratios. If the planner has, as in Table IV.7, the enrollment structure for future years, the outlay O_j^i in any level i and in any year j would be:

$$O_j^i = R_j^i \cdot Q_j^i \cdot P_j \cdot E_j^i$$

R_j^i = per-pupil/cost ratio,
P_j = factor to account for price rises between present and year j, (5)
Q_j^i = factor to account for raise in quality of inputs per student,
E_j^i = enrollment in year and level.

If R is based on past per pupil expenditure data, any of the current expenditure ratios (CU/EN, CU/ADA, CU/ADM) can be used, depending on the data available. The relative merits of the ratios have been discussed.

E represents enrollments in level i in year j, as in Table IV.7. If the enrollment structure for future years is not complete and the planner has only the number of graduates, enrollments can be estimated from the ratios of grade enrollments to graduates, worked back through the grades.

P is a factor introduced to account for price rises that will occur during the future years. Usually, the planner has nothing more detailed available than a general price index which relates past and current prices. The index can be pushed ahead to deflate future year costs to current year money or to inflate future costs to reflect rising prices. If the price index is 100 in base year O and 120 in future year j, then the future year budget could be expressed in O year money and the factor P would be .833. In j-year money the factor would be 1.2. There is no way of knowing, however, how well the index will represent future price movements generally or prices relevant to the educational level i specifically.

Q is a quality factor introduced to take into account improvements in the system to increase output, efficiency, and measurable achievement. It would reflect changes that come from reducing pupil/teacher ratios, improving teacher qualifications and hence salary-schedule positions, increasing inputs of supplies, materials, equipment and books. The factor Q highlights the weakness of using cost per pupil ratios for future year estimates. To derive Q, each component input to the educational level must be costed and related to projected increases in efficiency or output. If this can be done there is no need to use general ratios in the first place. However, in most countries there is a way around this by the use of model schools or subsystems that already exist in the country. Within any given educational system in a developing country, there is a wide variation in quality and output. School A, which has the output that the system is aiming for in future years, can be studied and the cost of inputs determined. The ratio of this cost to the general system can be calculated. If School A has the output to which the national system aspires in future years and if per-pupil expenditures in A are twice that of the other schools, a Q factor of 2 can be introduced. Again, the method is rough, because A may offer extra services that the country does not need and that do not affect output. If A is a private school the costs may also be influenced by the scale of the operation. Output might also be influenced by some esprit de corps that can not be related to the richness of inputs. Ultimately, the planner must go through a component by component analysis of the factors which influence cost and output.

If the ratios are used, the total current expenditure budget for all of the i to k levels and kinds of programs within the system for the years O to n will equal:

$$\sum_{j=0}^{n} \sum_{i=0}^{k} O_j^i \tag{6}$$

Per-pupil costs may differ by grades within levels. The upper three grades in primary school may cost considerably more than the lower three. Hence, there would have to be as many subdivisions by levels and kinds of programs as there were relevant cost groupings. Cost per pupil ratios appear simple and they are the bases of many plans, but if they are handled in adequate fashion they grow just as complicated as cost-component analysis.

The outlay budgets for future years can also be based on price-quantity indexes. Price-quantity indexes take the planner a step further toward the costing of quality components in education. Subindexes can be computed for each major input category (instruction, supplies, plant . . .). The subindexes can then be moved into future years, in accord with estimated increases in quantity (larger enrollments), quality (richer inputs directed at securing more output), and price rises. The subindexes can be multiplied by expenditure weights and built into a general index for the entire educational system.

Wasserman (1963) worked with indexes based on weighted averages of price relatives. His objective was to devise a general index for all inputs to an educational system. The general index or any combination of subindexes can be useful as an analytic and descriptive device for studying changes over past periods or for revealing trends and relationships of educational inputs and costs. However, Wasserman points out that the index does have utility for estimating future-year expenditures:

> An educational price index based on some fixed standard of education can be projected into the future to estimate the degree of change in expenditure levels that will be necessitated by any anticipated price level changes. For example, suppose that officials in a school district conclude that prices of supplies, materials and most other educational inputs will increase by about 1 percent a year for the next three years, but that across the board increases of about 5 percent a year will have to be made in teacher salary levels in order to maintain the quality of the teaching staff. An education price index, based on a fixed schedule reflecting current-year education inputs can be projected over the next three years in the appropriate sub-index groupings to measure the effect of the anticipated price changes on expenditure . . . other effects, such as changes in numbers of pupils in the elementary and/or secondary schools, also would have to be considered in arriving at estimates of total expenditures.

In Table VI.2, Wasserman illustrates the method by compiling a price subindex for office supplies. The price subindex is based on a sample of three items taken to represent all office supplies used in the system. The prices of these items are followed over three periods and the prices

TABLE VI.2
Calculation of Price Subindex for Office Supplies and Accessories by Method of a Weighted Average of Price Relatives
(Period 0 = 100)

Item	Price relative in period 0 $\left(\dfrac{P_{0i}}{P_{0i}}\right)$ x100	1 $\left(\dfrac{P_{1i}}{P_{0i}}\right)$ x100	2 $\left(\dfrac{P_{2i}}{P_{0i}}\right)$ x100	Expenditure weight (dollars) w_i	Using absolute expenditure weights Price relative X weight 0 $\left(\dfrac{P_{0i}}{P_{0i}}\right)$ x100 w_i	1 $\left(\dfrac{P_{1i}}{P_{0i}}\right)$ x100 w_i	2 $\left(\dfrac{P_{2i}}{P_{0i}}\right)$ x100 w_i
1	100	150	170	1,500	150,000	225,000	255,000
2	100	140	180	300	30,000	42,000	54,000
3	100	150	200	200	20,000	30,000	40,000
.				2,000	200,000	297,000	349,000

Index values: For base period $= \dfrac{200,000}{2,000} = 100$

For period 1 $= \dfrac{297,000}{2,000} = 148$

For period 2 $= \dfrac{349,000}{2,000} = 174$

Using relative expenditure weights

					0	1	2
1	100	150	170	.75	75	112	127
2	100	140	180	.15	15	21	27
3	100	150	200	.10	10	15	20
				1.00	100	148	174

SOURCE: Wasserman, William, *Education Price and Quality Indexes*, Syracuse: Syracuse University Press, 1963, p.21.

Index values: For base period $= \dfrac{100}{1.0} = 100$

For period 1 $= \dfrac{148}{1.0} = 148$

For period 2 $= \dfrac{174}{1.0} = 174$

are expressed as a percentage of the price in the base period. If item one, paper, were $2.00 a ream in period 0; $3.00 in period 1 and $3.40 in period 2, then the price relative computations would be:

Item 1	P_0	P_1	P_3		P_0	P_1	P_3
	$\dfrac{\$2.00}{\$2.00} \cdot 100$	$\dfrac{\$3.00}{\$2.00} \cdot 100$	$\dfrac{\$3.40}{\$2.00} \cdot 100 =$		100	150	170

The same thing is done for all items in the sample. All items are not equally important in the expenditure budget for the school and, hence, must be weighted to reflect the importance of each item in the over-all price change. To weight the items the absolute or relative expenditures must be incorporated into the index. This is shown in the w_i column of Table VI.2.

The subindex for teacher inputs is shown in Appendix E. The subindex for office supplies, the subindexes for teacher and other inputs can then be incorporated into a general index of expenditures for the system as a whole.

The Price Index and Future Year Estimates

The general educational price index can be used to make future year expenditure estimates. The simplest application would be to estimate some trend from the three historical periods and incorporate this as the P factor in formula (5). On the basis of the three historical periods the index might move an average of 30 per cent a period, and this could be carried into future periods, with interpolations for intervening years:

P_0	P_1	P_2	P_3	$P_4 \ldots$
100	135	160	190	220

This is a crude and risky procedure without some examination of reasons underlying the changes observed and assumed, but it would probably yield better results than the use of a general price index previously suggested for equation (5).

The difficulty when the price index is applied to future estimates is that several things will change at the same time. First, quantities will change as enrollments grow. This factor would be manageable whatever formulation is used. In equation (5), E is simply raised. Second, trends based on past price movement may not continue into the future. In the example, the average gain observed may not continue into the future. A much more searching study of the movement of the prices of educational inputs would be necessary and this is usually beyond the competence of the planner. More than this, however, changes in quality and changes in the technology of education may make both the sample of items chosen for the subindexes and the expenditure weights unrepresentative of the situation in future years. Some items may drop out of the budget entirely and new ones may come in. The proportionate use of, and expenditure on, items may shift.

To use the price index for future expenditure estimates, the planner would have to begin with a projection of enrollments as in Table IV.7. He would then construct a model of inputs necessary to educate the students at some standard of quality. He might then, on the basis of the inputs identified as necessary, study the movement of prices of key items in past periods. Then, constructing a price quantity index and moving it into the future, he would be able to estimate an expenditure budget that reflected changes in quantity, changes in quality and changes in price. The planner would have to make a component-by-component study to derive the relative expenditure weights for the future. In the formula for the index, the expenditure weights would have to reflect the technology planned in year *n:*

$$\left(\frac{\Sigma_i \dfrac{P_{ni}}{P_{0i}} \cdot 100 \cdot W_{ni}}{\Sigma_i W_{ni}} \right) \cdot E_n \tag{7}$$

In such circumstances using the index at all might be questioned; and in any case the planner is driven to a component by component analysis of inputs to the system.

ESTIMATION OF COSTS BY DETAILED ANALYSIS OF EDUCATIONAL INPUTS

To the professional educator, the setting of program quality and the estimation of the costs of the components necessary to achieve standards are the sum and substance of educational planning. Once the goals of the educational system are translated into curricula and the curricula into courses, specifications can be written on staff, books, equipment, plant, and supplies. The specifications will determine unit costs. Costs multiplied by the numbers of students enrolled will provide total expenditure estimates.

One prime requirement is a set of rubrics for classifying the component inputs to education. Rubrics for classifying educational income and expenditure are set out in Table 1 of Chapter VII. A more detailed breakdown, which the U.S. Department of Health, Education, and Welfare devised for standardizing educational program accounting, is shown in Appendix L. For planning in developing countries, a less elaborate system suffices. Table VI.3 outlines one possibility.

Table VI.3 arranges educational activities, resources, and input components in a form for use of the linear program model in Chapter V. The cells of the table are input coefficients, i.e., the amount of some resources *b* that is necessary to give a year of education to a student or group of students at some level *x*. With an estimate of resources available in some future year *n* and input coefficients appropriate for that year, the feasibility of handling any given enrollment structure or producing any number of graduates can be tested. The program can be

TABLE VI.3
A Basic Programming Matrix (Cost Classes X Educational Levels)

	Primary					Secondary					Semi Professional		Higher B	Higher A		Total Resources
	x_1	x_2	x_3	x_4	x_5	x_6	x_7	x_8	x_9	x_{10}	x_{11}	x_{12}	x_{13}	x_{14}	$x_{15}... x_n$	
Current																
Salaries (retirement, benefits, etc.)																
1. Administrators (central) (line and staff specialists)	a_{11}														a_{1n}	$\leq b_1$
2. Principals																$\leq b_2$
3. Supervisors-Inspectors																
4. Teachers (Sched. Class A)																
5. Teachers (Sched. Class B)																
6. Teachers (Sched. Class C) other instructors, etc.																
7. Service employees, other																
Current Purchases																
8. Texts, curriculum materials						a_{ij}										
9. Library-audio																
10. Expendable supplies																
Plant Operation																
11. Maintenance																
12. Rental																
13. Utilities, services																

Additional Services
14. Health
15. Nutrition (lunch, milk)

Capital
16. Building, land
17. Debt service
18. Equipment
19. Trained Personnel

cont.
.
.
.
m

C_1 C_2 C_n

$a_{mn} \leq b_m$

made dynamic and moved over several time periods. Return coefficients can be attached to the activity levels, and optimal programs can be generated.

The difficulties of the linear program model are discussed in Chapter V, but here one important point should be noted. Even if the problem is not taken to a linear program stage a component by component study of the inputs to educational programs is a fundamental requisite for educational planning This is the route that must be taken to relate standards to quality, and quality to cost, and cost to resources.

The inputs, represented by the row rubrics in Table IV.3, can be combined in any way that seems relevant for the planning at hand. A two-row classification might suffice for some purposes. Inputs could be classified as Capital and Current. Or the classes, Instruction, Administration, Capital Outlay, and Debt Service might be used. Capital outlays and commodity purchases might be distinguished as to the portion requiring outlay of foreign exchange rather than local currency; and in developing countries where such exchange is short this distinction is often made. The inputs are subclassified just as thoroughly as is necessary for the planner's purpose.

Table VI.3 has all of the 15 grades of the three-level system model of Chapter IV. The columns can be regrouped and reduced in number to reflect the output of graduates at various significant levels of the system. Input coefficients can be computed on the basis of the amount of any resource necessary to produce a graduate or group of graduates from a given level or type of educational program. As in the system schematized in Appendix H, secondary programs may be broken down into First Cycle Secondary, Preparatory, Normal, Industrial, Agricultural, and Commercial. The Higher Education level may have to be subdivided into Higher Technical, Social Science, Education-Arts, Engineering, Agricultural, Doctoral (Medical-Scientific), Doctoral (Arts-Education). Whenever inputs and program costs differ, subclasses can be set up to reflect the differences. Even primary-level education might be classified into Rural and Urban when programs and costs are significantly different for the two.

Usually, the coefficients are expressed in money terms (e.g., constant dollars). Coefficient a_{45} would represent the input of teacher salaries to provide a year of education at grade five for one or a cohort of students. Or if the columns are grouped to indicate completion of certain significant program levels (graduates of fifth grade, 10th grade, etc.), the coefficient a_{4j} would be the input of teacher salary necessary to product a graduate at some level j. The coefficients and constraints need not be expressed in money terms. Resource 19 might represent the number of trained teachers available for allocation to the system. The coefficient a_{19j} would be the number of teachers of some category required to produce one or a group of graduates at some educational level.

Even if no linear program were run the coefficients and the aggregates of Table VI.3 would be useful for planning.

$$\sum_{j=1}^{n} a_{ij}x_j = \text{Amount to be allocated to administration at all levels; it would be less than } b_1, \text{ the amount available.} \quad (8)$$

$$\sum_{i=1}^{m}\sum_{j=1}^{5} a_{ij}x_j = \text{Amount to produce primary school graduates.} \quad (9)$$

$$\sum_{j=1}^{n}\sum_{i=1}^{m} a_{ij}x_{ij} = \text{Total cost of producing graduates at all levels and kind.} \quad (10)$$

$$\sum_{j=1}^{n}\sum_{i=1}^{m} a_{ij}x_{ij} \leq \sum_{i=1}^{m} b_i \quad (11)$$

This relationship is the fundamental test for planners. The amount required to offer a specified amount and quality of education to a specified number of students must be equal to or less than the total resources. The comparison indicates whether or not a program is feasible.

Per-pupil average costs, educational price quantity index numbers and component input coefficients can be worked in various ways to yield estimates of future expenditures. The advantage of cost coefficients, apart from their possible application in mathematical program models, is that they permit the planner to do a component-by-component analysis of inputs to the system. Quality is tied to cost in a much clearer fashion.

Costing Categories: Instruction Costs

Instructional staff covers classroom teachers of various quality and salary schedule levels, special subject teachers, teaching principals and principals that devote full time to administration of a single school. In some schools it might also include guidance and testing services. In many developing countries, 80 per cent of current expenditures and 60 per cent of total expenditures go to instructional staff costs.

The prime determinants of instructional costs are:

1. The number of students to be handled by the staff.
2. The ratio of staff to students set for the various programs.
3. The salary schedule for the staff, i.e., remuneration by hourly or annual rates according to preparation, position, or years of

service. The product of staff numbers by pay rate sets the instructional cost, which is the largest portion of the current budget in any school system.

For the planner the significant facts for future years are the number and kind of teachers who will be available and the resources that will be available for paying their salaries and benefits. Both the availability of teachers and their costs can be built into the program model. The input coefficients for teacher costs and teacher bodies will depend on some variant of pupil/teacher ratios. The output of the system is planned at a level sufficient to produce the required teachers so that the system can replace teachers (who die and retire) and still expand to meet the target requirements set.

The usual formula for inputs of instructional staff is a simple one in which a ratio of teacher bodies to student bodies is struck:

$$\frac{2,000 \text{ teachers}}{60,000 \text{ students}} \quad R = 1:30$$

Given an increase in students to 240,000, the number of new teachers necessary on this simple ratio is:

$$\frac{180,000}{30} = 6,000 \text{ (without allowing for wastage,}$$
$$\text{teacher death, retirement, etc.)}$$

Given an increase in teachers to 4,000, the maximum number of students that can be handled is 120,000.

The problem of planning necessary inputs and growth limits with such a simple stroke is obvious:

1. The ratio may not hold over all the system. Ratios are usually lower in rural than urban areas because of thin population distributions. Hence, a distribution of ratios by kinds of schools (at least rural and urban) might better be made and then projected according to the populations which are to be enrolled from these areas.

2. Basing ratios on what exists instead of on what should exist to assure an adequate program is merely planning to institutionalize inadequacies. A more sensible approach is to plan on the basis of a teacher force sufficient to accomplish minimal curriculum goals. Ratios can then be computed on this standard. A teacher/pupil ratio that holds for all places and levels and kinds of education cannot be set with one simple stroke. It is determined in general terms by measurement against quality

norms and the pattern or organization. Team-teaching, instead of self-contained classroom organization, will change the way ratios are computed for primary schools.

3. Ratios often take no account of the level of training of the teachers. One teacher body is counted equal to the next. Once goals are set, a distribution of teachers by levels of training is required. Teachers below a minimal level should not enter into the ratios at all. Provision should be made to train them in service or replace them. Teachers with higher levels of training should be counted differently. An example of how a team teaching arrangement can affect both numerical ratios and levels of quality, where team teaching and a non-self-contained classroom is the pattern, is shown in Figure VI.1 for the six grades of a primary school of 600 pupils. Stone and Bahner (1962) offer the scheme.

TEAM LEADER (TL). An experienced, mature, 'master teacher' of unusual talent, who has had at least 10 years of teaching experience, who possesses at least a master's degree, who has had training in supervision and human relations or educational sociology, and who is a specialist in an area of elementary education. Furthermore, this person would have demonstrated satisfactorily ability to work with teachers in a leadership role. It is anticipated that about one-third of this person's school day might be 'released' for such purposes as observation and training of subordinates, planning, curriculum development, research and evaluation, and parent relations.

SENIOR TEACHER (ST). An experienced, mature person with above-average talent comparable to the well regarded career teacher today. In addition, this person would have some degree of specialized competence in a particular area.

TEACHER (T). This category is seen as including two types of personnel:

(a) competent, experienced teachers of broad general training; and

(b) teachers of relatively little experience.

The status of this position is regarded as equal to the status of the typical teacher today.

INTERN (I). A trainee in a program of teacher education doing full-time supervised teaching in a school for one semester. The work of the intern is usually directed by a master teacher working with the training school supervisor.

TEACHER AIDE (TA). A mature person who enjoys direct contact

FIGURE VI.1
Sample Organization for Team Teaching

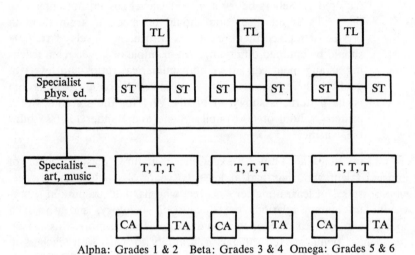

Alpha: Grades 1 & 2   Beta: Grades 3 & 4   Omega: Grades 5 & 6

with children. A teacher aide does not qualify as a teacher but can supervise or work with pupils in noninstructional situations: e.g., supervise bus arrivals and departures, recess and lunch periods; operate mechanical aids to instruction, 'housekeeping' tasks; correct objective tests. Specific tasks are defined by the particular demands of each team. Each team has 33 hours of teacher aide service per week.

CLERICAL AID (CA). A person for whom no professional preparation is necessary. This person assists with the routine nontechnical aspect of team operation: typing, duplicating, filing, and recording attendance.

There is no suggestion that any country, much less a developing one, should follow this pattern of organization. However, an appropriate pattern of organization which will determine future instructional staff inputs can be developed along this path far more effectively than by striking a simple ratio of teacher bodies to students. The planning for instructional staff inputs can be better done by school units (grouped by size) than by simple and often meaningless ratios of total staff to total enrollment for the system as a whole. For example, a six-year rural school might require the arrangement in Figure VI.2. The objective would be to optimize the assortment, taking advantage of limited numbers of trained and specialized people and the relatively greater numbers of lesser trained or untrained people who could serve as assistants.

Instructional staff inputs should be planned along with buildings and curriculum, even at the primary school level, instead of being computed as separate simple ratios. The team structure may affect the quality of the outcome significantly. Specialized teachers are more efficiently employed; lesson planning is improved; students are more effectively grouped for learning and people of lesser training receive in-service training and relieve shortages of highly trained and skilled teachers. It goes without saying that salary schedules for instructional staff will have to be more differentiated, so that rewards and incentives are provided for increased responsibility and improved performance. Measurement of teacher performance and award for merit is grist for another mill.

Generally, building principals are counted in with teachers to derive instructional staff ratios and inputs. Most countries specify, according to the number of classrooms, whether schools require a teaching principal or a full-time director.

The a_{ij} coefficients, representing instructional input per graduate, should be built up from the various school units within a given level and kind of education and then aggregated on a system-wide basis.

FIGURE VI.2
Alternate Organization for Rural and Urban School Team Teaching

(a) Six-year rural, partially graded school

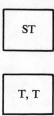

(b) An urban school with six grades and one class for each grade

(for purposes of comparison with Chart 5)

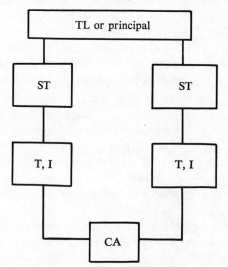

Ratios for each school are set according to the strategy indicated by the system output model in Chapter IV. Retention and survival in the upper grades of each level are to be maximized.

To express system-wide teacher to graduate input coefficients, various ratios are possible. The simplest is:

$$\frac{W}{P/T} \qquad \begin{array}{l} W = \text{years in level} \\ P/T = \text{Pupil-Teacher ratio (T always 1)} \end{array} \qquad (12)$$

The common way of setting teacher inputs in a six-year level, where the average pupil/teacher ratio is 30:1, is: $\frac{6}{30} = 1/5$. The coefficient of teacher input to graduate would be .20. When multiplied by the average annual salary of a teacher in the system, say \$1,000, the teaching cost for the graduate would be \$200, i.e. $\frac{6 \times 6 \times \$1,000}{6 \times 30}$. If put into a linear program model, the input-per-graduate coefficient could be expressed as \$200 or as .20, depending on whether the resource constraints were expressed in money or numbers of teachers available. The teacher input for one year of education would be \$33.33 in salary terms and .033 of a teacher.

In developing countries, the ratio should be modified to account for wastage and dropout. One simple way to do this is to make the numerator the average number of years of education that must be given to produce a graduate, rather than the legal number of years specified for the level. Instead of six years, the actual number of years to produce a graduate may be 15 (Cf. Chapter IV). In a system where the pupil/teacher ratios is 40:1, the situation would be: $\frac{15}{40} = .375$. Data from a small sample of primary schools in Nicaragua showed the pattern given in Table VI.4.

TABLE VI.4
Ratios of Years to Produce a Graduate to Pupil-Teacher Ratios ($n=7$)

1.	$15/40 = .375$
2.	$14/38 = .368$
3.	$13/36 = .361$
4.	$12/33 = .364$
5.	$10/32 = .313$
6.	$8/30 = .267$
7.	$8/28 = .286$

At issue is not an attempt to make anything of this shameful sample of seven schools. Other factors, in addition to teacher ratios, were favorable in the schools where numerators (fewer years to produce graduates) were small. But these 'mean' data do suggest that the planner might use some program such as this to set up coefficients over the years of a plan period:

		Year		
Base Year x	$x + 5$	$x + 10$	$x + 15$	$x + 20$
.375	.361	.313	.267	.286
(15/40)	(13/36)	(10/32)	(8/30)	(8/28)

This plans for cutting wastage and reducing pupil/teacher ratios.

The ratios can be converted to money terms, by taking into account the likelihood that salaries will rise as teacher preparation improves. From the outset, a qualitative assumption is made that 'teachers' have acquired a minimal level of training and education and are not merely bodies pressed into service. This format may be appropriate:

TABLE VI.5
Planning Schedule for Teaching Inputs

		Year			
	Base Year x	$x + 5$	$x + 10$	$x + 15$	$x + 20$
Teacher Input	.375	.361	.313	.267	.255*
Salary	$1,000.00	$1,500.00	$1,800.00	$2,000.00	$2,200.00
Money Input	$375.00	$541.50	$563.40	$534.00	$561.00

* improved

This scheme may also be useful to indicate to Ministries of Education that raising salaries, assuming comparable raises in teacher efficiency, does not materially increase the cost of producing graduates, which are, after all, the true issue of the system. System productivity, which is in large part teacher productivity, should be measured against students reaching some significant level of school achmievement.

Input ratios may also be expressed in terms of blocks of 100 or 1,000 graduates if this makes it easier to manage and if the other inputs are scaled accordingly. From Table VI.5, base year x, the input for 100 graduates would be 37.5, and for 1,000, 375. Unweighted pupil/teacher ratios serve well enough at the primary school level for getting future year estimates of instructional costs. For secondary and higher levels, staffs must be planned on the basis of instructional or contact hours and for each separate field of study. If future enrollments could be planned by optimally sized school units, as in Figure VI.2 for example, the cost of the instructional team (plus principal) could be forecast and future gains of enrollments broken up into 600 pupil units can be costed. Schools do not often come into being in this way in developing countries.

Other Instructional Staff (Principals, Supervisors, Inspectors)

Ratios for inputs of principals, supervisors, guidance counsellors and the like can be handled in the same way as teachers and need not be treated separately. Coefficients will be much smaller per graduate, as there are far larger numbers of graduates per principal or supervisor. The supervisory staff necessary to handle the programs envisaged must be built up in the same way as teachers, i.e., aggregated from within the system by school units.

Higher Administration

Administrator/pupil ratios can be handled in the same way as the Instructional Staff. In a balanced and efficient system, the ratios or co-efficients should be small. As a rough ratio, the number of principals should be not more than 1:6 and not less than 1:12 of teacher numbers. In money terms, because administrators receive higher salaries, the cost ratios may run 1:4 to 1:8. Supervisors and inspectors may run 1:20 of principals. These ratios are illustrative of method and not normative, but they should never be left out of the calculations or roughed into a pupil/teacher ratio in a way that suggests that all staff will be committed to classroom teaching.

Instructional Staff Ratio for Secondary and Higher Education

For secondary and higher education, it is more difficult to fix instructional ratios and input costs. The base unit is generally class hours, and if the plan deals in graduates, and not enrollment or attendance, hours per course and courses per program must be calculated. The simplest approach is to set up an adequate administrative-instructional staff for a school of a given size (800 or 1,000 pupils) and to cost this model staff. This was the approach taken by the IIME (Michigan State-San Carlos) planning staff in Central America (1964). Instructional hours may have to be classified as lecture, laboratory, conference, section meeting. Each may have a different yet appropriate instructional ratio. There are varying ways to arrive at the appropriate aggregates.

One possible way is outlined in Table VI.6 which has a four-subject program with a total of 78 hours of instruction:

TABLE VI.6
Teaching Hour Schedule

	Subject A		Subject B		Subject C		Subject D		Total
Lecture (IR = 1/40)	16	(400)	12	(300)	4	(100)	0	(0)	32
Laboratory (IR = 1/20)	8	(400)	0	(0)	4	(200)	0	(0)	12
Section Meeting (IR = 1/5)	2	(200)	10	(1,000)	6	(600)	0	(0)	18
Seminar-Conference (IR = 1/5)	0	(0)	0	(0)	0	(0)	16	(3,200)	16
	26	(1,000)	22	(1,300)	14	(900)	16	(3,200)	T = 78

The ratios can be expressed as fractions that must be imputed to the total program or to any of the major subjects within it. Calculations of ratios by subjects to be taught is esesntial at this level. It is necessary to plan for more than mere numbers of teachers to man programs. The assortment of teachers (specialities) is indispensable knowledge for planning secondary and higher programs.

Fractional ratios can be computed, but the easier way is to deal with units of 100 or 1,000 graduates and compute teacher man hours in the various subjects. For cell one, first row, first column, the calculations would be $\frac{16 \times 1000}{40} = 400$ instructional hours to produce 1,000 graduates in this kind of class and in this subject. The other values are filled in within parentheses in Table VI.6.

The data can then be used to estimate the number of instructors in different subject fields. If the total program runs five weeks, and an instructional load is 20 hours a week, then 10 teachers are required for subject field *A;* 13 in *B;* 9 in *C;* and 32 in *D;* a total of 64 to produce 1,000 graduates. The average ratio, for whatever it might mean, would be between 1:15 and 1:16. These ratios can be readily converted to money terms by multiplying into the salary schedule.

A factor may have to be introduced to convert enrollments to graduates. This requires analysis of each situation to scale enrollments to meaningful production, i.e., graduates. Fifty students may enroll in a class for every forty who graduate.

The numbers dealt with at the secondary and higher levels of education are sufficiently small (India and a few other countries are notable exceptions) that staffs can be analyzed and studied at all institutions and then summed. There seems no excuse for dealing with system-wide averages in secondary and higher education. It may be necessary in the primary school, where numbers are great and the teacher preparation and pay do not differ markedly.

A Further Note on Staff and Planning

In the United States, where education is administered in local units, it is common to lump administration and instructional staff under one rubric, Professional Staff Members, and to express this as a ratio to students. A ratio of 50 professional staff members to 1,000 students is generally held to be an adequate one. This staff may be further characterized by the percentage of professionals who hold higher degrees (Masters and up). In those systems generally characterized as 'excellent' in New York State, over 50 per cent of the staff hold higher degrees. Critics of 'professional' education would say that the analysis should go further and consider the kind of study program some of these higher degrees represent. The planner can read Conant (1959), Rickover (1960), and Bestor (1953) and take his own stance.

The appropriate rubrics for classifying instructional and administrative staff will vary. Formal educational background is a common basis for ranking, i.e., preparational schedule. Type of post is another, i.e., positional schedule. Length of service may be yet another salary schedule basis. A schedule with all three, positional, preparational and seniority is shown in Table VI.7.

Once categories are set up they can be arranged into salary schedules, multipiled by numbers of staff required in each class, and converted to cost. A great many country plans project teacher requirements for future years, without taking into account the fact that as the system grows and teachers increase, supporting professional staff must grow apace. Projections do not reckon with this and assume all staff increases will go into the classroom and directly handle a piece of the pupil load.

School Buildings and Capital Outlay

In the rapidly expanding school systems of developing countries, capital outlay for school construction (including the purchase of land for site and the costs of financing) may range from 10 to 35 per cent of the total expenditure on education. The size of the expenditure on school construction and the finality of the commitment when a school is located and built and the duration of the obligation that is undertaken in its financing—all make the programming of capital outlay for school building a central task for planners in developing countries. In the

TABLE VI.7
Model Salary Table
(Preparation, Seniority and Position)

Level	Salary: Range or Median	Formal Education and Training	Seniority Increment (3% on base rate for each 5 yrs. of service)	Likely Posts
Class One	***	University Education and Training	Steps 1.5	University, normal or secondary teachers; Ministry or Provincial officials; principals of large units.
Class Two		Higher Normal School Graduate	Steps 1.5	Secondary teachers, Ministry section head; provincial inspector; sub-inspector; principal; guidance counselor
Class Three		Lower Normal (Secondary level)	Steps 1.5	Primary school teacher or principal; sub-inspector, Ministry workers
Class Four		Secondary Graduate with some in-service training and certification	Steps 1.5	Usually same as class three
Class Five		Less than secondary or normal	Steps 1.3	Classroom teachers, primary and especially rural (sometimes greater than 50% of staff)

United States the field that is called 'educational planning' consists almost completely in estimating future need for buildings, determining the location, writing the educational program specifications for the school, translating these into the physical space requirements and arranging the financing of the venture. A voluminous literature on the subject has been produced by school administrators, urban planners, architects, engineers, and fiscal experts and some of the representative selections are listed in this book where the subject is explored only from the standpoint of how it enters general schemata and models.

In programming cost in developing countries, outlay on original construction is often the only factor explicitly examined. The common pattern is expenditure out of the revenues of the central government or from a long-term low-interest loan or grant from abroad. A reckoning of what the true cost of financing the project would be is not often made, although a cost-benefits comparison of the project with some other allocation might be attempted. Maintenance costs scarcely enter the calculations at all, and rarely is any budgetary provision made for maintenance and minor replacement in future years. Still, maintenance may shape the design of the facility, as when chicken wire is used instead of window glass and drinking water is provided out of a pipe and tap placed out of the reach of 'destructive' children.

The general planning which precedes a building program in a developing country is, in simple form, much the same as the study that goes forward in a richer one. Requirements, usually measured in terms of numbers of students in level and kind of program, are estimated. Existing facilities are surveyed. This covers the adequacy of the present location, the capacity of the plant and its condition. Plant and site are evaluated according to minimal standards of safety and sanitation. A canvass of potential sites is made; simple plans for building on them are drawn, and the costs estimated.

A building survey form used in Latin America is outlined in Appendix P. This schedule is shown not to exemplify a good form but rather to illustrate the primitive level of the facilities with which a developing country makes do. If a North American administrator were completing the form, almost every school would be classified as totally inadequate in site and structure.

Educational planners usually are consulted only to the point of determining the need for a specific size of facility in a neighborhood, district or area. At that point the Ministries of Education and/or Public Works prepare the preliminary plans. Usually in national systems these are stock plans with four or five variants according to the climate and materials in the specific area. The Ministry of Public Works engineers usually make the studies of topographical and soil maps and the test borings and surveys that underlie the selection of the specific site according to its size, shape, topography, subsoil, and availability.

Ministry of Education officials may, in larger projects and for secondary schools, have a chance to express their opinion on minimal specifications when the preliminary plans are drawn. Architects and engineers, often in Public Works offices, prepare the working drawings, construction specifications, and the cost estimates. Educators may have no further voice in the matter until the completed building is turned over for Ministry use. This is not the most desirable procedure but it is one that is widely prevalent.

A planner in a national office, located in the executive and outside the sectoral ministries, may attempt to establish some exchange of views between the educators and the builders, but the general lack of communication among functionaries is almost a characteristic of developing countries. Some great educational monstrosities have been founded because of this. Location is one of the most important aspects of site selection and accessibility is fundamental to location. In one country a new school was built on the wrong side of a gulley that became a rushing torrent in the rainy season; the children lived on the other side. The Public Works engineer's response to a query on this fact was: "I'm in the department that builds schools. You'll have to see the man in charge of highways."

At Highways the answer was: "You want the man in charge of bridges."

This man was out.

International standards for school facilities do not exist. Even within the United States, experts do not agree on the standards for measuring the area and volume of buildings. The 'architectural area' (of the American Institute of Architects) and the 'gross area' (of the American Standards Association) will yield slightly different estimates of plant capacity. If this fundamental metric differs, then standards for instructional space per student will also vary. And if these seemingly readily quantifiable measures are not standardized, it is quite impossible to set up norms for more qualitative relationships between space and learning efficiency. Masses of studies on the influence of physical surroundings (illumination, ventilation, work space, color, noise level) on learning and teaching have been carried out over many years; and yet the increment of efficiency that comes with improvement beyond certain minimal levels is not known with certainty. One suspects that the architects and educators are making perfectly good sense when they state that certain kinds of physical arrangement, over and above the basic minimum of comfort, will influence school performance. Cramped quarters and monotonous forms and drab and restrictive borders to the physical horizons may tend to cut down inquisitiveness and exploratory behavior and promote rote and routine response. Possession of individual work space may promote security and enhance powers of concentration. But finely shaded relationships between physical plant (and the resulting costs) and learning are difficult to establish. One must take a position half way between the budget officer who sees no need for a school plant that provides any more than the barest shelter, and the architect who favors beauty galore. Facilities that would appall North American educators serve quite well in developing countries. For the planner the best that can be offered is that minimal standards of comfort must be provided, and beyond that it depends on what the country can afford.

Some of the planning data required for school location planning have been treated in other sections. Population data which show the numbers and ages and locations of students who will attend are fundamental. The pinpointing of attendance loads in specific localities brings one more level of difficulty beyond the national and subnational projections. The common bases for location planning is a census of school-age and pre-school-age children, birth rates from local registries, number of women in child-bearing ages, fertility rates, and net migration.

National census data will often furnish the population by age and sex for the sub-area or district, but the vital rates (natality, fertility, mortality) may not be available, and even the local registries on which these rates can be computed may be missing or imperfectly kept in rural areas. The national census will also give a general basis for determining whether the area is undergoing net in-migration or out-migration, but precise information on the age and sex composition of migrants will not generally be at hand.

Rough estimates based on rates computed for other similar regions and applied to the specific area under study may be the best that the planner can hope for. However, in the rural areas a local census for school planning purposes is usually simple to run and inexpensive, and the teacher or district inspector may know the setting so well that fair guesses about the future can be made. There is usually no restriction imposed by the extent of open land available and the economic or physical factors that would affect population growth and shifts can be fairly well determined. One of these is the driving of a new road through a rural area. Population will tend to string out along it. Another problem that makes planning difficult is that the building of the school itself will attract people with children. Still, building is generally so simple and land so readily available that no costly mistakes are likely in rural areas. Buildings can be expanded or schools moved, and if the structure is of any quality at all it can be adapted to other purposes or sold.

For school construction planning in developing countries and for the critically necessary redistricting and consolidation of rural schools that are too small to operate efficiently, local district maps are necessary. These maps need not be elaborate or expensive, but they should show schematically the numbers and locations of school-age children, existing school facilities, natural barriers and transportation routes and district boundaries. The rude map in Appendix K illustrates the essentials. The number of children in each district could be included, and the map could be scaled and designed as an overlay and keyed to a map of a larger area.

District reorganization and consolidation is a necessary step before school construction programs are planned and buildings costed. In the United States, the number of school districts has been decreased from 127,000 in 1932 to 31,700 in 1963. In the decade 1951–1962, the number of school districts was halved, and by 1960 the number of districts was being reduced by 5 per cent a year.

In urban areas better data are available for planning, but the margin for error is small and mistakes in location can be costly. One of the great weaknesses of educational organization in developing countries is the absence of well defined neighborhood and community organization and the demarcation of school attendance areas and fixed districts. In the rural areas, the village center or a main highway usually provides a reference point around which the school attendance area can be established.

In urban areas, the quarter or neighborhood serves to keep primary school age children in some kind of district bounds. In fact, the mobility of poor residents of the neighborhoods may be very slight. In the middle grades and in secondary schools, however, urban districting is usually chaotic and children pour in from all quarters to crowd the few good schools. Establishing attendance areas and districts in the urban areas is one of the first requisites for planning. The data and the maps on which to do this vary in coverage and quality.

Population and vital data are generally available for districts in the older and settled parts of the cities. The *favelas, vecindades, barrios,* and slum settlements around the edges of the city or on the marginal lands (in gulleys and on steep banks) may be uncharted and unenumerated wastelands in which people from country areas come and go. But for the established areas, city planning offices usually have data on residential housing (housing censuses are run as part of the general census). These records cover age, condition and type, and may give some estimate of the permanency of occupancy. Permits for new units and units under construction furnish another source of data. A land-use map of the attendance areas in most parts of the city can be prepared. Urban planning is far enough advanced so that the major factors that control location can be determined. The planner can map where the children live, where the restrictive (natural and man-made) boundaries are, where the open land lies and how this is controlled, if it is, by zoning ordinances. The major traffic patterns can be sketched in as well as utility extensions and commercial and industrial hazards. From this, the probable directions of residential, commercial, and industrial growth for the area can be schematized. With all of this and a knowledge of land values, school locations and site acquisitions can be planned as far in advance as is practical in view of the one great restraint on future expansion, i.e., funds. In the settled and older areas of the city all facilities that are necessary to satisfy the neighborhood requirements, along with dwelling-unit saturation, may make neighborhood saturation planning possible up to the point where the long-term cycle of change sets in. Complete and permanent installations can be built with a reasonable expectation of an adequate service life.

In the flux of the nonpermanent areas where migrants are flooding in and out and no orderly patterns of urbanization have been established, the planner can only suggest flexibility in physical facilities. This may call for planning relocatable facilities, but not of the kind that the U.S. has used. In the United States in 1962, there were 36,000 nonpermanent school facilities. These were of various kinds, but the main classes were Portable (total structure could be moved on flatbed of a truck), Mobile (trailer-type), Divisible (large modular building components designed to fit together) and Demountable (designed in modules so that, if the building is disassembled and reassembled, a high recovery of the building components is possible). Inasmuch as most of the areas where relocatable facilities might be needed are also relatively inaccessible and disordered, the mobile and portable facilities are not likely prospects.

A study of almost a third of the relocatable facilities in the U.S. showed costs ranging from $4.50 to $30.00 a square foot. Facilities averaged out at about $13.00 a square foot. This is initial inplace cost and does not include costs for site preparation, disassembly, transportation, and relocation at another site which could run 10 per cent of the initial cost, depending on the type of facility (demountable facilities cost the most to relocate), the distance, the condition of the new site, and labor costs. This would put them out of the range of purses in most developing countries.

With infant industries and the scarcity and cost of skilled workers and materials, developing countries could not produce facilities as cheap. Very cheap construction, with local materials, climate permitting and security minima established, might be more likely. Tents are another alternative, although security is a problem, as with thatched roof shelters. The present common practice is shacks, either government-owned or rented, that represent small outlay and commitment. Even with the structure provided, there is often no site preparation and no utility connections for light, water, and sewage. The need for flexible, expansible, convertible, and versatile facilities is great in urban slums and for nomadic rural people, but the construction industry has not yet devised an economic alternative that provides minimal security for such meager school materials as exist, other than cheap and wholly unsatisfactory construction of wood, stone, and earth.

However pale the resemblance to the school houses in richer countries, the developing country must plan its facilities on the same basis. The facilities must fit the culture and customs of the community and reflect them in the educational program. (The present overriding consideration is fit to the economy and the budget it permits.) The school building should also provide for the best possible implementation of the present and future curriculum. Finally, the school should take into account the developmental characteristics—physical, social, and emotional—of the age group it will serve. It would be cruel to recommend that the educators in developing countries write the specifications for a plant that would satisfy even their own modest hopes for an educational program; but some attention to making the building fit the culture, the curriculum, and the developmental levels of the children is necessary.

Primary school facilities should, insofar as possible, be dispersed in neighborhoods, rather than built into very large central facilities of twenty classrooms or more. The travel radius for primary children should be less than a mile and should not be interdicted with hazards, natural or man-made. The primary school student will probably, and for some time to come, be served in the self-contained classroom. This should provide some individualized work space and some room for storage. There should be ample play space, which usually comes at small cost, and has an important contribution to learning as well as providing pleasure and healthful exercise.

Water connections and sanitary facilities are minimal, but many schools do not now have them. Ventilation and illumination are fundamental. Artificial illumination also offers the possibility of multiple use of the facility in the community for meetings and night school. It is not an added trimming.

U.S. schools, with their libraries and instructional materials centers, administrative and guidance facilities, teachers lounges, dining, assembly, and play spaces may average 100 square feet of space per child enrolled, and offer a minimal instruction space of over 25 square feet. In the developing countries, the schools may have little more inside the walls than classrooms, an office space, and a storage room which in some cases serves also as a place to prepare and serve a light meal. The minimal instructional space in the classroom should be one-and-a-third square meters. All of this may seem incredibly modest to educators from countries of plenty, but these minima are not even widely met. Lightless, cramped, waterless, foul little dungeons that do not meet these minima are called 'schoolhouses.' This, in itself, is damaging nomenclature and planners might begin by removing it from the records and calling them 'provisional space.' There is something in a name when it refers to anything so central in a community as its school.

Upper-middle and secondary-school facilities planning, addressed as it usually is to a variety of curricula and programs, is more complicated. Still, minimal specifications can be written. The location should usually not be more than two miles distant for commuting students, unless transportation is furnished. The building should provide individual study space in a homeroom base, although the classroom will not be as self-contained because of the variety of activities that must go forward. It should have two meters of instructional space minimally. There should be a library with reading room space for 10 per cent of the student body and nine or ten volumes per student enrolled.

If a vocational or industrial program is offered, the shop area should provide minimally 30 feet of space per trainee and go up in size, according to the program. Buildings should have varied sized rooms for varied size classes, ranging from small groups of 10–15 to large assembly groups of over 100. The more individualized study space that can be provided the better. More than anything else, the classroom and study space must be so designed that noise is minimized and scholarship possible. The constant observation that only rote and routine learning go on in the classrooms of developing countries is in part attributable to the fact that in the babble that prevails nothing but rote tasks can be attempted in school; and at home no privacy is possible.

These are only rough minima for the planner, and each facility has to be planned by experts on laboratories, shop programs, and libraries. In secondary schools, the provision of multi-use and flexible instructional work and study space is critical. One cannot hope for 10-acre sites with cluster and campus arrangements of buildings, but the lot must provide some space for recreational activities, e.g., a few hard-surfaced areas or courts and a turf-and-dirt area that provides space for the team sports of the country.

There are yardsticks for evaluating the adequacy of school facilities in the United States, but the minimal standard on these forms is so much higher than the maximum one which prevails in many countries—or that will prevail when education is opened up to greater numbers—that modifying an existing U.S. schedule or check list is depressing and useless. Each country must develop its own, in the light of its own capacities and educational program expectations. When these are developed, those components of the program that are established as minimal necessities can be costed. This is not to say that in developing countries some show-case facilities are not as elaborate as the best in the United States or Europe. Some are more elaborate and much more costly. But if educational opportunity is to be widened in accord with country development plans, there must be a leveling toward a middle package that the country can provide.

While North American authorities may recommend writing the educational program specifications first and making the building space fit them, the administrator in developing countries may have to accept the use of stock architectural plans which use relatively inflexible construction modules. Conditions of employment and import, and exchange restrictions may force the use of labor-intensive construction projects, rather than more advanced materials and methods from abroad. The result may be a row of coops or barracks in which all consideration of aesthetics have been sacrificed to economy, but learning may still go on there. The restrictions under which educators operate in developing countries are so great that no other course is open.

A typical component cost schedule from the U.S. cannot be applied. Yet there is merit in showing one, if only to introduce factors which must be considered in planning and costing. Appendix Q shows the comparison formula devised by Englehardt (1958). There are others, slightly different and equally useful. Each country must devise its own and the planner must assist in this task, along with the variety of educators in special areas and fields, the architects, engineers and physical space planners who are the true specialists in the work.

In Appendix Q, Component Column 1, some of the equipment, e.g., draperies and stage lighting, might be dropped. Special professional fees are not as likely, inasmuch as these services will be provided by attorneys, architects and engineers regularly employed by the Ministry of Education, Ministry of Public Works, or national or local planning offices or commissions. In general, these permanently employed specialists cost more and yield less, but that is the way the system operates in most developing countries. For countries in tropical regions, heating costs are saved, but air conditioning and ventilation are larger problems. Elevators are not a common feature.

In Component Column 2, correction factors are, of course, set on U.S. areas and indexes, but the developing country should borrow the notion. Regional differences in costs can be quite marked. So, too, is it necessary to take into account fluctuating price indices. The per-pupil standards are U.S. and must be modified to the reality of the country. Whether or not all areas in Column 5 would be classed as Educational Area, e.g., the swimming pool, depends on the educational philosophy and program of the country. The form is quite easy to modify for any given country, and the usual manner of modification would be simplification.

Cost Formulas for National Planning Models

The calculation of costs for buildings usually follows the straightforward formulation:

$$\frac{T}{P/CR} \cdot X$$

T = Total of students to be accommodated in classrooms (same for new and replacement of rental and inadequate) (13)
P/CR = Pupil to classroom ratio (CR taken as 1)
X = Per-classroom cost

This gives a rough measure of capital outlays required in future years. Cost coefficient per graduate will take into account, as instructional outlay did, the actual number of years it takes to produce a graduate within the level:

$$a_{ij} = \frac{WX}{YZ}$$

W = Number of years to produce graduate in level
X = Cost per classroom
Y = Building life in years (14)
Z = Average student load in classroom

Coefficients can be weighted to reflect different costs for different kinds of facilities within level, e.g., for rural and urban classrooms which often differ markedly in costs and pupil load.

$$a_{ij} = p\frac{(WX)}{YZ} + q\frac{(WX)}{YZ}$$

p = proportion needed rural (15)
q = proportion needed urban

Data from Guatemala showed:

$$a_{ij} = .6 \frac{(2000 \times 10)}{30 \times 30} + .4 \frac{(3000 \times 10)}{30 \times 40}$$
$$\$13.33 + \$10.00$$
$$\$23.33$$

Though classrooms in urban areas cost more, they can be more fully utilized because of favorable densities of student populations. By scheduling double sessions, the per-student cost can be halved in the city; but this is not likely in rural areas.

The use of the factor $\frac{2000}{30}$ in the above calculation is tantamount to using a straight line method of depreciation, with an assumption of no salvage value at the end of 30 years. It does not take into account the cost of the money put into capital expenditure.

Wasserman states that building life can be viewed as without limit; but this does not seem to be in accord with the facts in developing countries where cheaper construction, inadequate maintenance and shifts in population put a definite life limit on most facilities. This may not be 30 years, but it is some number under 100 and the planner needs an estimate of it. Countries may devise a school plant life table to summarize the data gathered from basic survey forms. Table VI.8, or

TABLE VI.8
School Plant Life Table

Age Interval Bldg.	*(1)* No. C.R.'s	*(2)* Total Capacity Students	*(3)* Average Years of Life Remaining	*(4)* Life × Capacity (2) × (3)
0–5				
5–10				
10–15				
15–20				
20–25				
25–30				
30–35				
35–40				
40–45				
45–50				
over 50				

variations on it, serves as an inventory and a base for projection into future years. Dividing column 4 by the number of years necessary to produce a graduate in the level will give an estimate of the plant capacity in graduates, and indicate how many classrooms must be added on to meet graduate output targets in future years. Column 3 will depend on other things, in addition to the age of the buildings, i.e., condition, construction, location. . . . The table is filled on the basis of a building survey of existing plant, and reports of completed construction and may serve as a continuing inventory. (Cf. Appendix P)

Capital Outlay for Future Years

In actual practice, the capital input per graduate is of less use in planning than the total investment or outlay on buildings to accommodate enrollments for future years. The capital outlay for buildings for education level i in year j can be estimated on the basis of enrollments, teaching, and other space required for a pupil place, and unit construction costs:

$$B_j^i = \left[\frac{E_j^i}{U_j} - \left(\frac{E_O^i}{U_O} - \frac{E_R^i}{U_R}\right)\right] \cdot [{}^tS_j^i \; {}^tC_j^i + {}^lS_j^i \; {}^lC_j^i] \qquad (16)$$

where:

$\quad {}^tS_j^i$ = Per-place space, teaching

$\quad {}^tC_j^i$ = Construction cost space, teaching

$\quad {}^lS_j^i$ = Per-place space, lab, library, other

$\quad {}^lC_j^i$ = Construction cost, space library, lab, other

$\quad B_j^i$ = Capital outlay buildings

$\quad E_j^i$ = Enrollments, level i, year j

$\quad E_O^i$ = Enrollments level i, base year

$\quad E_R^i$ = Enrollment space lost through replacement of facilities

$\quad U$ = Use of space ratio

The rather pretentious equation can be simply illustrated:

Enrollment projected in level i, year j is 200,000.

Enrollment in base year is 120,000.

Enrollment space that must be replaced during period is 40,000.

In the base year 30% of the space gets double use; the double use in the space that is to be replaced is 20%; and the double use in the projected year will be cut to 10%. Hence the use ratios will be 1:1.3; 1:1.2; and 1:1.1.

The teaching space per pupil place is 1.6 square meters.

The cost is $75 per square meter of teaching space.

The space per pupil for other (lab, library, etc.) is 2.1 square meters.

The cost for other space is $100 per square meter.

The future building outlay is then:

$$\$40.2 \text{ million} = \frac{200,000}{1.1} - \frac{120,000}{1.3} + \frac{40,000}{1.2} (1.6 \times \$75 + 2.1 \times \$100)$$

The cost per student enrolled can be converted to a cost per graduate by taking wastage into account.

The formula can allow for both quantitative expansion and qualitative change. The space per pupil can be expanded if enrollments in the base year and replacement space is modified. The construction unit costs can be raised to reflect price changes, according to a construction cost index, and also to reflect improvement in quality of construction. The use ratios can be reduced as the school day is lengthened and double sessions are cut back. The schedule for replacement of facilities, derived from a plant life table in the base year, can also reflect improvement in quality, as older and less adequate facilities are scheduled for replacement earlier.

Financing Capital Outlay

In the United States, the common pattern of financing capital outlay for school construction is through bond issues. The problems of getting the citizenry to approve the bond issue by vote are special burdens for the U.S. administrator. The interest rate on these bonds has risen steadily from 2 per cent and now is between 4 and 5 per cent. If the financing is over a 30-year period the financing cost may now come to 60 per cent of the principal. In the developing countries the cost of money on the open market may be much higher, and failure to include financing charges in plans leads to a serious underestimate of capital costs.

When resources are scarce and many alternative uses and investments are possible, formulas (13)–(15) underestimate cost. If a charge for money through a capital recovery factor is made (in which depreciation and interest are charged), the costs per student will come out considerably higher. The cost will depend on assumptions about rate of interest and life of the property and different sets of these will be appropriate for different circumstances.

The formula used here is:

$$\frac{W}{Z} \cdot R \qquad \text{Where } W, \text{ as before, is the number of years to complete level and } Z \text{ is student load handled in the facility.} \qquad (17)$$

R is the Equivalent Annual Cost: $\quad R = P \left[\dfrac{i\,(1 + i)^n}{(1 + i)^{n-1}} \right] \qquad (18)$

Within the parenthesis is the capital recovery factor. It can be directly obtained from tables of compound interest functions where values are tabled according to the interest rate i and the number of years n. This factor when obtained from the table is multiplied by the initial outlay P, and the result is an annual equivalent cost figure which takes into account interest and depreciation over the life of the investment.

An example is appropriate. In this example the construction costs per classroom, classroom use pattern, and years to complete level (i.e., graduate) are as before. The equivalent annual cost is computed over the life of the building, taken as 30 years, as before. The interest rate used is a low one based on availability of long-term soft loans (30 years at 2 per cent). This rate does not take into account the true or social rate which would prevail in the country which would be much higher (and much more difficult to estimate).

$$\text{Urban:} \ (p = .40) \frac{W}{Z} \cdot R = \left(\frac{10}{40}\right) (\$3000)(.04465, \text{ from table}) = 33.49$$

$$\text{Rural:} \ (p = .60) \frac{W}{Z} \cdot R = \left(\frac{10}{30}\right) (\$2000)(.04465) \qquad = 29.77$$

$$a_{ij} \text{ coefficient for system} = \$31.25 \text{ (weighted by } ps\text{)}$$

When the difference (between $23.33 and $31.25) of $7.92 is multiplied by the thousands of graduates that the system must produce the result is vast; yet it would seem that some allowance must be made for the capital used. An interest rate of 2 per cent is not very likely, even for long-term development loans.

In calculating capital costs for the school system, the method of amortizing outlays will influence the coefficients or ratios. Various sinking fund or bond retirement schedules may be appropriate, and different coefficients may prevail in different parts of the system, in accord with the way the financing is set up.

THE COST AND MAINTENANCE OF EXISTING FACILITIES

The handling of existing facilities is again a matter of option. The planner may be primarily concerned with future outlays, and existing facilities may, at the beginning of the plan period, be taken as a free good, with provision made only for maintenance through the life of the plan. The costing of maintenance in developing countries is widely ignored. So is maintenance itself. The cost of maintenance will depend on the quality of the original construction. With better design and construction and the replacement of older facilities, costs for maintenance as a per cent of total have been dropping in the U.S. Currently, maintenance and replacement, as a per cent of total has dropped to about 3 per cent. This covers recurring repairs, replacements, and improvements, which total about $.30 per square foot of construction a year. In the developing countries maintenance allocations may be so small as not to appear in the budget at all, and the effective life of the facility is drastically cut.

Equipment Costs

Outlays for equipment can be costed in the same way plant was. In the upper level of an educational system equipment outlay is large for the kinds of education most closely related to increasing the productive capacity of a developing country: vocational and technical training, and professional education in engineering and the sciences. Severe underestimates of cost and subsequent malfunctions of the system come from scrimping on equipment outlays. Mere shells of laboratories and shops proliferate and are inoperable because of a lack of equipment. Costing of these outlays is reserved for a later section.

Textbooks

Now, and for some time to come in developing countries, large expenditures will have to be planned for the purchase, production, and distribution of textbooks. A shortage or absence of standard textbooks characterizes schools of developing countries, above all in the primary school and literacy programs. Country educational plans continue to appear, without any provision for textbooks in the primary level or reference and library volumes for the upper levels. In almost all of Latin America, until very recently, no provision for textbooks was made in ministry of education budgets. The fortunate children whose parents could buy books had a motley collection of poorly designed, written, and manufactured books which sold at steep prices. In West Africa the situation was scarcely better. In a situation where every child in the class had a different, but equally bad, book, a standardized curriculum was impossible. Not that one would recommend a curriculum that was standardized and machine-precise in every detail; but a course of study with some common core of learning for all is necessary. Mexico and the regional educational materials center in Central America, which this writer planned, have made provision of adequate books at moderate costs. In countries where teacher qualifications, even with great good luck, can only be raised to minimal standards in the next 20 years, a great burden falls on the textbook. This situation is likely to persist for some time, despite the optimistic promises of teaching machinery for the future.

Textbook outlays cannot be costed until curriculum plans are established and the number and kind of books determined. Curriculum development is a central educational problem and deserves more than the space that can be given to it in an outline of this sort.

Patently, the public school curriculum should reflect, or at least not be in conflict with, broad national goals—political, cultural, and economic.

In those countries which are attempting to provide universal primary education in the face of manifest economic difficulty, on the grounds that it is an essential step toward nation building, the curriculum must not be inconsistent with the national culture and national social and political aspirations. School text books should embody these goals, or certainly not contradict them. Yet in any number of countries text books openly diverge from what might be presumed to be national aspirations and culture. Governments also differ on how much they wish elements out of their own cultural heritage to be used in school books. In one African country, the use of national folk material and legend for primary school books was approved; in another it was rejected with a curt reminder that children should learn about rockets and electrons. Bridging from one culture to another is a delicate business for curriculum planners.

The fundamental decisions to be made on curriculum and the text books and teaching materials that embody it are these:

1. The language of instruction for the schools, and hence the language in which the books will be written. More than one language of instruction may be used at different levels in the educational system, e.g., a local vernacular to begin literacy, a national language to carry primary education forward, and an international language (English or French) in secondary and higher education. The merits and defects of such a program do not need rehearsal at this point. Often the outside language is used per-force because there are no advanced texts in the national language. This was in part the case in Ethiopia where English was substituted for Amharic in the middle grades.

The language of instruction will affect the way the curriculum is developed and presented. The language embodies, as Whorf (1950) has observed, a *weltanschauung* which determines how phenomena will be observed and classified and conceptualization shaped. On the more practical side, the language will also materially affect costs of writing and manufacturing school books. Exotic syllabaries and alphabets may entail the design of special linotype machines or the use of calligraphy and

207

photo offset; and the size of the market, which is limited by the language, will affect the cost of book production.

2. The elements of content that are to be built into the text, and the kinds of skills that are presumed to be generated.
3. The melding of content and language into some pattern of grading presumed to be articulated with the level of school in which the book is to be used.
4. Programming of material in the case of programmed texts.

Other matters of format (type, illustration, pagination, margination) all have their effect on costs, but for those who have planned and produced text books the first three points are the fundamental ones.

Though the wealthy countries, notably the United States, shy away from too standard a set of text books, the time for planning a profusion of books within one level has not come to most developing countries. A rather simple scheme may be all that is required. One such scheme for Central American primary schools is illustrated in Table VI.9, using the enrollments data from Table IV.4.

If the $120,920 is divided by 4,977, the total of graduates, and if these cheaply manufactured soft-cover books have an estimated life of three years, the cost per graduate in this system, where 15.6 years of instruction are necessary to produce a graduate, would be $8.07. If progress were perfectly regular through the grades and it required six years to graduate a student, the price could be much lower: $3.10. The planner, over a period of years, would program expenditures on books running from a high of $8.07 per graduate and tending toward an optimal level of $3.10. This figure would be approximated but perhaps never reached in future years.

As with improved instruction, better text books would make for a more efficient system. A higher proportion of entrants might stay in school to graduate and per-graduate costs would not rise as much as one might presume on the basis of simple arithmetic. The sturdier the book, the higher the original manufacturing price; but, if storage is adequate and weather normal, the life of the book should be longer and the unit cost per graduate may be lower. This assumes multi-year use, but this is not necessarily a sound educational or social policy. In areas of low literacy, where the school book may be the only printed material coming into the home, the government may wisely choose to manufacture cheap, expendable editions with a one-year life. The additional cost, if there is one, may promote indirect social benefits.

TEXT BOOKS FOR SECONDARY AND HIGHER EDUCATION. To calculate outlays for text books in secondary schools and to derive coeffi-

TABLE VI.9 (abridged)
Curriculum Areas and Primary School Text books

Grade	Curriculum Area	Book Title (General)	Unit Price	Copies	Cost
1	Language Arts-Reading	Primer (Basal Series)	.15	26,867	4,030.05
		First Reader (Basal Series)	.20		5,373.40
	Mathematics	Arithmetic	.25		6,716.75
2	Language Arts	Basal Reader	.18	15,195	2,735.10
		Extra Reader	.22		3,342.90
	Mathematics	Second Arithmetic	.30		4,558.50
	Science	Environment-Health	.30		4,558.50
3	Language Arts	Basal Reader (Development)	.25	12,812	3,203.00
		Reader (National folk lore, legends)	.30		3,843.60
	Mathematics	Third Arithmetic	.30		3,843.60
	Science	Science (Gen.)	.30		3,843.60
	Social Studies	Social Studies (National History, Geography	.30		3,843.60
					49,892.60*
4	Language Arts	Basal Reader	.35	10,178	3,562.30
		Reader	.40		4,071.20
		Grammar (Usage)	.35		3,562.30
	Mathematics	Mathematics	.40		4,071.20
	Science	Science	.40		4,071.20
	Social Studies	Social Studies	.35		3,562.30
					22,900.50*
5	Same	six books	av. .55	7,111	23,466.30*
6	Same	six books	av. .75	5,487	24,691.50*
					$120,920.90

* Sub-totals added to obtain total amount.

cients, more specific information is necessary by course than in primary schools, where all children within a grade can use the same basic books. Text book inputs are better built up by planning outlays for each program separately. System-wide averages are much less stable and useful. With the much smaller number of institutions and enrollments at secondary level in developing countries this is not a difficult task. Inputs have to be determined for subjects and fields.

At higher educational levels, students furnish their own books. The problem for the planner is not so much the outlay for government purchase of text books as it is to determine whether the highly specialized books that will be required in technical fields are available in the language of instruction used in the country.

LIBRARY HOLDINGS AND AUDIO VISUAL AND EQUIPMENT OUTLAYS.

In secondary and higher education, library holdings of reference and resource books must be provided. On the purely quantitative side, there are minimum standards which set the necessary number of volumes for secondary school, college and university libraries. Quality and relevance are assumed. The American Library Association sets a minimum standard of 50,000 volumes for 600 students, for a four-year liberal arts college library, and adds the proviso that there should be 10,000 additional volumes for every additional 200 students.

This norm will provide cold comfort for college and university libraries in developing countries. As a matter of fact, less than half of the U.S. colleges meet this standard. The University of Santo Domingo in 1960 listed holdings of 158,719 volumes. By the above standard, it was about 65,000 volumes short for its enrollment of slightly more than 4,000 students. Many of the students were part-time, taking only a course or two, but many of the volumes were so dated as to be useless. The kind and quality of the books is more significant than the numbers, especially in countries where nothing is ever thrown away. Accessibility is another important feature of libraries. Books that are locked away from the students serve no useful purpose. Specialized texts on the design of library facilities and the management of services provide a starting point for planning, but the advice of experts is required to fit the general models to the individual requirements of the institution. Decisions on central collections and special school and departmental holdings will affect costs. The American Library Association (1955) covers the planning of facilities at all levels of education. Architects and librarians in the individual countries can scale the standards on buildings and book holdings to fit the local setting and purse. Again, outside standards furnish only the barest starting point.

Library holdings are better planned by courses, fields, and faculty requirements, and then totaled. A holding of half of the one listed above could provide a perfectly adequate library for a university in a developing country, if the holdings were appropriately selected. In Mexico, a holding of 200 modern statistics books in the data-processing center of a university seemed more than equal to a holding of 10,000 musty volumes in a law library. At least the 200 had a wider circulation than the 10,000 during any given year. Planning for library facilities and the acquisition of books is only a start. The collection of serial publications and documents is equally necessary. Administrators of higher education in developing countries make scant provision for the purchase of scholarly journals required for keeping faculty members in touch with current scholarship. At least one hundred journals and reviews are required for minimal coverage in the fields of science and the arts. Outlays for these must be programmed in library budgets.

Library acquisitions require detailed planning and costing, but short-cut general estimates are possible. A ratio of 50 volumes per student enrolled may be useful as a rough rule of thumb, but ultimately it will depend on the kind and quality of the books and the degree to which they match the study programs and are used. Developing countries must face the fact that an input of over a $1,000 in library books alone may be necessary for every new potential graduate taken into the higher schools for some years to come. These books are (in countries with appropriate controls) fairly durable assets, and eventually this outlay will fall sharply as multiple year use is made of books. But book prices will likely rise.

The American Library Association, through the U.S. office of Education, provides a book price index which provides a basis for projecting future year costs for books in English.

Educational Machinery and Equipment

Outlays for standard laboratory equipment (work benches, sinks, stoves and utility connections) are usually included in the basic capital costs of the plant. Even major items (refrigerators, microscopes—in some ratio to students, usually 1:2—and basic glassware and chemicals) can be budgeted. Outlays for scientific equipment have to be fitted to the educational program planned.

For the newer programs in science, e.g., PSSC (Physical Science Study Committee), BSCS (Biological Sciences Curriculum Study) and Chemical Bond, costs are listed either in commercial catalogues put out by the companies that market the materials or in handbooks produced the designers of the programs. For those developing countries that elect these programs, the quoted prices, plus shipping and less the equipment that can be home produced, furnishes sufficient guidelines for estimating future expenditures per pupil. In an appendix to the BSCS Biology Teachers Handbook, everything from laboratory facilities layout to budgetary allocations for expendable supplies ($500 per year per class) are detailed. A laboratory facilities check list is provided to cover all necessary detail.

Various plans and studies, e.g., Hurd (1954) and Johnson (1952), provide guidance in the design and arrangement of facilities for science programs. Purchase guides and price lists, e.g., CCSCO (1959), and the catalogues of large equipment supply houses like CENCO provide price data for converting to cost estimates and coefficients per student for future year programs. Standard texts in science provide lists of main suppliers. The general planner must work closely with the subject specialist to fit the final estimates to estimates of resources available.

Calculation of total costs and per-student coefficients may be quite time-consuming, but there is nothing complex in the methods by which they are computed. While educators in developing countries, aided by the designers of the newer programs, can produce domestically much of the equipment, some of the precision instrumentation must be purchased abroad. Such outlays must be minimized.

Visual and audio equipment (projectors, films, records) are costed in the same way. Schools in developing countries have little of this equipment anyway. But this will change in the future, hopefully. Administrators soon gain experience in the conventional costing and planning for expenditures on this kind, although the budgeting procedures for large future year outlays are not very systematic.

The Newer Gadgetry

The question of investment in the newer hardware (educational TV, language-laboratory equipment, and teaching machines) offers vexing problems. At international meetings, and Santiago was one, the drums have beaten over loud on the possibilities of major breakthroughs in educational technology. Planners have had to convince their ministers of education that books and teachers are not likely to be replaced with teaching machines in the very near future. In a country where trained teachers are scarce, and are likely to stay scarce, where salaries for instructional staff eat up major portions of budgets, despite the low unit costs for individual teacher salaries, the possibility of replacing man with machine holds considerable fascination for development planners. Economic development advisors are struck by real or fancied analogies between educational and manufacturing operations where advances in technology have made the machine a cheaper and more productive substitute for the man. An educator's resistance to an automated classroom or his seeming reluctance to consider a machine as a teacher substitute, appears stubborn and hidebound. Yet, it is not clear yet just how much teacher time—if any—can be saved by the machines.

Successful experiments with television and teaching machines are cited as evidence (e.g., the conference at Santiago) that education is on the verge of a technological revolution in methods. The arguments ignore the high initial outlays that may be necessary for such hardware, almost all of it in scarce foreign exchange; ignore the labor-intensive nature of the country, which prevails in education as well as agriculture; ignore the fact that little has been done in costing these programs, and ignore the fact that the machine is only as good as the program that is fed to it. Program development is costly and requires highly skilled people who are likely to be even scarcer than classroom teachers. The problem of technical maintenance of complicated instrumentation is crucial in countries where even bare classroom buildings are not kept up.

Certain materials lend themselves effectively to linear and branching program models, e.g. rudimentary language instruction (phonology up to syntactics but not stylistics) and some of elementary mathematics and science. Programmed materials have accomplished great things in occupational training in technical fields. Aesthetics, ethics, and human relations have not come through the machine in very handsome fashion.

Though time may be on the side of the technocrat and his wonderful teaching machine, cost analysis to date by Klaus and Lumsdaine (1962), Kopstein and Cave (1962) and Carroll (1963) do not furnish enough evidence to justify programming high machine inputs and low instructor costs for future years.

First, and for the present foremost, there is the problem of large initial outlay. A six-position language laboratory set up with pre-taped foreign language lessons would cost a country $3,800, almost all of it in precious foreign exchange. But the country would be tempted to go for a 12-position arrangement which would double teaching capacity for less than 60 per cent in additional expenditure. This $6,000 would pay for 4 rural classrooms with a presumed capacity of 160 children.

Second, the high cost of the facility would demand efficient scheduling in a setting where scheduling is not efficient. For 120 students, requiring five hours of instruction a week, to receive half their program, the six-position facility would have to be used more than eight hours a day or more than five days a week.

Third, it is not at all certain that if half the class load were taken by the facility, live instructor time could be halved, even over time. The 120 students would require a minimal staff of 4 teachers working 30 hours a week at a 20:1 student teacher ratio. If the machine could take 300 of the 600 hours and the instructional staff be halved it might pay for itself, but it is not at all certain that this substitutability prevails.

The Kopstein-Cave study did not demonstrate machines could replace teachers, if the Table in Appendix F and the footnote mean what they seem to say. Instruction through conventional and machine means were compared for cost, but in the machine program the same human instructional costs were present, although they were not counted. Nevertheless, the table is useful as a model for cost comparisons.

The Carroll analysis in Appendix G is even more useful because it shows not only the money costs of program development, but also the trained and skilled human resources which are necessary. In what could serve as a model for clear cost analysis of program developments of this type, Carroll lays out the requisites under five headings: I. Machine Outlay; II. Program Development Costs; III. Program Reproduction Costs; IV. Tryout, Revision and Recapitulated Unit Cost; V. Human Resource Requirements. The unit in the Carroll analysis is a per-frame cost which can most readily be aggregated into a total course price.

Kopstein and Cave have presented general formulas for cost comparisons analysis in four basic identities:

$$C = \frac{A}{S.h}$$

C = Cost comparison index   (19)
A = Dollar sum of all expenditure on a given course
S = All students in course
h = Total number of hours spent by each student in attaining specified proficiency.

The A is further broken down:

$$A = a_1 + a_2 + a_3 \qquad (20)$$

The a_1 is that portion of the costs related to programming the subject matter, and it is fixed and complete at the outset of instruction up to the time revision is necessary. As S, the number of students that can be handled under the program, becomes very large, this component shrinks as a unit cost.

The a_2 is the cost of storing the instructional information and it is further analyzed:

$$a_2 = \frac{S \cdot a_c}{n}$$

n = Number of users per unit of storage   (21)
a_c = Dollar amount per unit of storage
S = Students

If the unit cost of storing cannot be reduced, it is wise to make n as close to S as is practicable, i.e., get the maximum use out of each unit stored by having the largest number of students share the use of a unit. Obviously, this is limited by time, the number of hours in a day available and the amount of time a unit must be used.

The a_3 is the cost of necessary presentation devices, quite large in the AVID device used in the Carroll experiment and low when the Mark II auto-tutor was used in the situation analyzed by Kopstein.

Kopstein analyzes a_3 in this way:

$$a_3 = s \cdot R \cdot o \cdot h \qquad \begin{aligned} s &= \text{Number of students per course} \\ R &= \text{Number of course administrations} \\ o &= \text{Operating cost per hour per device} \\ h &= \text{Course length in hours} \end{aligned} \qquad (22)$$

With an auto-tutor that can accommodate only one student ($s=1$), R would equal S; the device would have to be used as many times as there are students.

Cost Coefficient for Program and Machine Teaching

An example, using cost data for teaching machines, will illustrate that formula (22) and index (19) must be modified before they make sense for cost comparisons.

In one course an auto-tutoring device with a rental or amortization cost of $0.20 an hour is used to give 40 students a 200-hour program.

Formula (22) would yield: $1 \times 40 \times .20 \times 200 = \$1600$.

If the same program could be given to the same number of students with a film that cost $6.00 an hour for equipment and projectionist assistant, the cost would have to be computed: $40 \times 1/40 \times \$6.00 \times 200 = \$1200$.

The student/hour index for the first program would be $\$1600/8000 = \$0.20$.

The student/hour index for the film program would be $\$1200/8000 = \$0.15$.

Teachers' salaries or any other instructional cost can be handled in the same fashion, and the costs of future programs can be estimated on the basis of student-hour instructional costs.

To calculate per-graduate inputs for hardware, a different formulation is suggested.

First, there is the matter of determining A, the amount, for program development, storage and presentation. In view of the kind of scarce personnel required for program development, it might be far cheaper for most countries, where they can, to purchase already developed programs that are being marketed. But, whether or not the program is purchased or developed, the cost coefficient is calculated in about the same way.

$$a_{ij} = a_1 + a_2 + a_3 \qquad (23)$$

Program   Storage   Machine Presentation

$$a_1 = \frac{A}{S\,T_h} \qquad a_2 \text{ negligible} \qquad a_3 = \frac{A}{S\,T_h} \quad (24)$$

A = Cost of development or purchase of complete program (tapes or frames) or device

S = Number of students who can use program or device simultaneously

T_h = Total life of program or device in usable hours

H = Total number of hours to complete course

An example of the language laboratory and a programmed tape mentioned earlier can illustrate the calculations.

$$a_3$$

Purchase of console and six-station laboratory (and installation) $ 3,600

Students served simultaneously   6

Life of facility in hours use   32,000
(8 hours by 5 days by 40 school weeks by 20 yrs.)

Class hours to graduate course
(5 weekly by 40 weeks)   200

$$a_3 = \$3.75$$

This would not include cost of lab attendant or maintenance on equipment, but such calculations would be made as recurrent costs of instruction and maintenance. With older students, little attendant time would be necessary.

$$a_1$$

Purchase of program tapes $ 200

Students served (assuming six positions above)   6

Life of program until ruined or revised (same above, 10 years)   16,000

Class hours to graduate course   200

$$a_1 = .42$$

Again this assumes that tape gets maximal use by six-position facility.

$$a_2$$

The cost of building rent would be negligible and usually included under other plant cost. If calculated separately, it would entail perhaps apportioning the cost of rent of one room of the building.

It is apparent that the coefficients could be much lowered if:

1. The number of students using the facility in one session could be raised, e.g., by buying facility with more positions, working off same tape and console.
2. More hours per day and days per week could be utilized.

A variety of alternate routes could be taken to make the same calculations, but the research of Carroll and Kopstein and Cave indicate that machine instruction is still fairly expensive per graduate, whether the programs and machines are purchased or developed.

In the case of other equipment not so directly related to instruction, e.g., a mimeograph machine for reproducing lesson materials, the proportioning of cost against a student base is not so clear-cut a procedure and such fixtures should best be treated in total school charges.

Expendable Supplies

Expendable supplies do not represent a significant portion of per-pupil costs at the elementary level. The costs are relatively easy to calculate for the elementary school programs as a whole, involving no more than chalk, copy books and paper and pencils. In many situations these costs do not run above $0.50 per pupil per year. Yet failure to provide even these minimal supplies may markedly reduce learning in the developing countries. Expendable work books may cost, but if they are well designed they relieve the teacher of a considerable burden of drill and test. It may well be worth the cost to provide them in rural schools where two teachers handle six grades. The difference between the workbooks, which can be programmed for auto-tutoring and drill, and the cost of a full teaching staff, is significant. These are the simple kinds of economies planners and administrators must search for in developing countries.

In secondary education, especially in technical and vocational programs, the costs of expendable supplies in stock consumed and hand tools broken, strayed, or stolen may run very high. Many vocational and industrial arts programs have been begun by outside groups in developing countries, only to languish and die because the local government cannot take over the high costs of expendable materials. Lab programs often fail to function completely, for want of small allocations for glassware and chemical materials. Calculations of such costs and apportionment according to student load presents no special problems for cost models.

Use of Cost Coefficients in Program Models

Once derived, coefficients of costs can be used in a variety of ways. They can be incorporated into the program models of Chapter V. They can be added to get more stable per-pupil costs and then multiplied by future estimated student load. They can be varied according to assumptions made about future educational programs and used to test efficiency and sometimes outright corruption in educational purchases. The great advantage over per-student costs is that they reveal most intimately the connection between program quality level and cost, so that quality and price can be varied in future years and the result costed more effectively for planning.

VII

Resources Available for
Educational Development[1]

IN A LONG-TERM PLAN FOR HUMAN RESOURCE DEVELOPMENT THROUGH education and training, two major constraints operate in developing countries to set the upper limits of expansion and growth of the schools.

1. Fiscal limitations which govern how much a country can devote to current and capital expenditures on education and training in present and future years.
2. Present supply and future output of trained human resources to serve as educators and trainers; and, in the upper levels of the system, as students.

The limits imposed by (2) are broken by strategies which raise output within the system. Countries may also import trained teachers and staff from other countries; or, in some cases, ship students abroad to be educated. Essentially, however, and in the long run, the planner undertakes to break through this constraint by using the output of the system itself, and his success depends on provision of fiscal resources to expand the system so it can replace itself as well as supply the society and the economy with the necessary numbers of educated people. The human resource deficits can be calculated as part of the system output necessary in the general demand model.

The educational planner, insofar as he can, must shape the system to meet the deficits sketched out in the general models of Chapter II;

[1] The assistance of T. David Williams in thinking through the issues involved in such a section and in compressing the material into reasonably non-technical presentation was so marked that he should be listed as coauthor of this section.

but the estimation of likely future resources is more appropriately the province of the economist and the development planner. Whatever the differences in approach and method, estimation of future fiscal resources will be based on projections of product and income, and assumptions about future government revenue and budgetary policy and practice.

The problems, statistical and conceptual, in the handling of national income accounts are severe ones. The problems, political and again economic, in the design of programs of taxation and public finance are also formidable. Educational planners are usually more than content to drop the problem of financing at the doorstep of the economist and public administrator. In past planning efforts, educators have made up their shopping lists, attached a price, and handed it to economists and administrators. Whatever the planner and politician could 'scare up' in future-year money was usually inadequate to cover what the educator was asking for. Once formulated, the educators' requests became sacred, and difficult to scale down and square with other competing demands.

The educational planner must have some notion of how much money is likely to be available, when it may come, and the soundness of the base on which these estimates of resources are made. He will not generally have to run economic growth projections, but he will have to be on speaking terms with those who do, understanding the models, the assumptions (which in turn are often based on estimates of human resources and their productivity), and the limitations of the data on which most economic analyses are based in developing countries. From these data and models will come the fiscal constraints within which the planner must operate. That there will be constraints, because of short finances and many competing demands, is in the nature of developing countries.

In most countries, the burden of providing for the education and training of the citizenry will be laid to the public fisc, either at the national, provincial or state, or local level. When calculating the resource potential of a country, all of these sources must be considered. Characteristically, in developing countries, the burden of educational expenditure is attributed to the central government. Resource estimates for future outlays are calculated according to national income, the portion likely to be available to the central government in tax and other revenues, and the portion of this total amount that will be expended on education rather than on some other government activity.

Only recently, as the state and local governments have acquired stable and formal structures, has any accounting been made of potential resources from these levels. In developing countries, local and community efforts can provide land, labor, and local material for rural school construction, and this can, and must, amount to a considerable portion of the primary education outlay. More than purely fiscal advantages come from local self-help and community development efforts. This may be the only way in which the motive force of vast rural populations can be related to country development goals; and the advantages of community contribution cannot be measured solely in money terms.

Also, in developing countries, a fair portion of such education as has been offered came from private sources, mission-supported and privately organized schools that run on endowments and fees from individuals and societies within and outside the country. In a great many countries, schools are supported by mixed sources of revenue: fees and endowments, combined with government subventions and grants. Grants may be made under many forms: capital grants for buildings and facilities, grants for current expense apportioned according to students in average daily attendance, provision of teachers, provision of ancillary services, and in the form of scholarships which pay student fees. In short, in a great variety of ways.

The contributions of governments, private groups and individuals to formal school programs are not the only resource with which the planner should reckon. In developing countries, money goes to agricultural education and research through extension programs. Lewis (1955) estimates that this should be as high as 1 per cent of national output. In countries which are industrializing, large outlays may also be required for vocational, technical and in-service programs. Private or government-run industries may have to furnish a substantial portion of the funds. These sources are only sometimes tapped in developing countries. It is done more effectively, or inexorably, in those countries where things are under government control. Yugoslavia has a highly developed system of factory-assessed contributions deducted from pay rolls and paid into municipalities for educational programs. In Latin America, industry has not yet shared this burden, except in a few countries and in large foreign firms.

Some of the methods of forecasting fiscal resources likely to be available have been mentioned. Gross national product and national income are used for estimating outside limits of resources, or for furnishing norms against which to test the adequacy of present or future outlays on education.

Under the Alliance for Progress, countries have pledged themselves to raise educational expenditure to an annual outlay of 4 per cent of the gross domestic product. This would seem to suggest a simple model for forecasting the fiscal resources available for education in future years. The gross product, under appropriate assumptions of growth, is forecast for future years and, by simple arithmetic, the resources for educational outlay in these years is obtained. The use of this method has some rough, normative utility, despite the underlying statistical problems in estimating such massive aggregates, and basing inferences on them.

A second method is to relate educational expenditure to some percentage of the national budget. National budgets for past years are generally available. The percentage of the total budget devoted to educational expenditures is calculable. Increases in the total budget are projected. (The basis for this is again an assumed growth in product or income or increase in population or some other economic or demographic variate). Educational outlay is then calculated as some percentage of the extrapolated general budget.

Along this route the planner must use caution. The published request budget, which is not an accounting of actual expenditures, is usually all that is available, and it may not be a very stable base for estimating outlays. The common practice of using only the Ministry of Education budget as a reflection of educational outlay leads to underestimates. School construction, renovation, and repair may be carried in large part under Ministry of Public Works budgets. Considerable expenditures on extension and even rural day education may be in the Ministry of Agriculture budget. The Ministry of Economy or the development agency or Central Bank may carry portions of technical, industrial, and even commercial education and training. The military, e.g., in Guatemala as in Uruguay, work on school buildings, print literacy materials, and conduct adult education classes. The Ministry of Health may educate nurses, sanitarians, medical orderlies, and laboratory technicians.

If budgets are to be used as resource guidelines, they must be combed for every educational outlay. Even so, large outlays on education, which might be included in supplemental budgets are overlooked. And the published budget may not reflect actual expenditures, after all, because all kinds of transfers and finagling of funds go on during the year. In most countries there is nothing comparable to the U.S. Treasury's Statement of Receipts, Expenditures, and Balances, or the Daily Statement of the U.S. Treasury.

The problems of untangling fiscal, academic and calendar years and breaking down aggregate expenditures may be formidable. Fluctuation in prices across years may make comparisons over time, using money values, rather difficult. In many of the budget documents it may be difficult to distinguish between capital and current expenditures on education. Skilled administrators may get buildings built out of the salaries of 'phantom' teachers carried on spurious roles, year after year.

Determining what one country should spend on the basis of what another seems to spend can be almost pernicious. To the best that this can be accounted for with the statistics available, most countries in Latin America spend between 10–20 per cent of their national budget on education. Some African countries appear to run much higher than this, with statements that 25 or 30 per cent and even more are so spent. In the United States in 1958, only 1.3 per cent of the total federal budget was spent on education, the bulk of support coming from local and state sources. Mexico, in 1964, spent 25.461 per cent of the budget on education—and was proud of it right down to the third decimal.

The use of a percentage allocation to education based on the gross national product, offers a very simple model for the planner to follow:

1965	1970	1975	1980	1985
$P(GNP)$	$P(GNP)$	$P(GNP)$	$P(GNP)$	$P(GNP)$

or in projection terms: nPx. $n(GNP)x$. The conceptual and statistical problems which underlie this are not simple.

There are two sets of problems which require discussion. The first is the definition of categories—when, for example, we refer to 'educational expenditure as a proportion of National Income' we should have a reasonably good idea of what we mean by the basic terms we are using; the second is the establishment of targets, as for example 'educational expenditure should be P per cent of National Income in year N'. In this case we want to know what is likely to happen to National Income and why P or P' is an appropriate percentage.

There are a number of conceptual and accounting problems involved in the development of National Income data. The first thing that has to be resolved is what it is that one is trying to measure. Most English or American economists would say that one is trying to measure the total amount of physical goods and services produced during the year. Marxist economists, on the other hand, exclude services, since they are not 'productive'. The issue is not, however, simply one of ideology.

McClelland (1961) has argued that, if one tries to go beyond measurement of physical production, one gets involved in complex problems of measuring "satisfactions," which can not, at least at present, be handled in a satisfactory manner. Indeed, attempts to use National Income data for welfare comparisons—to argue that a country with a high National Income is necessarily better off than one with a lower income—has come under very heavy fire from a variety of sources. (e.g., S. H. Frankel's work on national income comparisons reflects one critique, while the virtual impossibility of finding an adequate and generally acceptable set of criteria for ranking different states has long been a feature of welfare economics.)

Apart from the assumptions that have to be made in interpersonal or intertemporal welfare comparisons there is the problem involved when the 'what' to be measured is decided in terms of whether or not it involves a money transaction. If a man builds a home, it adds to national wealth irrespective of whether or not anyone pays him for doing the job. At one level, one can deal with this problem by 'imputing' the value of work which does not enter the market. This raises some technical difficulties which will be discussed below, but it does not touch the conceptual problem at issue here. If a certain type of transaction normally enters the market in country *A* but not in country *B,* should the transaction be 'counted' in comparative data? What usually happens is that economists trained in Britain or America count, or try to count, those transactions which enter the market in Britain and America, but do not count transactions which are not to be found in Anglo-American markets.

If one reaches agreement on what is to be measured—and the point of questioning the conceptual framework is not to suggest that it is too shaky to allow any reasonable agreement to be reached but to emphasize that there is a significant range of error possible in comparative income studies under the most favorable circumstances—one has only begun to tackle the problems of measurement.

The remaining difficulties turn on the location of production (of goods and services) and on the *weighting* of production. The first arises because in all economies, but particularly in the less developed ones, there is production which does not enter the market but which it is agreed 'should' be counted. In the United States, for example, farmers consume some part of their own produce. An attempt is made to impute the value of this consumption by weighting the reported quantity by the market price. In an underdeveloped economy the problem is aggravated by two factors. In the first place, there is likely to be much activity which is not adequately reported: the Central Government Statistical Agency may, quite simply, not be aware of what is going on in many areas. In the second place, its attempt to provide a realistic imputation of values for activity about which it has knowledge is greatly handicapped by the fact that extra-market activity is likely to be large in relation to market activity.

Perhaps an example will make the point clearer. If the American farmer, in the example given above, consumes 5 per cent of his own product and the other 95 per cent passes through the market, the imputation assumption that his consumption should be valued at market price is reasonable, because even if he had put all his produce on the market and then bought some of it back the additional volume of transaction would be small compared to those already taking place and would not be likely to cause any great change in market price. If, however, one 'imputes' in an economy where the extra-market transactions are much larger than those in the market, one has to be very bold to assume that prices would remain the same even though transactions increased several fold. There may, as a variant of this problem, be a large number of more-or-less closed markets. There may, that is, be a different price index for several different cities and rural areas, between which there is little traffic. The problem then becomes one of deciding which index to use for imputation purposes.

There is yet another problem. The prices which are used as weights in Anglo-American accounting are those of the 'free market.' The rationale for this is that these prices reflect in some meaningful way the 'real' costs of production and the 'real' desirability of products. Government output has, in this tradition, been measured at cost, because there has been no other way of dealing with the problem—no one can say whether or not a road or a battleship should have a higher or lower market price. Hopefully, if people feel that the government program as a whole has been unjustifiable the government that sponsored it loses office and this, therefore, provides a sort of market check on government expenditures. But whenever the government can 'fix' prices at will, the stated amount, composition, and movement of national income becomes a matter not only of the amount of production that is taking place but also of the weights that the government may arbitrarily choose to attach to various types of production. One supposes that in the long run a government which sets prices which do not reflect basic economic realities will run into very severe problems which could not be concealed by any amount of fiddling, but in the short run—five to ten years—National Income may be a poor guide to what is really happening.

There are, to summarize, three basic problems. The first is that there is room for disagreement about what 'should' be counted; the second is that there may be errors—even gross errors—in estimating what is, in physical terms, being produced; the third is that physical output may be weighted in a variety of ways, and that apparent changes in output may reflect the method of weighting rather the output itself.

The final tables of national accounts may appear in various formats. Ruggles (1956) describes two of the major formats, the one schematized in Appendix J-1 prepared by the United States Department of Commerce, and the one schematized in J-2 developed by the United Nations. The United Nations format is widely used in developing countries because it is felt to be simpler and offer greater comparability. In any given country, however, the accounts may follow no standardized form, but merely reflect the methods of some national account statistician who worked there and modified the system according to his own methods. The various national accounts methods, including input-output arrangements, may have differing advantages depending on the economy in which they are developed, the economic analysis to which they are applied, and the data available to put them together.

One must go behind the summary tables, in any case, to make a judgment on the adequacy of the aggregates. Product for one series may be derived from inferences based on a different but related series. In the production statistics for Mexican industry, for example, the output of bakery and pastry product is inferred from the production of milled wheat which in turn is derived from series on the domestic wheat crop and import and export figures. There is obviously a limit on the detail with which an educational planner can examine the economic statistics which underly estimates of product or income. Yet, if he is following a simple model which fixes educational revenues as a percentage of national income, he had best know that the only thing simple in the situation is his method of estimating.

Estimates of educational expenditure may also be fixed on a percentage of the national budget. It is, therefore, important to know something about the way in which budget figures might obscure the reality that the planner is attempting to study. The first point is that the share of government activity in the economy varies greatly. To say that educational expenditure should be *P* per cent of the government budget has, for example, different connotations in a country where government activity is largely confined to basic activities of defense, internal security, and education, and in one (otherwise similar) which has extensive government welfare programs, government investment in roads and basic industries and even in distributive industries. Changes in the education percentage of the budget may reflect nothing more than changes in the level of government activity in other places.

A second point is that budget expenditure may differ radically from total expenditure 'inspired' or stimulated by the central government and differ still more from total public expenditure. There may be autonomous agencies established or encouraged by the central government, but not dependent on annual budget allotments, which undertake significant expenditures. Substantial public expenditures may be undertaken by local authorities. In this last case, the expenditures may be mandatory or they may be subsidized in one form or another. In the first instance, they will not be featured in the budget; in the second instance, the subsidies may receive attention in the budget, but not under the heading of education.

To summarize, first, the total budget figure depends very largely on the government's view of the range of its responsibilities and, second, budget expenditure may differ substantially from total public expenditure.

This leads to a third point. 'Educational expenditures' should, one supposes, include all items of expenditure on education. There is, however,—to start with—the problem of deciding what is 'education.' An apprenticeship program, for example, if it is conducted within the formal educational system, will be counted; but if it is conducted by a Labor Department extension program, or in the Armed Forces, probably will not be. Literacy courses given by private firms, a government department, or the army may not, probably will not, be counted. Many of these educational expenditures outside the formal educational system will be a part of some other program, so that even if one wanted to count them, it would be difficult to know how much should be described as education. But insofar as education is a process of preparing a person for dealing effectively with his environment, these programs should be classified as education. The problem is an old one. We are all familiar with the people who claimed that they went to the College of Hard Knocks (in Britain, it is the School of Hard Knocks, but that just reflects another problem of nomenclature).

Supposing that one agrees about the types of activity that will be classified as educational, there are other difficulties that have to be met. The first is that some expenditures will be undertaken by the central government under annual allotments, (some of which will be disbursed through the Education Department and some through the budgets of other departments), while some will be through autonomous or semi-autonomous public authorities. The second is that some will be from central and some from local public agencies, and the accounts of the local agencies are rarely available for inspection. The third is that various private agencies, of which some will receive formal recognition and some will not, will also be active in this area. This is not simply a matter of deciding how large the program is. One may feel, for example, that the government 'should' increase its program by, say, 50 per cent. If the government is entirely responsible for the program, this is straightforward. But if, as is usually the case, the government is providing x per cent of the cost of the program—let us say 50 per cent—then a doubling of government expenditure will only lead to a doubling of output (assuming that buildings, staff and competent students can also be doubled —a glib assumption) if there is also a doubling of extra-government expenditure. To pursue the example: If we suppose that private or local sources cannot increase their expenditure, a doubling of output would require a tripling of government expenditure.

This is not mere 'nit-picking'. The data on which estimates of government expenditure on education are based are crude to a degree which anyone who has not worked in the field (literally as well as metaphorically) would find incredible. Almost all of the information provided on the subject by national or, even more so, by international agencies is worthless where it is not positively misleading.

Estimation of the current status of product, income, and budgetary outlay on education has all the problems mentioned, and a few more. Estimation of probable future patterns of change brings new complications.

ESTIMATION OF FUTURE NATIONAL INCOME AND OF REVENUES AVAILABLE FOR EDUCATIONAL PURPOSES

There are two related questions, or sets of questions, that concern us here. First, the methods used for estimating the change in National Income during the planned period: What are these methods and how accurate are they likely to be? Second, the additional revenue that may be expected to become available for educational purposes as National Income increases: What is the institutional arrangement which converts 'potential' resources into 'actual' resources?

There are many different ways in which estimates of future National Income may be obtained, and there may be significant differences in the result according to the method used. The educational planner should have some awareness of the probable 'range of error' of the estimates that are handed to him by the economic experts. If he accepts an overly optimistic figure as the basis for his own calculations, he might find that he has encouraged his department to commit itself to a program which cannot be carried out and, since there is little benefit to be derived from partially completed educational programs he will, unwittingly, have encouraged a wasteful allocation of resources. If, on the other hand, he accepts an unduly pessimistic figure he will, at best, have delayed the implementation of useful programs.

Furthermore, many estimates of future National Income depend, implicitly or explicitly, on certain assumptions about the quality of the labor force which, in turn, depend on assumptions about the nature of the educational system and on the relationship between various types of education and efficiency in working situations.

The methods used to estimate income are substantially the same as those used to estimate human resource requirements which are described in Chapter II. The simplest method of estimation is that of projection. This assumes that the future will in an important way repeat the past. It may be done by simple linear extrapolation or by fitting other trend lines or curve functions to past data. This method is most likely to be useful when over-all experience during the plan period is expected to be similar to that of the period to which the trend refers. A point, of very minor theoretical, but often great practical, importance which the planner should bear in mind is the significance of the precise dates chosen to find the trend. If either the base year or the final year is one which is characterized by atypical behaviour the resulting 'trend' may be grossly misleading *even* as an indication of the changes which took place during the period which the trend is supposed to represent.

A second method is to make use of a comparative model, i.e., the product of country *A* is projected on the basis of previous development in country *B,* on the assumption that country *A* will develop in the future as country *B* did in the past. Many of the Puerto Rican projections in the 1950s were based on the assumption that Puerto Rico in 1970 would be similar to the United States in 1950. Estimates of this sort may be made on the basis of one model country or by running a regression analysis with a large number of countries. Ths method, though attractive in its simplicity (in its first variant, at least), suffers from the fact that detailed information is available for only a small number of countries and most of these are manifestly unsuitable in the immediate future as models for presently developing economies. There is some danger that enthusiasts for this method will adopt models which not only have different economic structures but which are characterized by radically different folk ways and social institutions.

A third method is to estimate the capital/output ratio by sectors, and project National Income on the basis of anticipated capital investment. There are two serious drawbacks to this method. The first is that capital/output ratios are liable to substantial variations, and the second is that it is very difficult to obtain a reliable estimate of private investment, even in the short run.

The capital/output ratio—that is, the annual increase in output expected to occur as a result of a given addition to capital stock—has been used in several U.N. assessments of required capital investment in underdeveloped areas. It may have some usefulness as a yardstick when many sectors in many countries are taken into account, but it is a very crude instrument for measuring specific changes. The capital investment of the government can be estimated with some accuracy, on the hopeful assumption that the political climate remains unaltered, and one might reasonably assume that there will be no great changes in the gross level of investment in traditional and some of the semi-traditional sectors; but there is a large area for which the estimates are bound to be very loose. In any case, the unpredictability of specific capital/output ratios makes this method most hazardous although it might be useful as a rough check on the reliability of estimates reached by other means.

A variant of this approach is the use of 'labor productivity.' The essence of this method is to estimate present productivity in each sector, and to assess both the sectoral changes which would take place and the changes in productivity within each sector during the planned period. The simplest assumption that could be made would be that inherent productivity would not change—that is, all changes would be due to changes in the composition of the labor force. One could first take present labor force and subdivide it by sectors, industry, occupations, age, sex. The next step would be to project—from demographic data and assumed labor force participation rates—the age/sex composition of the labor force at the end of the planned period, and distribute this among the assumed occupational industrial, and sectoral groups. A slightly more complex method would be to add in the anticipated changes in educational level (some of which would be due to the anticipated changes in age/sex composition and some to the changes in educational structure) and estimate the effect that this would have.

A further refinement would be to account for the changes due to shifts in the labor-capital 'mix'. It should, in any case, always be remembered that additions to the "modern" labor force require, if productivity is not to fall, a substantial increase in capital. (Some estimates are of the nature of $1,000 per worker). Changes in skill may come from increased familiarity with 'modern' work routines. Different types of people will come in to the modern work force, from traditional or semi-traditional areas. It is unlikely that any estimate will in fact reach this level of sophistication. The educational planner should, however, be careful to note the type and plausibility of assumptions made in the cruder models.

Another method is to relate the estimate of over-all growth to growth of certain 'key' sectors, such as power, transportation, or heavy industry. The rationale of this method is that growth in these sectors spontaneously generates development in other areas. Transportation facilities are improved, trade is facilitated, and inert traditional peasants become aware of the opportunities open to them—if they abandon their traditional roles. Sources of power become cheaper and new methods of production become feasible. As heavy industry expands, the possibilities of an indigenous construction industry and a variety of indigenous manufactures are enhanced. One difficulty is to choose an exponent of expansion. One might select that experienced by a particular country that one is attempting to emulate or use a larger sample with some type of regression analysis. The drawbacks to this method may seem so obvious that it is scarcely worth mentioning them except for the fact that many people do use the method. The educational planner should, however, be aware that there is no serious empirical support for this kind of speculative estimation.

A basic problem in all the underdeveloped nations is that the data on which planning estimates are made are, at best, based on aggregative industrial or sectoral information. This may mask the most significant movements in the economy. If one is really serious about the process of estimating future National Income one should attempt to locate the 'growth-cones' in the economy.

This means looking for those areas—classified by location and activity—in which there have been significant changes in the recent past, and making a judgment as to whether or not such changes indicate a dynamic force which might continue and become progressively more important in the future. This procedure differs from the one mentioned above in connection with National Income estimates, though it is related to it, in that it is concerned more with the apparent psychological propensities of particular groups of people than with the change in observed production of entire sectors. It may, for example, be the case that semi-traditional farmers in a particular region have shown an awareness of market opportunities, and a capacity to adapt them, which suggest that this particular group possesses a high degree of entrepreneurial capacity. Meanwhile 'agriculture' (or some subdivision of it) may appear, over-all, to be stagnating.

To find out where, if anywhere, such changes are taking place requires an intensive general analysis of the economy. If a general analysis cannot be carried out at frequent intervals because resources are not available, a thorough examination of a particular area or sector should be relevant for several years, and it may be adequate to carry out such a survey every five or six years. The first general analysis that is undertaken should, however, attempt to trace previous developments as well as examine the current status; since a static analysis would not reveal the changes which were taking place. The approach is mentioned because there may be especially high 'pay-offs' attached to the improvement of educational facilities in areas where there has already been evidence of successful entrepreneurial activities, even though these might have been on a very small scale.

It does not necessarily follow that provision of improved education will have the desired result. There are two factors most likely to thwart optimistic expectations. The first is that success in one type of operation may be a poor index of the likelihood of success in different types of work, so that a group may have shown considerable innovative capability in one area—in trading or the development of cash crops, for example—but have a low competence for different work, such as, for example, small-scale manufacturing. The second 'danger' is that previous success as innovators may have been, in a sense, forced on them for lack of alternative routes of self-achievement. In these circumstances, more widespread opportunities due to growth may simply draw the sons of the innovators into different types of activities where they may respond in a conventional (i.e. noninnovating) way and show no more interest in entrepreneurial activity than do the sons of conventional fathers.

In practice, National Income projections are likely to be made up by using several of these methods and adding a considerable measure of optimism. Government contributions to changes in National Income are likely to be estimated precisely (although not necessarily accurately); a 'reasonable expectation' developed for expansion of the private 'modern' sector and trend rates used for agriculture and petty trading.

Whatever method is used, estimation of the resources available for educational expenditure involves some degree of circular reasoning. Any reliable estimate of National Income depends on assumptions about the quality of the labor force. This depends, in part, on the system of education. In other words, the estimate of National Income rests on certain implicit or explicit assumptions about the general pattern of educational expenditures. In the short run this does not present a serious problem, because it takes some time before students become effective members of the labor force. If, however, the output of the schools represents a substantial addition to the stock of graduates at various levels—and this is typically the case in developing economies—the new graduate may bring about significant changes in the quality of the labor force (although the nature and force of the change is still a matter of conjecture).

Fortunately for the educational planner, he is not usually expected to make the critical decision as to which method or combination of methods will be used to estimate future National Income. If this brief review of the various crude techniques employed by the economists— although the educator should not hold them to blame for their lack of elegance, since his own methods in the spheres where he is held an expert will be equally rough—serves to provide him with a shield of skepticism, it will have done some service. If it encourages him to adopt an aggressive but informed doubt about the reliability of the estimates handed on to him in the expectation that he will simply accept them, then the authors' own hard-earned experience will have borne some fruit.

The next problem involves the revenue available for educational purposes when the resource base of the nation is known. It might appear that this is a straightforward matter: the wealth of the country grows by P per cent, then, given an unchanging commitment to the pursuit of education the amount of resources available for educational purposes grows by P per cent. The question is, however, a more difficult one than this sort of answer would indicate.

One problem was mentioned in an earlier part of this chapter: if part of the money comes from central government funds and part from private or local authority funds, one has to demonstrate the fact that *all* parts of the expenditure rise. If this is to be the case, all expending groups must experience a rise in income.

The problem is, indeed, even more involved than this. It is not enough to know (if one can 'know') that National Income will increase. Even at the central government level, one must know whether government income—gained through varoius forms of taxes—will rise proportionately. In many underdeveloped countries a large part of government revenue is based on foreign trade. Imports and exports *may* increase proportionately to the increase in National Income, or more or less. It would be a 'fluke' if they increased proportionately. If they rise by less, the government must find other sources of revenue if it is to base its educational expenditures on changes in national income.

Appendix M shows in summary form U.S. government receipts and outlay for 1953. On the sources side, most of the major categories (corporate profit taxes and income taxes) could be expected to move with changes in National Income. The allocation side reminds us that in the United States the national government is not the chief support of education. Sources of income at the local and state level are more significant.

Table VII.1 illustrates the situation at the local level, where income and expenditures have been projected over a five-year period for a school district. Many of the significant items (e.g., property taxes) may not move in accordance with National Income. Rates may have to be increased, assessments re-evaluated and amount of improved property increased in order to move this source of revenue forward. This is not

TABLE VII.1
Estimated Annual Receipts and Expenditures
Foxcroft School District
1960–1965

	1960–61	*1961–62*	*1962–63*	*1963–64*	*1964–65*
INCOME					
Beginning balance	$ 35,755	$ 17,468	$ 20,164	$ 30,265	$ 32,165
Property taxes	615,652	813,332	913,274	963,365	995,028
Delinquent taxes	48,851	33,043	34,118	33,295	31,070
State appropriation	121,315	156,790	185,793	222,983	212,590
Tuition	24,112	1,871	41,798	21,187	17,720
Interest	..	..	..	..	..
Temporary loans and bond sales	70,000	102,117	100,000	..	..
Sales, real estate and materials	..	6,492	1,668	1,747	3,577
Real estate transfer tax	70,000	80,000	93,000	126,000	164,000
All other sources	40,710	31,128	98,443	79,184	51,012
Total receipts	$1,026,395	$1,242,241	$1,488,708	$1,478,026	$1,507,162
EXPENDITURES					
General control	36,510	41,644	47,054	53,307	59,652
Instruction	491,148	597,848	718,855	724,022	797,417
Auxiliary and coordinate	47,839	49,961	165,124	140,241	128,491
Operation	83,450	86,184	106,159	114,167	130,018
Maintenance	64,646	77,525	106,982	87,382	121,491
Fixed charges	12,410	25,641	39,091	45,123	41,126
Total current exp.	736,003	878,803	1,183,265	1,164,242	1,276,195
Debt service	97,924	105,824	125,678	140,619	142,333
Capital outlay	175,000	237,000	149,500	141,000	75,500
Total expenditures	$1,008,927	$1,221,627	$1,458,443	$1,445,861	$1,496,028
Balance	17,468	20,614	30,265	32,165	11,134

SOURCE: Ovsiew, L. and W. Castetter *Budgeting for Better Schools*, Prentice Hall, 1960, p. 172.

always easy to do. In developing countries a cadastral survey—in which property is charted and rated—may be a critical first step toward an adequate revenue system based on property taxes.

When one moves to the private schools, the situation becomes more complex. Funds available from invested bequests, for example, may decline in value, if, as is likely, there is a tendency towards a rising price level during the period of economic growth. The planner may have to concentrate on detailed analysis of publically supported education only, and make some rough assumption about how much of the burden will be covered by private effort.

Even if the educational planner knows what the total of resources will be, on the basis of aggregated income, he does not know what resources, in aggregate or type, will be available to him, unless he also examines the institutional framework which determines the actual distribution of resources in the economy. Regional differences are important, both in terms of the differing economic capabilities of the regions and because of various arrangements for channeling funds into education.

When resources can be forecast with any degree of accuracy, they can be apportioned to the program models for resource allocation.

In Model I, Chapter V, the resources are the b coefficients.

VIII

THE FUTURE AND THE GUIDED LEAP:
INFORMED GUESSING

MODELS, SCHEMATA, AND PROJECTION ROUTINES PROVIDE THE PLANNER with methods for fashioning some image of future possibilities in human resource development. Crude routines, they do not shape the future and they may not reveal it very accurately. They may even be harmful if they exude such an air of bogus authenticity that the planner becomes pre-occupied with elementary algebra and arithmetic and has no time for an occasional creative speculation on what the future may hold.

The final exercise, then, is just such a speculation. One, it is true, that departs from a base of reality and goes beyond the statistical portents and their limitations. Post-secondary education, has been chosen as the subject of speculation and this choice itself rests on the likelihood that for developing countries this level will be the major concern during the next two or three decades, even though the imme-diate concern is the great secondary school bottleneck.

Hosts of students will be seeking admission to post-secondary schools. By 1970, over seven million will be packed inside the walls of U.S. colleges and universities (it is quite possible that there will be more); Britain expects half a million and Mexico a quarter of a million; in countries like Togoland, 5,000 would represent just as much of a burden on the public fisc as the greater numbers in the richer countries.

In the developing countries, everything that could influence future enrollments in higher education shows an upward trend. The base pop-ulation is on the rise, as mortality rates are cut, births stay steady or rise and natural increase edges up over 3 and beyond 4 per cent in some countries. The age structure of the populations shows huge bulges in the school-age groups, with peaks coming at the post-secondary ages in the mid and late seventies. As the drive for primary and secondary education acquires quality as well as quantity, retention will be maximized; and larger cohorts will sweep along to fill the post-secondary entrant pool.

The incentives in the work force and the demand for education and training which they influence can only exacerbate the matter. Primary school certificates will not command what they once did in the job market; nor will secondary. Post-secondary education will be the level preferred by employer and employee alike. Automation and technological advance will nudge educational requirements even higher in industry, and consumer preference will opt for 'university men' in the service sector.

Students

The vast numbers of future students will not merely make post-secondary education different in bulk; changes in substance and structure are inevitable too.

The student body in post-secondary school will not merely be larger. It will be different. If resource constraints on the expansion of places in higher education could be banished, what percentage of an age cohort has the capacity for study at first degree level (college or *professional*)? There is probably a limit, lying somewhere beyond 50 per cent, as capacity is defined by present measures and reflected in present norms. But is this merely a matter relative to the present and the immediate past and the cultural deprivations they reflect? Is there any limit, short of a small group with marked motor, social, psychological, and intellectual disabilities? Could entire cultures be shifted upward on the intelligence scales? However this may be resolved in the far future, in that future which is amenable to sensible projections and plans there are very likely to be differences because a bigger cut is taken into the stock of 'prepared' talent.

Should this bigger cut be taken and should the places at university level be without limit and should all who have a modicum of talent and motivation be allowed to continue to tertiary level? What happens when the country's economy does not develop rapidly enough to provide places for all those who have the training and the expectations which higher education generates? India is perhaps in this situation at the moment, as thousands of university graduates flood out to an uncertain future as clerks. The planner cannot make the decision to cut down university opportunity and increase second level technical training, but he should ponder the consequences of the problem. Is there such a thing as an overeducated population? Or is it merely a structural problem, i.e., a wrongly educated population? Is mass tertiary education a contradiction in terms? In any event, the masses are coming.

Teachers

Not only must there be more staff to handle student loads in future years and to press the search for new knowledge, but the teachers, researchers, and administrators must be different. Prevailing patterns in one country or part of the world may shift to other quarters, and this shift will not merely be from developed to underdeveloped countries. As Latin American universities press a desperate attempt to cut part-time teacher-professionals and increase full-time staff, institutions in Europe and the U.S. may be forced to take on greater numbers of part-time staff.

The nonfaculty member of Kerr's (1963) multiversity, who is a writer-researcher-entrepreneur-consultant-world traveler and a sometime teacher, will be more tolerated in the big and rich institutions, not because administrators and scholars find him tolerable, but because a seller's market in the physical and social sciences makes it necessary that he be catered to. Up to a point, that is. What happens when he reproduces masses of his own kind? Or perhaps the wily fellow is preventing just that by his chronic absence from the classroom.

In the smaller schools, and especially at subcollege and subprofessional level and particularly in the applied sciences, the teachers are more likely to make their home in the new research industries out along the perimeter of the city and come into school to offer a class or lab or two a week. And they will be welcome, above all for specialized technical schools that cater to the peculiar economy and manpower needs of a subnational area.

Finances

Increased tuition fees are almost inevitable for those who can pay for higher education in developing countries. The public fisc will be hard-pressed to carry the burden of primary and secondary education and extend universal opportunity steadily upward.

Even with fees, government outlays for higher education can only be greater as priorities are given to expensive scientific and technical education which have far higher per-pupil costs than the traditional studies of law and the arts. Scholarships in the form of grants-in-aid for tuition and living costs must grow as the poor and talented come through the system with short family and personal resources. Endowment and private benefactions will probably increase. For national fortunes are being made in developing countries, and conspicuous consumption within the extended family is becoming less admired, and in some countries even dangerous. But it is not likely that this source will furnish a significant portion of the revenues necessary for higher education, although buildings, facilities and other plaque-bearing memorials, may be covered from this source in an increasing number of cases.

In the United States, Harris (1962) estimates that government revenues as a source of funds for higher education will decline relative to tuition between 1958 and 1970 (government going from 53 per cent to 38 per cent and tuition from 25 per cent to 40 per cent). Given certain political trends, the shift could occur but it is unlikely, unless it comes in the form of tax exemptions which the individual citizen, through the grace of his government, immediately pays out for higher tuitions for his children. Even so, the proposition is doubtful and rests mainly on the indisputable fact that individual tuitions do not pay or come close to paying the present costs of higher education. Why they should in the United States but not in other countries is not clear.

Even in schools of the U.S. Ivy League, government support seems likely to increase, especially in the form of research grants for graduate programs; and it probably will continue to increase as the supply of large endowments and benefactions falls or becomes tied up in foundations which dispense their largess in projects grants, much in the manner of government agencies. The unrestricted private gift which enabled the old and august institutions to accept government aid selectively and even suspiciously may grow harder to come by. The U.S. government and its agents and agencies may have to become a great deal more flexible, making more general-purpose grants, being less stingy in its overhead provisions and less restrictive with qualifications—from security clearance to loyalty oaths. While U.S. government support through grants may have to increase and become less restrictive, Great Britain may go through an opposite experience with the government taking a closer look at the expenditures in the face of constrained resources. In the developing countries, governments have had the complete responsibility for supporting higher education, with almost no authority to examine its productivity. This may become a thing of the past. Universities in Africa may have to find some way to protect themselves from unwarranted intrusion and abridgment of academic freedom by megalomaniac national leaders; whereas Latin American universities must come to terms with responsible government officials and private leaders, who, after all, must be the source of future funds for expansion.

In developing countries, as in the developed ones, the contributions of private businesses and their foundations—especially to scholarship, equipment, and building funds—can only grow, as industries increase in scale, become conscious of their public image, and move to guarantee their own supply of high-level manpower. In developing countries, this aid may be very significant at the post-secondary but pre-university technical level. But the universities themselves must be more responsive and responsible on the model of Instituto Tecnologico de Monterrey and the Universidad del Valle in Latin America.

Program Constraints

If the students change and the faculty changes and the basis of support for higher education shifts in future years, what about program, curricula, organization, and presentation methods, which lie at the heart of the matter? To say 'further education' is to picture first the university, the university college, or the college. This is almost reflex in the developed countries of the West, above all in Britain and the U.S., and also in the developing countries of Africa, Asia and Latin America.

Through most of the world, the aspiration to have and to hold a full-fledged university, complete with all faculties, and with every trapping down to the cap and gown and a sports program, seems to be a normal national desire. The British and Americans may merely have made an attempt to help satisfy this aspiration in developing countries, but whatever the case, the time is already late to point out that less formal and expensive patterns might be better.

There is a serious question, whether developing countries can, given resources and population, provide any significant portion of their citizenry with higher education on the university or college day-school model that prevails in the United States and Great Britain. The most obvious constraint on this development is fiscal.

Countries in the throes of development must allocate scarce resources to capital and current expenditures, with great skill and good luck, in order to provide the minimal social services of health and basic education, the necessary physical infrastructure that will insure power and transport, and still retain sufficient savings for stimulating productive investment and growth in industry and agriculture. At the same time, international credit status must be maintained and borrowing capacity husbanded. Most development plans project substantial gaps between future resources from national revenues and future year allocations for necessary economic and social development outlays.

The 1963/65 development plan of Nyasaland calls for expenditures of £12.8 million. Only a portion of this could be realistically scheduled out of scarce local revenue sources and development bond issues. The next source to which a developing country turns is external aid in the form of long-term soft loans or grants. Great Britain has committed substantial sums (£2.9 million) to Nyasaland under the Colonial Development and Welfare Act and Exchequer loans, and the U.S. has programmed a smaller sum through the Agency for International Development. In spite of this and most optimisitic forecasts of additional local revenue and market borrowing, a gap of over one-third remains to be financed. The extent to which external aid—from West or East—can take up the slack in future country plans remains very small. Should Nyasaland establish a costly university establishment? Nobody—much less the lending countries—can answer this. The decision rests with the people and government of the country, and in the matter of establishing a university no mere considerations of economics are likely to deter realization of a national aspiration.

Mexico faces innundation at the higher education level. Population is increasing by 3 per cent, the proportion of school-age children in primary is being brought toward 100 per cent under the 11-year plan, retention in the primary school and first cycle of secondary school increased over 10 per cent in a four-year period, and enrollments in the preparatory cycle increased at a rate almost double that in secondary terminal cycle (vocational, technical and agricultural); and all clamor for admission to universities which currently are close to the limit of capacity. At the same time, Mexican resources have been extended heroically in education. Over 25 per cent of the national budget is allocated to education, and the percentage of gross domestic product so allocated seems to be close to 4. In developing countries, what portion of product and national budget can be allocated to education generally and higher education specifically? Are there limits? Four per cent of output has been an arbitrary level set for education at all levels, but the likelihood is that countries may soon have to exceed that.

More critical than fiscal constraint for the developing countries are the restraints imposed by shortages of human resources. It requires university-trained people to administer and man university teaching staffs, and no amount of money or physical property can break through this limitation. Developing countries must face the problem of assigning extremely short rosters of trained personnel to rather long lists of government and private sector enterprises. The dilemma is clear. If the country allocates its few trained engineers to expansion of physical infrastructure and production, they will not be available in the faculties of the universities to multiply their own kind for future years. And yet if these allocations are not made, income and product may not be generated to support expensive programs in higher education. Into this gap have gone the new technical missionaries. It is critical to examine this pool and its likelihood of expansion in future years.

The need in the future is not for just any old university trained-body, but rather for representatives of certain fields and disciplines which are in short supply—not only in the underdeveloped countries but also in the 'mature' and still growing economies. Physical scientists, theoretical and applied mathematicians, engineers and social scientists are at premium even in the developed countries of the West. Not so apparent, although it soon will be, is the shortage of high-level technicians who must undergird progress and growth. The prospect of large surpluses of well-trained people in these fields is not good over the next 20-year period, the time of maximum need. Unfortunately, developing countries may even lose some highly trained scientists who come to developed countries for training and never return.

Salary increases alone will not prevent a drain-off of young scientists from underdeveloped to developed countries. The enormous outlays for machinery and equipment that must be used for research and teaching in order to keep a scientist happy and girded for a sortie from the frontier is already almost beyond the capacity of many developing countries. Students flooded through mere textbook *tour de force* and given paper credentials are not going to solve the problem but perhaps merely complicate it by blinding countries to their true level of shortage in critical fields.

What then are possibilities, and how will they shape the future of higher education in developing and developed countries?

First, it is apparent that fiscal and human resource constraints will make it unlikely that substantial proportions of the age cohorts in developing countries will be given a chance at higher studies in the next 20 years. If post-secondary education inevitably suggests day, full-time attendance at University or college, it is not even clear that this is a thoroughly bad thing. Determining the appropriate proportion of the citizenry that should have higher education is, of course, fraught with difficulties.

Japan and Russia showed about 10 per cent of the age group enrolled in university; England and Wales slightly less (8.2) in higher education, with different methods of classification and bases for proportions. Only 50 per cent of the Russian enrollments were in full day school attendance, 10 per cent were in night school, and 40 per cent in correspondence courses. The data are not so useful for a cultural comparison of East and West as they are in showing the possibilities of patterns other than full day university school for countries where less than 1 per cent of the relevant age groups are now enrolled in higher education. The data do suggest alternative patterns of organization for the future of higher education. Developing countries have instinctively turned to developed countries for their educational models and, for that reason, the future of higher education in developing countries cannot be assessed without reference to present and future experience in developed ones. One can recognize this pedagogical borrowing as a fact, without recommending it as a virtue. It is exciting to contemplate the possibility that developing countries will generate their own unique forms for higher education; and so they will. But when that time comes, they will not be developing countries any more. They will be developed.

Institutional Changes

In the developing countries, the expansion and upgrading of teacher training and normal schools offers one possibility of meeting future demand for higher education. Countries heading toward universal primary education establish large numbers of lower normal schools to produce the necessary teachers. As long as the demand for teachers is great and a fair proportion of the graduates enter the profession, these schools should be kept to their original mission. But overproduction of graduates coupled with the universally low salaries for teachers soon brings a situation where many of the graduates do not teach, and, to a certain extent, are being mistrained. In Turkey, 17,000 trained teachers work on the railroads. When such a point is reached, education officials might well think of changing the training institutions.

Lower normal schools can be upped to higher normal schools as the demand for primary teachers peaks and large numbers of secondary teachers are required. The training of secondary school teachers outside the university is not the ideal solution, but it has been one that has been forced on officials by the failure of universities to meet the demand of expanding public-school systems. The same lack of university flexibility that the U.S. and, later, New Zealand officials faced years ago is now a problem for ministry officials in Guatemala and the Sudan. Newer countries will be facing this problem later. When universities will not open programs to train secondary teachers in sufficient numbers, the higher normal school and pedagogical institute are the only answer.

There has been a tendency for higher normal schools to evolve into full degree-granting colleges, and no doubt this will happen in developing countries. As long as staff and program are reinforced to fit the new status, the development is a natural way to expand higher education in countries hard-pressed by rising enrollment. There is no reason why a training institution with established standards cannot, with appropriate improvement in staff and facilities, develop into a first-rate college or university. The cost of making such a transition might be considerably less than would be required to found a new establishment, and the educational product equal.

The evolution from lower to higher normal school and then to general degree-granting institution should be carefully programmed by education officials. Quite obviously a lower normal school should be held to its major task as long as vast shortages of primary teachers exist and as long as most of its graduates are using their training as teachers. When a higher normal school reaches the point where it can, with improvements, be made a full-fledged degree granting institution, the changes should be made and the step taken. Such developments offer ways of meeting the burden of higher education which is bound to come, and there is no good reason why one national university, often unresponsive to a country's development needs, should monopolize higher education.

A variety of other forms of higher education may also spring up in the developing country to relieve pressure from the national university and university college. Area, regional, municipal, state, and community colleges will offer some relief from the future pinch. The two-year community or junior college can only grow and may well spread in developing countries. This is a versatile institution because it can offer terminal technical and vocational preparation at the post-secondary level.

At the same time, by affiliation either on a formal statewide basis or through informal accreditation arrangements, the regional subuniversity can offer the first two years of higher education to students who may later transfer to universities or colleges. It can act as a maturing stage for the late-blooming scholar and it can also act as a screening and terminal device for students who simply do not have the capacity for going on. It can also meet the enormous social demand for education beyond the secondary that can be satisfied with something less than a full-fledged first degree. It is particularly promising when located in urban or suburban areas, because the majority of students can commute and save capital outlays on dormitory construction, or government subsidies for boarding expenses. Also, when located in urban areas, it can —in the technical fields—profit by use of part-time instructors and even plant and equipment loaned by private industry.

For the developing countries, the building of vocational centers—advanced shop and laboratory centers—jointly financed by industry and the education ministry may get at one of the critical problems in sub-professional and upper vocational education. These centers must stay abreast of the rapidly evolving technology. They must provide machines and work experience that are *au courant* with the present industrial situation, and not become, as so often has happened in the past in vocational and technical education, museums of antique equipment, and out-moded shop and lab practices. The equipment will be expensive and have quick obsolescence. Industry must contribute its share, and this may have to be enforced. On the other hand, public educators must not have the sole voice in curriculum development. Joint boards must govern, and the inhibiting and tradition-bound plans of the educators must be shaken and shaped.

The subprofessional institution is likely to grow in developing countries, because there will be no other way for educational demand to be met. Smaller institutions scattered in places where a university might not be located will offer a wider chance at post-secondary education to children who might not otherwise have it; and yet the scale of these institutions makes for certain limitations, particularly in the provision of laboratories and workshops for science and technology. When the institutions are in urban areas, where cooperative arrangements can be worked out with other institutions or industries for sharing technical staff and facilities, these schools may be more economical and at the same time just as productive educationally.

Apropos of these institutions, a great many may have to be terminal —and thus be higher technical schools which produce subprofessional technicians, i.e., engineering and science associates and assistants. Diagnosis of the problem is easier than the remedy. In countries where the formal university degree has enormous social status, parents and students might avoid such programs, even if they were created. This is not wholly unreasonable either. Industries may well not offer rewards and incentives for such technicians. The hierarchy may have no intervening steps between the professional engineer and the skilled workman. The development of such programs will require skilled social and economic staging in many countries.

It is probable that the in-industry contribution to technical training will increase in future years, as opposed to formal school programs. Equally desirable will be vastly increased cooperative programs between schools and industry. The ideal condition of the future may be schools flexible enough to offer advanced and specialized training, as new technologies evolve. Workers, technicians and scientists may go through a life time of retraining in joint school-industry enterprises.

Subprofessional institutes of technology may also evolve into full-fledged universities or university colleges, as years of study and advanced programs are added. There is a further stage, where the schools broaden out from concentration on science and engineering and offer heavier programs in social sciences and humanities. In developing countries there may have to be careful control exercised for a few years, precisely to see that this does not happen to the detriment of the very real need that such schools are designed to fill.

Part-time study (night, weekend, summer) at the post-secondary level, either in subprofessional or professional courses can only increase. It is likely to increase in the still-developing countries, because limited resources, facilities, and staffs will permit no other pattern. Furthermore, it is unlikely that vast numbers of the best educated youth can be fully withheld from the labor market for the period of time necessary to finish university studies.

Present patterns, where students spend seven or 10 years beyond secondary, stumbling through a professional training that should require four or five years at most, cannot long be maintained. The cost of the tuition is only a fraction of the true cost. Calculating opportunity costs of education through wages foregone has always been easier in theory than in fact, in developing or developed countries. But the fact that withholding large numbers of students from the labor force has a cost has never been challenged. This cost can be minimized if the students attend school for sandwich courses in cooperative or continuing programs and profit from both work and educational experience.

The size of correspondence schooling and its importance has never been made clear in educational statistics. There has always been a certain snobbishness connected with this, as with night school. Unhappily, these prejudices have been transferred to developing countries, and ministries of education have been most unsure of themselves in granting credit for such work. Countries may simply have to put these prejudices where they belong and take advantage of every access to further education that is possible. Programmed instruction through auto-tutorial devices may make home education far more effective than massively overcrowded classrooms.

In summary, full-time day attendance may be less likely in developing countries than more flexible part-time and correspondence work arranged on continuing and cooperative basis between industry and community institutions. This will be particularly so for technical training courses. Major blocks to more flexible and realistic programs reside in social prejudice and educational conservatism.

Fields of Study

However programs are organized, certain fields will receive greater emphasis in the future than others.

Relative reduction of enrollments in traditional fields is already well under way in developing countries. In Latin American universities, the rectors' pleas to reduce enrollments in law, and in some cases medicine, are now received as obvious and as clichés. Although admissions continue heavy in the Latin American 'traditional faculties' of law and medicine, enrollments are also growing in engineering and the sciences.

Within the fields of engineering, certain overstock is already appearing in the more advanced Latin American countries. Civil engineering, usually the first field to be established, shows signs of overproducing in the years directly ahead. However, subfields that may be associated with civil engineering at the post-graduate level, e.g., structures, strength of materials, still require expansion, both to produce teachers and researchers for the universities and to turn out research and development staffs for industry.

The output of chemical, mechanical, and electrical (electronic and power) engineers may be under or over the requirements, depending on the state of development of any given country. Electronics and solid-state physics programs are expanding in certain of the more rapidly developing countries, and nuclear physicists and engineers—still and most often trained abroad—are proving hard to absorb in the home country, and probably will be a source of leakage of high talent from developing to developed countries.

Industrial engineering—the management of the processes of production and distribution through controlled methods and the skilled handling of human resources—is only now developing. Courses of study in this area are going to cause problems when some of the more exotic dogma of human relations have to be introduced into other cultures. In the developing countries, productivity centers which offer short courses in management for middle-echelon executives are established and in some cases thriving and showing strong growth potential. Over-all, engineering programs are growing and will continue to grow, with some surplusses appearing in certain fields at the professional level (e.g., civil engineering) within ten years.

The need for post-graduate programs in basic and applied sciences is already apparent in the more rapidly developing countries. First, the graduates are required as professors. Second, university staffs are anxious to move into graduate-level research where they may generate as well as transmit knowledge. How much the programs will expand is problematical. In the short run, it is apparent that the few graduate students involved can be more inexpensively trained abroad. On the other hand, nationalism and the prestige of a science and research establishment may provide the fillip which brings countries to make rather large outlays to produce few graduates. Outlays will be huge, for buildings and equipment, staff salaries (with large instructor to student ratios) and fellowship aid.

Furthermore, parents in many parts of the world have not accepted the responsibility of supporting students, even at the first-degree level. Many of the parents could not offer graduate-level support for their children, even if they wished; and the burden of support for scholarships and fellowships is going to come down heavily on new countries.

On the other hand, industries and government may well wish to give relatively high-cost support, for economic reasons. Greater investment in research and development and more efficient industrial management may be necessary to generate new enterprises and to keep them viable.

The prospects for expanded programs of higher education in agriculture, and the sciences which undergird them, are bright. The first agricultural school developments were, as in primary teacher training, at the secondary level; and the status of graduates of such programs was low. Because of prodding and financial support from outside, the situation is changing in Latin America and Africa. University schools of veterinary medicine and agriculture are expanding, improving, and attracting higher calibre students. One could hope that this will raise the status of work in agriculture in countries that must inevitably depend on agriculture for a major share of product and foreign exchange. One can also hope that the graduates will not be piled up in the ministries of agriculture or in the agrarian banks, as white collar strategists scorning the fields and pastures.

The social disciplines which support agricultural development and rural improvement, the agricultural economists and statisticians, the sociologists and community development workers and researchers, also seem to be showing growth. The American land-grant pattern has been useful in upgrading the status of research applied to community service in rural areas.

The future of the land-grant model in developing countries is difficult to assess. The pattern has been more admired in developing countries than copied. In West and East Africa there has been much talk by politicians and statesmen about the need to break away from the British pattern to follow the American land-grant model. The Michigan State— Nsukka arrangement in the Eastern Region of Nigeria may be a move toward attempting this, although it is too early to tell how closely the pattern will be followed.

In Latin America, the rectors are exhorting their faculties to serve beyond the walls. The hundreds of *institutos* formed in Latin American universities to carry out applied research in special areas of the physical and social sciences reflect university responsiveness to extra-mural social need. For pedagogical reasons, it is perhaps unfortunate that these are not more directly tied to the basic *facultad* structure of the mother insti- tution, so that students might profit by work and learning affiliations that characterize North American and European research. But with the *facultades* operating as centers of conservatism and resistance to change, the *instituto* represents about the best a progressive rector can do when he operates in a situation of *facultad* autonomy (in many cases the *facultades* are governed by the rector's man and the dean's man, often working at cross purposes), and *consejo* and *Co-Gobierno* features (in which the faculty and university councils with student, alumnae, and professional representation sometimes play a powerful and unsettling role).

However the present structure of the Latin American university is defended by pointing to its lineage out of the Bologna, Salamanca and Sigüenza 'communities,' the truth is that it hasn't served well for effecting reforms and preserving standards. It is not as bleak as some outside commentators think, however, and student government of the university is being reduced to symbolic and representational status and confined to areas which should properly concern students. This trend will per- force continue in the future and when it has reached the point where the rector commands his ship; *institutos* will be reincorporated; *facultad* autonomy will be reduced to responsible levels; departmentalization will allow more efficient, inexpensive instruction; and the university will be more adaptable and responsive to changing social and economic demands in the country which supports it. The winds of change al- ready blow strongly through most Latin American institutions.

Withal, one would hope that the land-grant model would not pre- vail abroad, at least not without appropriately trained staff to make it work. Without strong supporting departments in the basic and applied sciences, the land-grant transformation abroad could produce a hodge- podge of arid courses catering only to the immediate needs of the market place and the shop.

One comes, at last, to the heart of higher education, or, indeed, of education at any level, the programs which, apart from professional applications, attempt to present learners with some basic portion of the arts and sciences cumulated to our times. One can predict with reasonable certainty that the basic corpus of knowledge not only will grow but the rate of acquisition will probably increase. The methods and instrumentalities for generating, storing, searching, and transmitting new knowledge are too powerful to allow it to be otherwise; and unless these mighty engines shut down for some reason that cannot be foreseen, knowledge will grow, and the rate of growth will probably accelerate.

The schooling which a society offers its members depends to some extent on how much there is to learn. As this increases, years of formal schooling tend to increase also. Schooling also increases according to the proportion of the population that demand, backed by the means of enforcement, some substantial portion of knowledge. The years of schooling which are offered and will be offered depend on both these things and also the efficiency with which the knowledge can be transmitted. It is not likely that the rate of improvement in efficiency of transmission will outstrip the growth of new knowledge or the increased number of people demanding access to it. Years of schooling then can only rise in the foreseeable future.

Professor Barzun (1959) envisages an uncertain future for the liberal arts college which in his view is being squeezed out of a job, as high-school courses step up in pace and university and college courses turn more quickly professional. This is happening and may indeed grow, but it can not be because there is less general knowledge and basic science and art to impart. Students who are treated to the elements of set theory, probability, and the calculus in their high-school programs still have a lot of mathematics left for their college days before they need be confined to special topics or professional applications. The four-year liberal arts cycle may be squeezed out simply because there is no demand for it and hence less impetus to make the outlays necessary to support it. This may be particularly so in the hard-pressed developing countries.

The liberal arts and basic sciences portion of higher education may also be reduced, because professional courses have become so solidly grounded in the substrate disciplines that there is less necessity of providing this grounding elsewhere.

The squeeze may also be on colleges, because the better scholars and teachers may wish to be in the universities. And lastly the squeeze may come because the basic fields have become themselves so vast that they have fragmented into very many little pieces that are difficult for any one professor to handle generally.

But the liberal arts will endure, as they have, and in some quarters they are being reborn and strengthened. Stages of basic studies to follow secondary school and come before professional studies are being planned. In Latin America, the two-year basic studies programs, inserted between the *bachillerato* and entrance to professional course work, is finding favor. To date, these basic programs are largely in science and mathematics but there is reason to hope that they will broaden to embrace the arts.

In the English-speaking countries of Africa the sixth form seems to present some very real economic and pedagogical problems in the sciences, when very small, upper-level installations are maintained as appurtenances to secondary schools. On the basis of efficiency these might better be detached and centered in institutions of third level where large outlays on equipment and plant have to be made and used to the maximum.

The defense of the sixth form sometimes offered is that it tends to maintain higher status for the secondary schools. Whether this will continue to be true in the crowded years to come is problematical, and whether new countries can afford the bookishness and verbalism of some sixth-form science is a question. One might make the argument that it is precisely the laboratory and work-shop experience in science and technology that schools in the new countries must supply, because it is less likely to be acquired incidentally through flivver-tinkering, as in the countries where machines abound. It is easy to recommend that one year be broken off the sixth form and put up at university level, where heavy dosages of laboratory and shop science could be better provided. In the next 10 years it is unlikely that this will happen in Africa. As a guess, one would predict that the sixth form pattern would not grow and that the junior college and basic studies sections of the universities would, along with the technological institute (subprofessional and professional), be more the pattern of the future.

In any case, the basic arts and sciences will continue to be offered somewhere, and it is difficult to conceive how this could be otherwise. The prospect of a conglomerate of technical fields, whose members are unintelligible to each other, is frightening to contemplate, but unlikely, as more multi-disciplinary and hybrid fields appear in the universities. Philosophy has been suggested as the queen and unifying force, but which of the systems can do the job? And one wonders if philosophy hasn't the problem of unifying itself first. In Latin America, there has begun a counter insurgency led by so-called philosophers who cry out for a balanced liberal education in the face of the encroachment of applied science and professionalism. One can sympathize with the movement without having a great deal of sympathy with the motives or respect for the intellects of the movers. A problem that is amenable to solution by no one discipline may be far more effective as a unifying force in science and arts than philosophical dialogue that is really monologue.

Educational Technology

Saved to last is a discussion of the ways in which advances in technology will affect higher education. Especially pertinent are the new teaching modalities and the part they may play in helping countries meet the crushing demand on higher education in the future. One suspects— despite the promises of the economists about planes or satellites endlessly circling overhead and beaming down teacherless educational programs— that the savings and efficiencies effected through new technical modalities will not be vast in the next 20 years, the time of maximal trouble for the poor, new countries. At the same time, technology applied to education will show progress in the developed countries and some of this will be exportable.

The design and building of functional and inexpensive facilities will progress a great deal in developing countries through the use of standardized modular units with all splendor cut away. The time will come when vast and elaborate—but empty—university buildings will be avoided by those who cannot afford them. Some years will pass before university classrooms will be sprayed up in plastic, but the signs all point to a lowering cost and an increase in accommodation, without sacrifice of anything but facade.

For those countries where even the cheapest building outlay hurts, the correspondence course, monitored by an occasional classroom instruction or test, is a possibility. These will reach further out into the provinces as basic communications improve and commuting and correspondence become easier. With population growth and improved travel, the number of full boarding facilities that have to be provided may diminish, although there are hidden cultural and pedagogical advantages to the well regulated intern study programs that cannot be duplicated by some day-school patterns. In those countries where a variety of subnational languages and cultures prevail, the central boarding facility has and will have some merit. But cultural homogeneity will come and the boarding facility will have less reason to exist, and improved national communications will level regional or tribal differences.

U.S. authorities have reason to suppose that the student-owned

automobile has a bad effect on academic performance, and other countries may note this for the future and organize accordingly. Remedies
for the automobile, as reported to Professor Seymour E. Harris (1962),
are designing campuses without access motor roads or parking lots,
locking the students into the establishment for a major portion of the
day, and providing long rounds of classes, cultural activities, and brief
fun and games. This latter course also maximizes the use of the facilities
and effects the kind of economies economists relish. 'High facilities use
ratios' is the term.

Provision of the increasingly complex equipment that science
courses require is going to be a problem for developing countries. The
blow may be particularly heavy because purchase not only requires
large, absolute expenditures but also because these outlays must often be
made in scarce foreign exchange. In Chile, university science and technology programs are building equipment for the secondary school
laboratories, but who builds for the university labs? In some cases,
Mexico for example, universities build their own equipment—up to a
point—as part of thesis projects. For countries where experience in
technical manipulation is necessary to supplement theoretical programs
in science, this is all to the good, pedagogically as well as fiscally.

Surplus equipment from the developing countries—where planned
obsolescence is a feature of the economy—may also fill the gap, but
countries should be wary that the gift they accept is both necessary and
costless.

The largest part of the running budget of any school establishment
goes for instructional staff, and efforts may be made to replace the
teacher with the machine. Too often, attention focuses on the presenta-
tional device—television set, radio, record player, teaching machine—
and away from the program that is projected by it. (Certain U.S.
scholars, usually classicists, already see the end of the book in sight, but
what exactly will replace it is not specified.) To get a return on the
large initial outlay, the device must be used as often as possible and
serve the widest number of students per use. Hence, the wide-screen
projection of a movie is likely to give a better return than an auto-
tutoring device that can serve only one viewer at a time; and if a language laboratory console is purchased the more booth outlets the better.
The staff that is required to monitor and reinforce instruction may not
be much reduced. The greatest problem, however, comes in the program,
which is central to the show.

Development of initial programs, whether in branch or linear
format or even in fairly sprawling old lecture style, are costly, not only
in materials and clerical time, but in the inputs of highly skilled writers,

animators, and designers. These skills do not abound in most countries. Programming, like the construction of objective test items, has a deceptive simplicity about it. Not all good teachers can do it. Purchase of gadgetry should never get out beyond the stock in the program library available to feed it.

Still the technics of programming can be taught and the use of programmed instruction will spread. It is not yet clear how much teacher time it may save. However, in countries where professorial talent is short and classes large, the advantage of canning the work of a good professor, for multiple showing to large groups, is obvious. For certain technical demonstrations, e.g., precision work on a lathe, or electronic mazes, cameras can bring the student into more intimate contact with all of the steps and the scene can be projected again and again. One would still hope that the lathe in material form would somehow later come into the student's program and that he would get the chance to tinker with tools.

It is apparent that some kinds of materials and some stages in the material will offer more possibility for machine teaching than others. Rudimentary language instruction can perhaps be even better done with language laboratory audio procedures than with a live instructor. The manipulations involved in mathematics, although not always the conceptualization, can be machined, as can the rudiments of science, with the same limitations. In the arts and verbal disciplines where appreciations are required, the machine will not be nearly as good as a sensitive teacher.

For home study the auto-tutor and even programmed books may relieve congestion in the classrooms, but a certain amount of follow-up lecture and testing would be all to good.

Technology will offer poorer countries ways of reducing costs and serving wider demands in higher education in the days to come, but excellent teachers, whether in front of the class, or at one remove working on the program, will be in just as heavy demand as always, and countries should reckon on the fact that they won't soon be replaced by machines.

Conclusion

The hosts of students in the future will be handled, but there seems to be a pitifully small amount of creative thought going into the planning of higher education for the future. There are, of course, only so many new directions possible in higher education. Program quality rests on great books, teachers, students, facilities, and some measure of institutional *Zeitgeist;* and there are only so many ways to recombine these things in any country. Still, the prevision that is directed toward the higher education of the future—and this section will serve as well as any to exemplify this—is not bold. In education generally there is little thought given to the future; much addressed to the past.

Poetry begins with a datum and ends with a quest; planning should do this, too.

Material in Appendix A is included to illustrate the first comprehensive application of the manpower schemata described in Chapter II. To conserve space, the tables—except for the final deficit table—have been abridged. There are five abridged tables showing the five steps taken to calculate the demand for educated people in the work force. The steps taken to calculate the supply can be described, and all the tables need not be shown here:

Steps Taken to Estimate Supply

1. The population is projected by age 1955–1975.
2. First-grade enrollments are projected 1955–1975.
3. Retention rates for grades 1 through 12 are calculated or estimated (Table A-6).
4. On the basis of entrants and retention, school enrollment from 1950–1975 are estimated for primary school, junior-high school, and senior-high school.
5. College and senior-high school graduates are estimated as a proportion of 12th grade enrollment.
6. The education level of the population (educational attainment) is estimated for 1950–1975.
7. Labor force participation rates by age, sex and education are estimated for 1955–1975.
8. The labor force classified by age, sex and education is given for 1955–1975.
9. The comparison of manpower supply and demand by education is given for 1955–1975. This Table A-11 is shown in full.

Step No.   *DEMAND*   TABLE A-1 (abridged)
1.   Income by Sector, 1950–1975
(constant dollars)
(million dollars)

Sector	1950	.. 1960	.. 1975
Total	705	1280	3176
Agriculture	172	178	273
Manufacturing	102	340	1435
Construction	31	48	157
Trade (Wholesale-Retail)	117	220	540
Transportation, Communications and Utilities	57	101	276
Services	111	216	506
Government	133	261	338
Rest of the World	−18	−84	−349

TABLE A-2 (abridged)
2.   Productivity by Sector, 1950–1975

Sector	1950	.. 1960	.. 1975
Total	1190	2120	3980
Agriculture	790	1200	1990
.			
.			
.			
Government	2660	4200	4450

Productivity is income divided by workers, i.e., income per man, on assumption that Puerto Rican productivity in 1975 will be approximately that of U.S. in 1950.

SOURCE: Commonwealth of Puerto Rico, Committee on Human Resources, Puerto Rico's Manpower Needs and Supply, San Juan: 1957, Appendix Tables

Step No.   TABLE A-3 (abridged)
3.   Employment by Sector, 1950–1975
(in thousands)

Sector	1950	.. 1960	.. 1975
Total	595	604	798
Agriculture	218	148	137
.			
.			
.			
Government	50	62	76

TABLE A-4 (abridged)

4. **Estimated Employment by Industry and Occupational Group, 1975**
(in thousands)

Occupational Group	Total	Agriculture	Government
Total	798	137	76
Professionals	55	—	9
Managers	67	—	8
Clerical Workers	100	—	33
Sales Workers	50	—	*
Craftsmen	90	—	6
Operatives	192	—	4
Private Household Workers	13	—	12
Service Workers	54	—	*
Farm Owners and Managers	39	39	—
Laborers	40	—	4
Farm Laborers	98	98	—

* Less than 500

TABLE A-5 (abridged)

5. **Employment by Occupational Group and Education, 1975**
(in thousands)

Occupational Group	Total	College	Senior High School	Junior High School	Elementary School	Five Years or Less
Total	798	49	246	158	248	97
Professionals	55	27	21	3	3	1
	55	27	21	3	3	1
.						
.						
.						
Farm Laborers	98	*	12	14	40	32

* Less than 500

Supply

1. Population projected by age 1955–75 (not shown here)
2. First grade enrollments, projected 1955–75 (not shown here)

3.
TABLE A-6 (abridged)
Estimated Retention Rates, 1950–1975

Grade	1950	1960	1975	United States 1950
1– 2 Grade	90.6	93.6	93.6	93.6
2– 3 Grade	93.3	99.2	99.2	99.2
3– 4 Grade	89.9	93.0	98.4	98.4
4– 5 Grade	88.4	90.0	93.5	98.1
5– 6 Grade	90.6	90.3	95.0	98.4
6– 7 Grade	89.2	87.7	94.0	97.0
7– 8 Grade	88.5	84.0	88.5	96.7
8– 9 Grade	91.1	86.0	88.0	91.8
9–10 Grade	79.3	88.0	88.0	89.4
10–11 Grade	87.9	87.0	87.0	86.8
11–12 Grade	83.7	86.5	86.5	88.5

(Steps 4 through 8 to complete supply side would follow here but are not shown.)

Final step   **TABLE A-11** (complete)
Comparison of Manpower Supply and Demand by Education, 1955–1975
(in thousands)

Educational Level	1955 No.	Excess (+) Shortage (−)	1960 No.	Excess (+) Shortage (−)	1965 No.	Excess (+) Shortage (−)	1970 No.	Excess (+) Shortage (−)	1975 No.	Excess (+) Shortage (−)
Total Supply	645	+106	702	+ 98	761	+112	806	+ 76	883	+ 35
Demand	539		604		649		730		798	
College										
Supply	14	−2	17	−4	24	−7	29	−18	37	−12
Demand	16		21		31		47		49	
Senior High School										
Supply	53	−16	100	−10	135	−13	179	−17	219	−27
Demand	69		110		148		196		246	
Junior High School										
Supply	46	−7	63	−20	74	−34	99	−31	112	−46
Demand	53		83		108		130		158	
Elementary School										
Supply	129	−20	146	−28	166	−30	160	−64	172	−76
Demand	149		174		196		224		248	
Five Years or Less										
Supply	403	+151	376	+160	362	+196	339	+206	293	+196
Demand	252		216		166		133		97	

Appendix B shows Cooke's schematization of the overall planning sequence outlined at the end of Chapter II. There are also specifications for staffing the planning sections to carry out the tasks schematized. Each one of the circled numbers in the overall diagram represents a subsystem which would have to be analyzed and broken into its component parts.

As an example, subsystem 7, Industrial Surveys and Analysis, is schematized and the activities and events are described. Cooke's Schemata are offered as examples of how the planning process might be analysed atomically. The schematization of all the component parts of the process is deliberately not given in this book. Planners often become so intrigued with models and schemata that they spend months working on pictures when they should be out looking at schools. For those planning staffs that have an underemployed draftsman, the preparation of such schemata might offer considerable aesthetic satisfaction. A substantial literature on PERT analysis is available as a guide.

Overall Planning Sequence[1]

Stage Descriptions

    I. Situational Survey and Negotiations Pursuant to Study Design
    II. Internal Management Planning
    III. Systems Analysis and Data-Collection-Reduction
    IV. Projection of Supply and Demand
    V. System Design
    VI. Feasibility Evaluation
    VII. System Re-design

[1] Arrows show activities of staff, not flow of information. Communication among staff members must be complete and well-coordinated, but such lines would unnecessarily complicate the schematic.

261

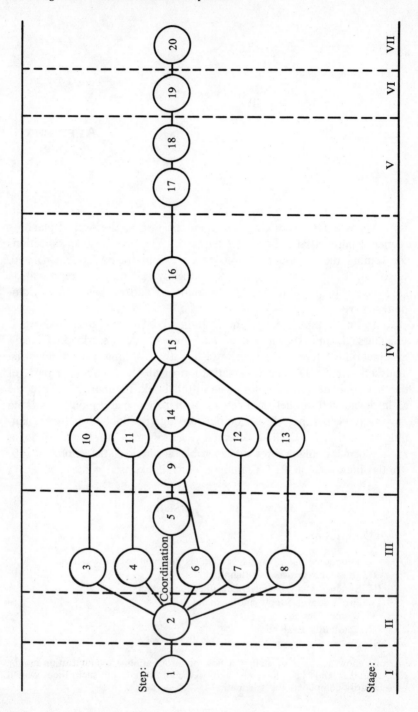

Notes on Staffing

a. Basic staff requirements and tasks are: Educational Planner and Project Director (1, 2, 5, 9, 14–20) plus coordination; Sociologist (3, 10); Demographer (4, 11); Industrial Survey Technician (7, 12, 14); Economist (6, 9, 14); and, Educational Systems Analyst (8, 13). All would cooperate in establishing service sector demand (Step 15) and total demand targets (Step 16).

b. The educational systems analyst should work with the project director from beginning to end; however, the sociologist, industrial survey technician, demographer and economist need only be available full-time during Stages III and IV, but should be available as consultants both in the preceding and final design stages. When a country is contemplating significant changes in its agricultural complex, an agricultural expert may be needed.

c. Since future measurement of the new system's output must be performed on a continuing basis by local officials, it would be advisable to include "counterparts" in each segment of the study, so that they may be thoroughly familiar with the operation of the system and can carry on without frequent technical supervision.

Step Descriptions

1. Establish study scope and sequence; survey existing data. *Note:* Scope will include targets set by home officials (over which the planner has no control) and economic development targets and specifics (which the planner must accept, at least until Stage VI is reached).
2. Determine staff requirements; recruit, organize and brief study staff.
3. Socio-cultural analysis to determine special conditions (e.g. religious restraints, literacy shortcomings, traditional family or village production patterns) which any future system will have to alter or circumvent.
4. Population study: Census tracts, birth and fertility data, life tables, migration, et cetera.
5. Data on employment in government sector and estimate of future needs, both state and local; *Note:* logical responsibility of project director since he is in closest touch with government officials; may require extra staffing.
6. Resource estimate: involves measures of national or regional product, sector or industry productivity, corporate and personal income; also, estimates of tax policies and revenues, as well as past practices in allocating resources to education; general analysis of existing economic development plans, including agricultural sector.
7. Industrial survey and analysis: establishment surveys to determine current status of workforce and future manpower needs; establish measures of efficiency in manpower utilization and performance; acquire data on current and planned in-plant or apprenticeship training programs.
8. Analysis of formal educational system (public and private): input-output relationships (e.g. supply of teachers and their distribution, as against output of graduates from various levels); efficiency measures (both those resulting from cost analysis and performance of graduates on the job); system structure and lines of authority and communication; current instructional content, techniques and sequences; hardware evaluation; legal bases for system; estimate of attitudes which might prejudice future system improvements (i.e. student, teacher and administrator).
9. Agricultural employment analysis, with reference to broad-scale development plans: rough worker projection in agricultural sector.

10. Set educational goals for non-workforce part of population, particularly women.
11. Perform necessary population projections.
12. Estimate effect of planned new industry on future workforce demand, by discrete steps to target year; add predicted need as ascertained from existing industries.
13. Project output of the formal educational system, all levels, public and private. *Note:* This is the output of the present system, if it continued to function unchanged until the target year.
14. Establish total future workforce requirements, in occupational terms, except for service sector; appropriate wastage factors should be used, as in 9 & 15.
15. Establish future workforce demand in service sector, by discrete steps to target year. *Note:* Those services connected with educational expansion and improvement can not be added in until end of step #16, and can not be made fairly exact until end of step #18.
16. Aggregate total workforce needed in target year, taking into account wastage; add in desired general characteristics of non-workforce; deduct projected output of present educational system; calculate gaps, in occupational and behavioral terms, which future system must fill. *Note:* Check percentages of economic sectors (e.g. service vs. production) against experience of similar countries.
17. Translate demand targets into educational terms (not necessarily years of schooling completed, et cetera). This partly depends on the prototype educational system which (from among many possible) is indicated by all of the preceding analysis. Therefore, final figures must await the actual system design.
18. Design optimal (ideal) system to fill gaps (as well as increase efficiency at current level of output), at lowest cost. *Note:* Sufficient cost analysis should be undertaken both to provide a sound basis for evaluation and to identify where and how much costs are increased (e.g. curriculum improvement, teacher training, laboratory equipment, et cetera). Thus, if cost-cutting is indicated in step #19, it can be done with full knowledge of how the quantity or quality of output will be affected in the re-designed system. Note that such factors will usually alter the assumptions and projections in step #13 and the final estimate of the "education gap" in step #17.
19. Test system designed in step #18 against estimate of resources available, both financial and human.
20. Re-optimize and re-design educational system to conform to financial, and other, realities.

Subsystem #7
Establishment Survey of Existing Industry
(Schematic)

Activities Leading to Circled Events

1. Start
2. Compile list of industries, classified by economic sector, ISIC and size. (Location may be also included if geographic factors warrant.)
3. Sample and Statistical Analysis Design

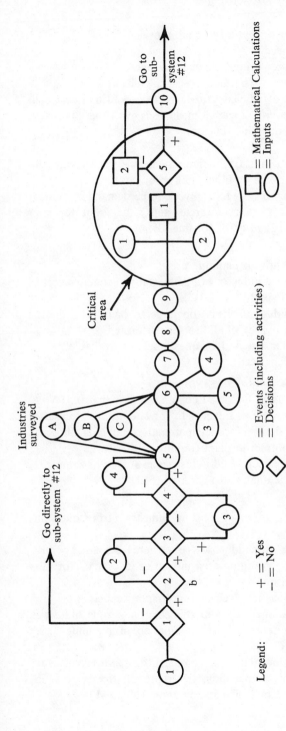

Legend: + = Yes
               − = No

A, B, C = Industries surveyed (may be sample)
Closed Curve = Part of sequence most crucial to successful outcome of sub-system.

a. Industry is defined here as emphasizing light and heavy production, but in actual practice the field staff will be able to gather data on such "industries" as retail businesses, hospitals, and so forth, although the master schematic shows others working in non-industrial sectors.

b. If complete industrial census data are available (⬦2), the sequence from ⬦3 up to (but not including) ◯6 will concern investigation of future needs, data on training programs, spot checks on census information, and bringing census data forward to base year x.

SOURCE: Cooke, Lot. Unpublished papers

4. Design questionnaires and personal interview forms
5. Conduct field survey
6. Classify work-force using following matrices:
    (a) Occ × Sector (b) Occ × Ed. Level (c) Occ × Age
7. Devise estimate of efficiency in large Occ × Ed. Level cells (may be productivity, if such a measure is available; otherwise, some management rating scheme)
8. Data processing
9. Profile of present industry, including efficiency of various sub-industry occupational or functional groupings
10. Report of projections for future work-force demand in existing industries, years x to n (discrete steps), as input for later calculations. Use IBM cards for final data.

DECISIONS (DIAMONDS)

1. Is industry presently in planning area?
2. Is listing of all local industry available, stating economic sector, ISIC coding and size?
3. Is number of industrial firms too large to handle in allotted time, if complete survey of all firms is performed?
4. Are personal interview and/or questionnaires available?
5. Was sampling plan used?

MATHEMATICAL CALCULATIONS (RECTANGLES)

1. Calculate gaps, using Occ × Economic Sector matrix. (*Note:* Hold off on Occ × Ed. Level data for later conversion, after general system design for occupational training is chosen.) Add wastage; subtract in-plant training.
2. Aggregate net gaps across all industries in survey or sample.
3. Perform statistical analysis to get final total.

INPUTS (ELLIPSES)

1. Future expansion plans of existing industry (from questionnaires and interviews).
2. Established "mix" for industries (elsewhere) not at stage projected for existing planning area industries in year n (for purposes of comparison).
    Important assumptions involved in any sampling scheme:
    (a) Are occupational mix and efficiency in sample industries same as in total industry population of planning area? (steps 6 and 7)
    (b) Are expansion plans (or some central tendency measure of same) of sample industries representative of total industry population of planning area? (ellipse 1)

Notes on Appendices C, D, E, F, and G

Appendix C is an abridged life table compiled by Vasquez for the Dominican Republic. On the basis of the mortality conditions shown in his table, Vasquez was able to enter the United Nations model life tables at the appropriate levels and to carry out a population projection for the Dominican Republic, using methods outlined in Chapter III.

Appendix D is an outline of the Stanbery (1960) formula for estimating population for future dates in subnational areas. The data in the example are from the United States, but the problem of estimating subnational populations will become increasingly important as planning progresses in developing countries. The country plans must get below the level of national aggregates, so that effective planning can be carried out for regions within the country that often differ substantially in level of development.

Appendix E outlines Wasserman's (1963) methods for calculating price subindices for instruction. The example of a price relative subindex for office supplies appears in Chapter VI of the text.

Appendix F is the cost comparison of automated and conventional teaching run by Kopstein and Cave (1962). It should be noted that the cost of automated instruction does not include the cost of teachers used to reinforce and direct the instructional program. Hence, the comparison does not indicate how much is saved on instructors' costs through use of the hardware.

In Appendix G Carroll (1963) describes the human and financial inputs to the development of an automated program for language teaching. Part V of the Carroll outline shoud be studied carefully by those who are pushing for rapid technological modifications in education in developing countries. The existence of real resources in the form of very highly skilled programmers must be established before the country launches into new technologies.

Abridged Life Table for Both Sexes, Santo Domingo, 1960

Age Interval	$_nq_x$	l_x	$_nd_x$	$_nl_x$	T_x	e_x
0–1	0.134516	100000	13452	90261	5369073	53.7
1–5	.078021	86548	6753	327863	5278818	61.0
5–10	.017259	79795	1377	395112	4950949	62.0
10–15	.008018	78418	629	390394	4555837	58.1
15–20	.010102	77789	786	387060	4165443	53.6
20–25	.013118	77003	1010	382638	3778383	49.1
25–30	.019719	75993	1499	376360	3395745	44.7
30–35	.022706	74494	1691	368274	3019385	40.5
35–40	.022706	72803	1653	360017	2651111	36.4
40–45	.032841	71150	2337	350131	2291094	32.2
45–50	.039609	68813	2726	337479	1940963	28.2
50–55	.051962	66087	3434	322364	1603484	24.3
55–60	.082906	62653	5294	300922	1281120	20.4
60–65	.113366	57459	6514	271523	980198	17.1
65–70	.150362	50945	7660	236169	708675	13.9
70–75	.216339	43285	9364	193406	472506	10.9
75–80	.281182	33921	9538	122659	279100	8.2
80–85	.373927	24383	9119	83102	156441	6.4
85 and over	1.000000	15264	15364	73339	73339	4.8

$_nq_x$ = probability of dying between the lower and the upper age limits of the age interval

l_x = beginning with a cohort of 100,000 live births, survivors to the beginnings of each age interval

$_nd_x$ = death occurring during each age interval

$_nl_x$ = stationary population in the age interval

T_x = stationary population in the age interval and in all the followings

e_x = expectation of life at the age corresponding to the lower limit of the age interval

The first value of this column is the expectation of life at birth.

SOURCE: Vasquez. Unpublished work sheets, Santo Domingo, 1963.

STANBERY FORMULA FOR PROJECTION OF THE CIVILIAN POPULATION OF AN AREA OF THE UNITED STATES BY DECADES[a]

Let A = Civilian population of area at beginning of decade

Let X = Civilian population of area at end of decade

Then $X = A +$ (total in-migration − total out-migration + natural increase during decade)

Let B = Arithmetical mean of civilian populations of United States at beginning and end of decade

Let R_1 = Projected rate of total migration of civilians into area during decade per mean civilian population of United States excluding civilian population of area

Let R_2 = Projected rate of total out-migration of civilians from area during decade per mean civilian population of area (arithmetical mean of civilian population of area at beginning and end of decade)

Let N = Projected average annual crude rate of natural increase[b] per 1000 mean civilian population of area during decade multiplied by 10 (years)

(Algebraic derivation is omitted here)

$$\text{Then, total in-migration} = R_1 \left[B - \left(\frac{A + X}{2} \right) \right]$$

$$\text{Out-migration} = R_2 \left(\frac{A + X}{2} \right)$$

$$\text{Natural increase} = N \left(\frac{A + X}{2} \right)$$

(Algebraic derivation omitted here)

---

[a] Projection, table and formula references in Appendix D may be examined in below source.

[b] Natural increase = excess of births in area over deaths of civilians (including in-migrants) in area during decade.

SOURCE: Stanbery, Van Beuren, *Some New Techniques for Area Population Projections,* Los Angeles: Haynes Foundation, 1960, p. 93.

Hence:
$$X = \frac{R_1 B + A\left[1 - \left(\dfrac{R_1 + R_2 - N}{2}\right)\right]}{1 + \left(\dfrac{R_1 + R_2 - N}{2}\right)}$$

Computation of Population Projections

Example of Computation of Population Projections in Table C-5 by Formula in Table E.

Series B Projection, July 1, 1960—July 1, 1970.

$R_1 = 0.45675 = 1950$–1960 rate of 0.0435 + assumed increase of 5%
$R_2 = 0.273525 = 1950$–1960 rate of 0.2605 + assumed increase of 5%

$$R_1 + R_2 = 0.3192$$
$$N = 0.143 \text{ (from Table C-4)}$$
$$\frac{R_1 + R_2 - N}{2} = \frac{0.1762}{2} = 0.0881$$

$$1 - \left(\frac{R_1 + R_2 - N}{2}\right) = 0.19119 \qquad 1 + \left(\frac{R_1 + R_2 - N}{2}\right) = 1.0881$$

$$B = 192{,}250{,}000 \text{ (from Table U-1, Series B)}$$
$$BR_1 = 0.045675 \times 192{,}250{,}000 = 8{,}781{,}019$$

Civilian population of California, July 1, 1960 = A = 15,530,000 (Table C-5)

$$A\left[1 - \left(\frac{R_1 + R_2 - N}{2}\right)\right] = 15{,}530{,}000 \times 0.9119 = 14{,}161{,}870$$

$$R_1 B + A\left[1 - \left(\frac{R_1 + R_2 - N}{2}\right)\right] = 22{,}942{,}826$$

Civilian population of
California, July 1, 1970 $= X = \dfrac{22{,}924{,}826}{1.0881} = 21{,}085{,}000$

Assumed military population $\qquad\qquad = \underline{\quad 300{,}000}$

Total population of California, July 1, 1970 $= 21{,}385{,}000$

$\qquad\qquad\qquad\qquad\qquad$ = Series B projection in Table C-5.

TABLE 2
Calculation of Price Subindex
For Personal Service Teacher Inputs

Utility stratum (level of preparation)	Price relative Base period $\left(\dfrac{P_{0i}}{P_{0i}}\right)$ x100	Price relative Period 1 $\left(\dfrac{P_{1i}}{P_{0i}}\right)$ x100	Expenditure weight w_i	Using absolute expenditure weights Price relative Base period $\left(\dfrac{P_{0i}}{P_{0i}}\right)$ x100w_i	X weight Period 1 $\left(\dfrac{P_{1i}}{P_{0i}}\right)$ x100w_i
1. Uncertified	100.0	105.4	46,000	4,600,000	4,848,400
2. Bachelor's	100.0	112.9	223,700	22,370,000	25,255,730
3. Master's	100.0	112.0	227,900	22,790,000	25,524,800
Total			497,600	49,760,000	55,628,930

$$\text{Index values: for base period} = \frac{49,760,000}{497,600} = 100.0$$

$$\text{for period 1} \quad = \frac{55,628,930}{497,600} = 111.8$$

Using relative expenditure weights

1.	100.0	105.4	.092	9.2	9.7
2.	100.0	112.9	.450	45.0	50.8
3.	100.0	112.0	.458	45.8	51.3
			1.000	100.0	111.8

$$\text{Index values: for base period} = \frac{100.0}{1.0} = 100.0$$

$$\text{for period 1} \quad = \frac{111.8}{1.0} = 111.8$$

Note: It may be helpful to rephrase these steps with the following notation. Each price relative $\left(\dfrac{P_{1i}}{P_{0i}}\right)$ times 100 is multiplied by its approximate weight (w_i); these arithmetic products are summed over the strata: $\sum_{i=1}^{n} \dfrac{P_{1i}}{P_{0i}} \cdot 100 \cdot w_i$, and this sum is divided by the sum of the weights, $\sum_{i=1}^{n} w_i$; hence, the formula for the price index is:

$$\frac{\sum_{i=1}^{n} \dfrac{P_{1i}}{P_{0i}} \cdot 100 \cdot w_i}{\sum_{i=1}^{n} w_i}$$

SOURCE: Wasserman, p. 44.

TABLE 3
Calculation of Price Relatives, General Method

Utility stratum (level of preparation)	Number of teachers in base period (1)	Total salary in stratum in base period (2)	Mean in stratum in base period (col. 2 ÷ col. 1) (3)	Number of teachers in stratum in period 1 (4)	Total salary in stratum in period 1 (5)	Mean salary in stratum in period 1 (col. 5 ÷ col. 4) (6)	Price relative for period 1 (col. 6 ÷ col. 3) × 100 (7)
1. Uncertified	6	$22,400	$3,733	6	$ 23,600	$3,933	105.4
2. Bachelor's degree	19	87,900	4,626	26	135,800	5,223	112.9
3. Master's degree	16	80,800	5,050	26	147,100	5,658	112.0

TABLE 4
Calculations of Weights, General Method

Utility stratum (level of preparation)	Total salary expenditure in[a] typical period (1)	Relative salary expenditure in typical period (2)
1. Uncertified	$ 46,000	.092
2. Bachelor's degree	223,700	.450
3. Master's degree	227,900	.458
Total	$497,600	1.0

(a) Typical period is the two-year period consisting of the base year and the year 1.

SOURCE: Wasserman, William, "Education Price and Quality Indexes," *The Economics and Politics of Public Education,* XII (Syracuse: Syracuse University Press, 1963) pp. 42–43.

SUMMARY COMPARISON OF COST INDICES FOR CONVENTIONAL AND
AUTOMATED TRAINING WITH VARIOUS ASSUMPTIONS AND BY THREE
METHODS OF ESTIMATION

$Cost per Student-Hour

I. Automated Instruction

Method I (Cost accounted on the basis of the contract to produce the materials)

Cost of Programming	
Nominal	.029
Corrected	.058
Cost of Program Storage	
Printed Booklets	.007
Microfilm (inseparable from cost of programming)	
Cost of Presentation Device	
Mark I AutoTutor	.215
Mark II AutoTutor	.060
Range of Estimates	.036–.273**

Method II (Cost accounted on the basis of manhours expended to produce materials)

Cost of Programming	
Low Estimate	.054
High Estimate	.064
Cost of Program Storage	
Printed Booklets	.007
Microfilm	.030
Cost of Presentation Device	
Mark I AutoTutor	.215
Mark II AutoTutor	.060
Range of Estimates	.061–.309**

Method III (Cost on basis of commercial charges for programmed materials)

Cost of Programming*	
Royalty-free Rights	.006
Absolute Copyrights	.041
Cost of Program Storage	
Printed Booklets	.007
Microfilm (prints only)	.116
Cost of Presentation Devices	
Mark I AutoTutor	.215
Mark II AutoTutor	.060
Range of Estimates	.013–.422**

273

II. Conventional Instruction

Mean Costs (estimated per AFR 172-7)	.370
Range of Estimates	.300–.450**

* Includes the cost of preparing the microfilm Master Negative
** As noted earlier, the estimated costs of automated instruction do not include the costs of instructors while such costs comprise a major portion of the estimated costs of conventional instruction. Normally, automated instruction will require fewer instructors, however in this particular study, the same number of instructors were used for each method of instruction.

SOURCE: Kopstein, Felix F. and Richard T. Cave, Preliminary Cost Comparison of Technical Training by Conventional and Programmed Learning Methods (Technical Documentary Report No. MRL-TDR-62-79) Wright-Patterson Air Force Base, Ohio, 1962, p. 14.

I. Machine Outlay

Engineering costs incurred in the acquisition and development of the two prototype models of the audiovisual presentation device used in this experiment ("AVID") were approximately $10,000. It may be estimated that production models of this device could not be made for much less than $1,000 each unless they were to be made in large quantities. In any event, the device should be redesigned rather completely before it is made in any large quantities, entailing engineering costs which might range between $10,000 and $50,000 dollars. Ultimately it might be possible to produce commercially a somewhat simplified and redesigned version of AVID for $300 to $500 apiece; exactly how much more than this would be a feasible sales price is difficult to say at this time. In any event, the kind of audio-visual presentation device which seems desirable for PSI in foreign languages will be fairly expensive. On the other hand, this expense may not be, in the long run, much greater than the expense presently incurred by many school systems in the installation of foreign language laboratories, and the learning attainable through PSI may be much greater and more efficient.

The other principal factor of cost is the cost of developing and producing programs. Certain cost estimates can be made on the basis of experience acquired during the present research. These are *net* development and production costs, rather conservatively estimated, and do not include overhead, travel, training, research, and other related costs. They are simply the costs that the investigator estimates he would incur if requested to prepare additional program materials similar to those already prepared for this research. They are estimated on the basis of the programming system as it evolved in the course of this research after a number of false starts, experiences with inefficient procedures, etc., that have not been detailed in the present report.

The estimates have been made on the basis of producing one "frame" in the present programming system. It should be recognized that the "frame" utilized in this system is more elaborate and is presented more times to the learner than the "frame" of the usual "linear" program. In fact, it may be estimated that for each frame of the present programming system, from 5 to 10 frames would be used in the conventional linear programs covering the same material.

Our experience is that about 100 frames are needed to cover the material of a typical lesson in a standard foreign-language textbook. The average number of lessons presented in such a textbook, suitable for a one-year standard college course or for 12 weeks of intensive instruction, is about 30. Therefore, it may be estimated that 3,000 frames would be needed to cover the material needed for an introductory language course. All cost estimates stated in terms of frames may therefore be multiplied by 3,000 to obtain total cost of a programmed foreign-language course.

Our estimates are based on the assumption that instructional materials (textbooks, grammars, etc.) already exist that can be adapted for programmed instruction by persons competent to do so. The programmers used in the present research were either experienced teachers of Chinese or (in the case of the writer) a psycholinguist with extensive experience in linguistics and language learning.

II. Program development costs (per frame):

Programmer time to plan and write the frame: (30 minutes, at $5.00 per hour)	$ 2.50
Supervision and review (10 minutes, at $6.25 per hour)	1.04
Typing of frame on a standard form for camera copy, including accompanying tapescript, with proofreading and checking (20 minutes per frame, at $2.10 per hour)	0.70
Cost of filming from camera copy, including labor and materials	0.10
Cost of making master tape (labor and materials) including native speaker, engineer, etc.)	0.25
Cost of making required copies of master tape and packaging in cartridges, including labor and materials (one Familiarization tape, one Learning tape)	0.15
Total per-frame cost for materials ready for try-out in AVID	$ 4.74
Total cost for one loop, 40 frames	$189.60

276

III. Program reproduction costs (per frame)

Filming from camera copy	$ 0.10
Production of a Familiarization mode tape and a Learning mode tape, in cartridges	0.15
Total per-frame cost for one extra set of materials	$ 0.25
Total cost for one loop, 40 frames	$ 10.00

Thus, it may be estimated that the total cost of the 22-loop program developed for this research was $4,171.20; the set of extra copies that was made represented an outlay of $220.00.

IV. Tryout and Revision

All these costs are prior to program tryout and revision. If unpaid volunteers are used in program tryout, the cost would be about $0.33 per frame on the following assumptions: that 10 subjects are used, that each S spends an average of 2.5 minutes per frame in all, that the supervisor is paid at the rate of $1.60 per hour, and that two subjects are run simultaneously. We have no data pertinent to the cost of program revision, but many of the costs of initial programs development would recur in program revision. Further, there would be the cost of analyzing data from the intial tryout. It may be estimated that the cost of program revision would not be less than half that of initial program development. that is, $2.37 per frame. To recapitulate the estimated costs for revised program:

Cost of initial development (per frame)	$4.74
Extra copy of program for try-out (per frame)	.025
Cost of try-out of initial program (per frame)	0.33
Data analysis and program revision (per frame)	2.37
Extra copy of revised program for try-out (per frame)	0.25
Cost of try-out of revised program (per frame)	0.33
Data analysis, compilation of data (per frame)	0.50
Total cost, revised program (per frame)	$8.77

If this cost is multiplied by 3,000, the estimated number of frames required for a standard introductory course in a language, the resulting figure is $26,310. Each extra copy of the program material would cost $750 if produced by the techniques worked out in the present project; some economies could probably be effected, however, if copies were to be produced on a mass-production basis and materials such as cartridges were acquired at more favorable discount prices than were encountered.

While the above costs may seem rather large, they must be evaluated in comparison to the cost of conventional instruction using live instructors. The above program costs are for the most part non-recurrent; sets of program materials could be re-used an indefinite number of times.

In view of the cost of developing material for programmed self-instruction in a foreign language, projects for such development should not be undertaken lightly. The above estimates of costs are on the conservative side, and do not allow for the profits that would be reasonably expected in a commerical enterprise or even the overhead that would have to be charged in a non-profit organization.

V. Human Resource

It may also be remarked that effective development, production and tryout of programs requires the gathering together of a competent and well-organized group of personnel. In addition to the person supervising the operation, the following types of persons are required:

PROGRAMMERS: Obviously, programmers must be familiar with the language to be taught, either as native speakers of it or as persons who have learned it quite thoroughly. In addition, they must be able to write materials in effective English where required. They must also be familiar with principles and techniques of programming; our experience, however, is that this familiarity can be acquired quite rapidly.

CLERICAL WORKERS: Needed for typing of program material on special formats for camera copy, often with exacting problems of layout, special characters, diacritical marks, etc. Also needed for analysis of data from tryouts, typing of reports, etc.

TECHNICIANS: Several different types of skills are needed: sometimes they are found in a single person. First, photographic skill is needed in setting up the camera, making films, developing them, and splicing them into loops. Second, competence in tape recording techniques is needed for engineering the production of master tapes and the copying of masters into endless-loop tape cartridges. Third, competence in simple electronic and mechanical repairs is needed for the maintenance of audio-visual presentation devices and associated equipment.

ARTISTS: If pictorial material is to be used in the visual presentation, an artist may be required to make suitable line drawings. (The use of such materials in the present project was extremely limited and should be increased in future work.)

NATIVE INFORMANTS AND SPEAKERS: Needed for checking over program material, for voicing foreign language material on tape, and writing on camera copy with special characters or scripts. Also, preparation of the master tape requires a person with a good English speaking voice.

TRYOUT SUPERVISORS: Needed to schedule and supervise volunteer subjects doing tryouts of program material.

SOURCE: Carroll, John, B. Programmed Self-Instruction in Mandarin Chinese. Wellesley, Mass. Language Testing Fund, 1963, pp. 50–52.

NOTES ON APPENDICES H, I, J, AND K

Appendix H shows as schematic of the Peruvian School System. It shows how much more complicated an actual system is, when all the fields and levels are entered, than the simple model systems with which planners generally work. Each of the 35 programs at the level of higher education may have to be planned separately because the outputs and the costs are different. Compared with systems that exist in other countries, the Peruvian system is simplicity itself.

Appendix I is an outline of the quantitative aspects of an evaluation of the Mexican 11-year plan for educational development. It gives the flavor of difficulty associated with planning on the basis of inadequate pupil accounting data.

In Appendix J, Table I gives the United States System of National Income and Accounts. Table II shows the United Nations system for Domestic Product and National Income. The difficulties of getting very precise estimates of future revenues based on product and income covered under such very general schemes is discussed in detail in Chapter VII.

In Appendix K are two maps used in planning school districts and educational services. The first map, used for planning rural schools on an American Indian reservation, illustrates that very simple and crude cartography may serve the planner.

In the second map, used for planning school development in Ciudad Guayana, an urban region of Venezuela, rather more refined cartography is necessary. The basic units for districting in Santo Tomé de Guayana are the *UD*s, i.e. the development units or parcels. All of the *UD*s are numbered and defined on the map. Some are housing and neighborhood areas, existing or planned; some are zoned for commerce and industry and require no neighborhood school services. The major traffic arteries, present and planned are also shown; as are rivers, gullies and other natural barriers and bounds. On the basis of this map and expansion plans for the city, six (cf. numbers on map) 12-room primary schools were scheduled for construction. School number 1 (*UD* 231) is in a well-defined area where new housing construction was just beginning when the map was drawn. It was simple to identify this as a necessary facility. School 5 (*UD* 115) is in an old and settled part of the city and will serve to replace existing facilities that are crowded and inadequate. The future growth paths of the city are clear, and the future school construction possibilities can be clearly identified. This map was keyed to a school census of the area, which showed a high proportion of children not attending in *UD* 144 and 145.

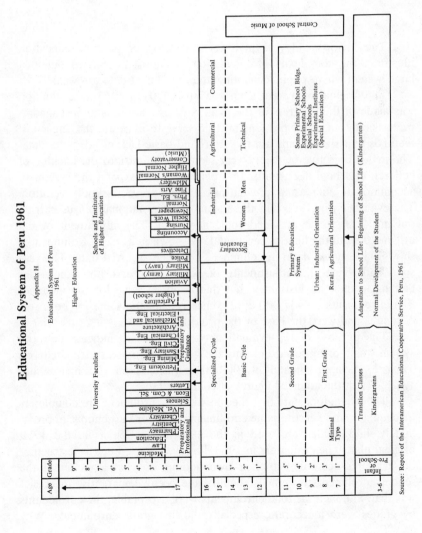

Educational System of Peru 1961

Appendix H

Educational System of Peru
1961

Higher Education

Schools and Institutes
of Higher Education

University Faculties

Source: Report of the Interamerican Educational Cooperative Service, Peru, 1961

281

The Mexican 11-year plan for expansion of primary education illustrates the complexity of calculation that must be carried out in a large system where pupil accounting and enrollment data are weak.

The original plan went from 1959 to 1970. In 1963 an evaluation was made of the progress of the plan. This evaluation is almost incomprehensible, but select portions of it do serve to illustrate the 'ingenous' methods that statisticians use to get around basic lack of adequate data. The major objective of the 11-year plan was to cut into the backlog of children of school age who had no places, and to expand the system to accommodate increasing populations and improved school retention. The evaluation in 1963 had the advantage of a national census carried out in 1960, which provided some new data. The adjustment of the original data in the light of census data is shown in Table I. Column (1) shows the original data; in column (2) are the adjusted data. The reasons underlying the adjustments of some data and not others are baffling in their inconsistency, but that is not at issue for the moment. The enrollments (4,437,000 approximately) are the same for both sets of figures and were the base of the projection.

The purpose of the evaluation of 1963 was to indicate how the system was moving toward closing the gap. This gap was estimated (cf. Table I) as approximately 1,700,000 in the column (1) figures and 1,978,371 in the adjusted figures of column (2).

The evaluators state that the statistics on enrollment are completely inadequate. And yet, the same enrollment totals for the schools, approximately 4,437,000, were used in the 1963 evaluation as in the 1959 original plan. The evaluators in 1963, however, started out to restructure these figures according to their own notions of what a model of the school enrollments by grades should have been. Apparently, the belief was that, although the total enrollments were acceptable, the enrollments by grades were inaccurate, especially the first-grade enrollments. Why

TABLE I

School-Age Population in 1959	*(1)*		*(2)*	
	Absolute		*Adjusted Data (1962)*	
1. Enrollments (of school age 6–14)	4,337,000		(4,337,000)	
2. Enrollments (15 years old or more)	100,000		(100,000)	
3. School-age population who have[1] already completed primary	140,734		(296,987)	
4. Six-year-olds not enrolled	266,967		(289,557)	
5. Deserters who will not return to the system	427,223		(650,669)	
6. Deserters (through causes that can be remedied)	367,928	Gap approx. 1,700,000	(560,104)	Gap (1,978,371)
7. Never enrolled (for reasons that could be remedied in the system)	1,288,135		(1,418,267)	
8. Never enrolled (but for reasons that can not be remedied in system— isolation, infirmities, etc.)	705,618		(620,480)	
	7,633,155		(8,273,064)	

[1] Inferred to adjust the table

SOURCE: Tables from Enriquez, Ernesto, *Estimacion del Progreso Obtenido en la Ejecución del Plan Nacional para el Mejoramiento y la Expansión de la Educación Primaria en México,* Mexico, Ministerio de Educacion Pública, 1963.

total enrollments should be much better than grade-by-grade enrollments is never made clear, but the construction of the model has methodological interest.

Step One: *First Grade enrollments for 1959.*

The model enrollment would be the total of six-year-olds entering school. The census of 1960 gave the number of six-year-olds as 1,143,-140. The school statisticians reduced this (by flat demographic rates) to 1,109,216 which they estimated to be the six-year-old population in 1959

a. Estimated six-year-old population for 1959 = 1,109,216
b. Minus 7.5 per cent (children who through illness or isolation could not attend) = 1,026,025
c. Plus 25 per cent of children repeating grade one from previous year = 1,283,000

The first grade enrollment for 1959 was then estimated at 1,283,000.

Step Two: *Restructuring enrollments in the other five primary grades.*

The statement was again made that the grade enrollments were inaccurate and had to be restructured. The steps for doing this were:

a. The number of children passing in each of the grades was said to be more accurate than grade enrollments because it was based on the records of year-end examinations. Children passing at each grade as a percentage of first grade were:

TABLE II

Grade	% Passing
I	100
II	64.4
III	47.6
IV	35.2
V	27
VI	26

These percentage relations were presumably derived from a great many studies of past patterns. The number passed in 1959 was 257,247. If this is equal to 26 per cent of first grade passers, then the numbers in column 1 of Table III can be generated. Also in Table IV the number of fails and hence total enrollments can be generated by the ratios in Table III of Fails to passers.

TABLE III

Grade	Fails/passes
II	35.9
III	36.4
IV	31.5
V	27.1
VI	15.3

* Note that in Table III, first-grade ratios are not used. But the total first-grade enrollment has already been built in Step One as 1,283,-000

These two sets of ratios were then used to build up the 'normal' grade structure enrollments.

TABLE IV

Grade	Passes	Fails	Total Enrollment	% of 1st Grade Enrollment
I	989,412	293,588	1,283,000	100
II	637,181	228,748	865,929	67.49
III	470,960	171,429	642,389	50.07
IV	348,273	109,706	457,979	35.70
V	267,141	72,395	339,536	26.46
VI	257,247	39,359	296,606	23.12
			3,885,439	

284

Step Three: *3,886,000 is taken as the model enrollment for the base year, 1959.*

The actual enrollment, given by school statistics for that year was 4,436,561. The difference between these two figures 550,561 was taken as the number of people out of the normal age-grade pattern (gap of past) who were being taken care of in the system in the base year 1959. Table V then shows how the plan covered the gap or deficit of 1,700,000 (gap of future).

TABLE V

Year	I Projection of School Population	II Increased by Improvement in Retention	III Actual Enrollment (+)	IVa Difference to Apply to Filling the Gap	IVb Places for Filling Gap Before Plan Year Began	V Enrollment by Grades of the Gap Numbers								VI Progress in Eliminating the Gap
						New Entrants	25% Repeaters	Total	Second	Third	Fourth	Fifth	Sixth	
1959	3,886,000	3,886,000	4,436,561	550,561	550,561									
1960	4,007,970	4,042,879	4,884,988	842,109	458,903	383,206		383,206						383,206
1961	4,134,276	4,206,295	5,368,247	1,161,952	279,069	468,164	156,155	624,219	258,664					851,370
1962	4,265,119	4,376,567	5,620,324	1,243,757	185,751	333,791	111,264	445,055	421,348	191,603				1,185,161
1963	4,400,612	4,553,929	5,895,324	1,341,395	103,349	336,607	122,202	488,809	300,412	312,020	136,805			1,551,788
1964	4,541,124	4,738,890	6,095,324	1,356,434	64,390	311,381	103,793	415,174	329,946	222,528	222,846	101,550		1,863,149
1965	4,686,699	4,931,626	6,295,324	1,363,698		319,958	106,653	426,611	280,242	244,405	158,885	165,418	88,137	2,183,107
1966	4,837,599	5,132,547	6,064,111						287,962	207,587	174,505	117,940	143,570	
1967	4,994,061	5,342,047	5,935,467							213,306	148,217	129,534	102,363	
1968	5,156,204	5,560,399	5,935,146								152,300	110,021	112,426	
1969	5,324,626	5,788,401	5,996,943									113,052	95,490	
1970	5,499,247	6,026,130	6,124,251										98,121	

(+) Up to 1962, statistical data; latest figures available at moment of preparing this table.

THE UNITED STATES SYSTEM OF NATIONAL INCOME ACCOUNTS, 1953

I. National Income and Product Account, 1953
(in millions)

Compensation of employees:		Personal consumption expenditures	$230,080
Wage and salaries	$197,980		
Supplements	11,081	Gross private domestic investment	51,408
Income of unincorporated enterprises and inventory valuation adjustment	38,444	Net foreign investment	− 1,866
Rental income of persons	10,596	Government purchases of goods and services	85,235
Corporate profits and inventory valuation adjustment:			
Corporate profits before tax:			
Corporate profits tax liability	21,144		
Corporate profits after tax:			
Dividends	9,365		
Undistributed profits	8,921		
Inventory valuation adjustment	− 964		
Net interest	8,435		
National income	305,002		
Indirect business tax and nontax liability	30,037		
Business transfer payments	1,016		
Statistical discrepancy	1,047		
Less: Subsidies minus current surplus of government enterprises	− 529		
Charges against net national product	337,631		
Capital consumption allowances	27,226		
Charges against gross national product	$364,857	Gross national product	$364,857

SOURCE: Ruggles, Richard, and Nancy D. Ruggles, National Accounts and Income Analysis, New York: McGraw-Hill, 1956, p. 90.

THE UNITED NATIONS SYSTEM OF NATIONAL
INCOME ACCOUNTS

Account 1. Domestic product

11. Gross domestic product at factor cost (2.9)
12. Indirect taxes (5.7)
13. Less subsidies − (5.2)

1.4. Private consumption expenditure (4.1)
1.5. General government consumption expenditure (5.1)
1.6. Gross domestic fixed capital formation (3.1)
1.7. Increase in stocks (3.2)
1.8. Exports of goods and services (6.1)
Expenditure on gross domestic product and imports
1.9. Less imports of goods and services − (6.3)

Gross domestic product at market prices

Expenditure on gross domestic product

Account 2. National income

21. Compensation of employees (4.5)
22. Income from farms, professions and other unincorporated enterprises (4.6)
23. Income from property (4.7)
24. Saving of corporations (3.4)
25. Direct taxes on corporations (5.8)
26. General government income from property and entrepreneurship (5.5)
27. Less interest on the public debt (5.6)
28. Less interest on consumers' debt (4.8)

2.9 Gross domestic product at factor cost (1.1)
2.10. Net factor income payments from the rest of the world (6.2)
2.11. Less provisions for the consumption of fixed capital − (3.3)

National income

Net national product at factor cost.

SOURCE: Ruggles, Richard and Nancy D. Ruggles, *National Accounts and Income Analysis,* New York: McGraw-Hill, 1956, p. 97.

Map of Longman Day School and Communities

Source: Student Planning Project, Harvard University

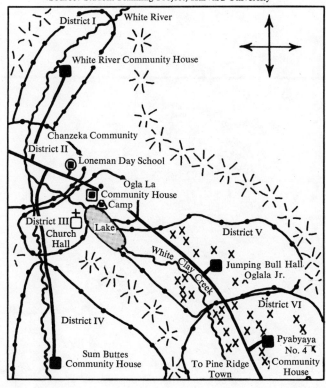

Key

⊙ Consolidated School

■ Community House

▣ Community House and Proposed Child Day Care Center

▲ Camp, Lakeside Camping Development

☀ Buttes, travel across impossible

— Bus Routes

•—• Community Districts

X Houses

⛪ Church Hall

School Development Plan

NOTES ON APPENDICES L AND M

Appendix L is a system for classifying educational expenditure accounts developed by the United States Office of Education. For the developing countries, a simpler set of rubrics will suffice. However, the U.S. system is useful. From it, the planner can devise his own system for studying inputs and making component cost analyses and the expenditure estimates outlined in Chapter VI.

Appendix M is a classification system for government receipts and outlay in the United States. It shows that the bulk of educational expenditures comes at the state and local level, rather than the national as in the case of developing countries. It is helpful for suggesting forms for estimating future year revenues and expenditures as outlined in Chapter VII.

CLASSIFICATION OF EXPENDITURE ACCOUNTS

U.S. Office of Education System. The numbers appearing to the left of the accounts are used primarily for identification purposes. They may be used also with necessary adaptations as an accounting code by local and state school systems with either machine or hand methods of accounting.

ADMINISTRATION 100 SERIES
110. Salaries
120. Contracted services
130. Other expenses

INSTRUCTION 200 SERIES
210. Salaries
    211. Principals
    212. Consultants or supervisors
    213. Teachers
    214. Other instructional staff
    215. Sec. and cler. assts.
    216. Other salaries for instr.
220. Textbooks
230. School libraries & audio visual
240. Teaching Supplies
250. Other expenses

ATTENDANCE AND HEALTH SERVICES 300-400 SERIES
300. Attendance services
    310. Salaries
    320. Other expenses
400. Health services
    410. Salaries
    420. Other expenses

PUPIL TRANSPORTATION SERVICES 500 SERIES
510. Salaries
520. Contracted ser. & pub. carriers
530. Replacements of vehicles
540. Transportation insurance
550. Expenditures in lieu of trans.
560. Other expenses

OPERATION OF PLANT 600 SERIES
610. Salaries
620. Contracted services
630. Heat for building
640. Utilities, except heat
650. Supplies
660. Other expenses

MAINTENANCE OF PLANT 700 SERIES
710. Salaries
720. Contracted services
730. Replacements of equipment
740. Other expenses

FIXED CHARGES 800 SERIES
810. Employee retirement
820. Insurance & judgments
830. Rental of land & buildings
840. Interest on current loans
850. Other fixed charges

FOOD SERVICES & STUDENT BODY ACTIVITIES 900-1000 SERIES
900. Food services
    910. Salaries
    920. Other expenses
    930. Separate fund or account
1000. Student body activities
    1010. Salaries
    1020. Other expenses
    1030. Separate fund or account

COMMUNITY SERVICES 1100 SERIES
1110. Recreation
1120. Civic activities
1130. Public libraries
1140. Custodial & detention care of children
1150. Welfare activities
1160. Nonpublic school pupils
    1161. Instructional services
    1162. Attend. & health services
    1163. Transportation services

CAPITAL OUTLAY 1200 SERIES
1210. Sites
1220. Buildings
1230. Equipment

DEBT SERVICE FROM CURRENT FUNDS 1300 SERIES
1310. Principal of debt
1320. Interest on debt
1330. Paid into sinking funds
1340. Schoolhouse authority
1350. Other debt service

OUTGOING TRANSFER ACCOUNTS 1400 SERIES
1410. District in the state
1420. Districts in another state
1430. Tuition to other than public schools

SOURCE: U.S. Department of Health, Education and Welfare, *Financial Accounting for Local and State School Systems.* Washington: U.S. Government Printing Office, 1957, pp. 27–35.

Receipt Accounts

Revenue receipts are defined as additions to assets which do not incur an obligation that must be met at some future date and do not represent exchanges of property for money. Non-revenue receipts are defined as amounts received which incur an obligation that must be met at some future date or which change the form of an asset from property to cash and therefore decrease the amount and value of school property.

REVENUE RECEIPTS 10–40 SERIES

10. Revenue from local sources
    11. Taxation and appropriations received
    12. Tuition from patrons
    13. Transportation fees from patrons
    14. Other revenue from local sources
20. Revenue from intermediate sources
30. Revenue from State sources
40. Revenue from Federal sources

NON-REVENUE RECEIPTS 50–70

50. Sale of bonds
60. Loans
70. Sale of school property and insurance adjustments

INCOMING TRANSFER ACCOUNTS 80–90 SERIES

80. Amounts received from other school districts in the State
90. Amounts received from school districts in another State.

SOURCE: U. S. Department of Health, Education and Welfare, *Financial Accounting for Local and State School Systems.* Washington: U. S. Government Printing Office, 1957, pp. 6–7.

GOVERNMENT RECEIPTS AND OUTLAY ACCOUNT FOR THE UNITED STATES, 1953
(IN BILLIONS)

1. Government expenditures on goods and services	$77.2	7. Tax and income payments by producers to government	54.4
a. Federal	53.7	1. Corporate profits taxes	21.1
(1) National security	45.8	b. Property taxes	9.1
(2) Agriculture and agricultural resources	3.9	c. Commodity and transactions taxes	16.9
(3) Natural resources	0.8	d. Licenses, fees, and other business taxes	4.1
(4) Veterans' services	0.9	e. Interest and dividends received by government	2.4
(5) Social security, welfare and health	0.4	f. Current surplus of government enterprises	0.8
(6) Education and general research	0.1	8. Tax payments by individuals	44.6
(7) General government	1.1	a. Income taxes	32.5
(8) Other +	1.1	b. Total social insurance contributions	8.7
(9) Minus: Government sales	0.4	c. Fees, fines, personal property, and other taxes	3.4
b. State and local	23.5	9. Transfer payments to government from abroad	0.1
(1) Natural resources	0.7		
(2) Highways	4.8		
(3) Public welfare	0.5		
(4) Health and hospitals	2.3		
(5) Education	8.9		
(6) Police, fire and sanitation	2.4		
(7) General control	1.3		
(8) Other +	2.6		
2. Subsidies and government interest	7.6		
1. Subsidies	0.2		
b. Government interest	7.4		
3. Capital grants to government enterprises	1.7		
a. Federal	0.2		
b. State and local	1.5		
4. Transfer payments by government to individuals	12.8		
5. Transfer payments by government to abroad	6.3		
6. Government surplus	−6.6		
Government outlay and surplus	**$99.1**	**Government Receipts**	**$99.1**

SOURCE: Ruggles, Richard and Nancy D. Ruggles, *National Accounts and Income Analysis,* New York, McGraw-Hill, 1956, p. 78.

NOTES ON APPENDICES N AND O

Appendices N and O are examples of the kind of reference tools that are useful for the general level of manpower planning outlined in Chapter II. Appendix O lists some ratios that can be applied to check the first approximation of occupational distributions. The percentages are for the major occupational categories modified from the ISCO (International Standard Classification of Occupations) system. This list was used to check the occupational distribution forecast for the Caroní district of Veneuela in 1975. The final column of the table in Appendix O shows the distribution forecast. In no case will the distribution come out the same as the one shown in some other country, but the other country distributions are useful for indicating where gross departures from an expected pattern occur. On the basis of unexplained discrepancies adjustments can be made.

Appendix N shows the education attainment distribution for a selection of occupations and professions. These were compiled on the basis of 1960 U.S. Special Census Report PC(2) 7 A. Appendix N has only two pages from much longer tables computed at the Harvard Center for Studies in Education and Development. The U.S. tables are handy as reference checks, but the coefficients should not be applied to any developing country. The educational attainment in the United States is much higher than would be necessary in any developing country. Educational attainment in the United States reflects the results of productivity as well as the causes of it. Still, the table is useful for setting targets in developing countries. The complete tables from which the Appendix N tables are taken are useful as a reference tool for planning.

Educational Attainment Levels for Some Detailed Occupations in United States

Detailed Occupation	Total	Elementary		High School		College		
		under 5	5–7	8–11	12	1–3	4	5 or more
TOTAL, 14 YEARS AND OVER	100%	5.94	12.33	38.04	24.3	9.56	5.34	4.39
PROFESSIONAL, TECHNICAL AND KINDRED	9.92	.31	.53	8.06	16.20	18.62	23.46	32.54
Accountants and auditors	8.7	.15	.47	7.43	19.87	28.51	34.06	9.51
Dentists	.19	.16	.46	.59	1.00	6.40	16.34	75.51
Designers	.12	.84	1.68	11.03	28.71	29.34	16.83	11.51
Draftsmen	.45	.16	.50	11.43	42.36	35.22	6.57	3.76
Engineers, technical	1.89	.22	.86	7.52	15.56	20.17	37.81	17.86
chemical	.09	.05	.31	1.95	4.99	6.69	5.06	35.42
civil	.35	.37	1.33	8.85	15.16	20.47	38.00	15.81
electrical	.40	.14	.53	5.82	14.51	20.52	39.23	19.19
industrial	.21	.06	.75	9.35	22.41	23.65	30.57	13.20
mechanical	.35	.29	1.28	10.06	15.70	18.85	37.66	16.14
metallurgical & metallurgists	.04	.21	.43	5.32	15.19	15.51	40.31	23.03
mining	.027	.68	.66	6.78	8.58	9.13	49.94	24.23
sales	.13	.03	.48	8.42	16.61	24.03	39.57	13.36
Natural Scientists	.30	.21	.42	3.65	8.75	11.12	32.55	43.44
Nurses, professional	.03	.86	4.09	19.94	25.52	28.14	8.42	3.03
Pharmacists	.17	.10	.36	4.47	6.22	30.00	42.36	16.51
Physicians and surgeons	.45	.04	.07	.31	.47	.87	5.73	92.51
Social Scientists	.09	..	.34	3.96	11.42	13.85	24.06	46.42
Teachers, Elementary Schools	.31	.07	.09	.88	2.15	10.79	37.30	48.73

SOURCE: Based On U.S. Census of 1960, Special Reports: Subject Report PC(2) 7 A Abstracted from larger tables computed at Harvard Center for Studies in Education and Development.

Educational Attainment Levels for Some Detailed Occupations in the United States (Continued)

Detailed Occupation	Total	Elementary		High School		College		
		under 5	5–7	8–11	12	1–3	4	5 or more
CRAFTSMEN, FOREMEN AND KINDRED WORKERS	19.64	4.71	13.34	45.67	28.45	6.38	1.48	.49
Cranemen, Derrickmen and hoistmen		7.14	20.56	51.10	18.85	2.01	.23	.09
Electricians		1.43	8.31	42.12	37.79	9.19	.93	.21
Excavating, Grading and Road Machinery Operators		5.95	19.06	51.15	20.32	3.05	.37	.06
FOREMEN (N.E.C.)		2.17	9.51	42.86	31.25	9.38	3.71	1.09
Construction		3.64	3.79	49.73	24.75	7.02	.83	.21
Manufacturing		1.81	8.05	41.61	32.49	9.95	4.41	1.37
Metal Industries		1.34	8.00	43.66	31.10	10.29	4.41	1.17
Machinery, except electrical		.98	6.90	41.38	37.40	9.39	3.20	.73
Electrical machinery, equipment and supplies		.68	3.93	32.35	40.15	14.16	6.31	2.48
Transportation equipment		.51	5.10	38.51	37.33	12.50	4.59	.66
Textiles, textile products, and apparel		5.71	16.35	43.19	24.34	6.30	3.56	.52
Communications, and utilities and sanitary serv.		1.89	8.57	39.16	35.97	10.03	3.73	.62
Machinists		2.30	11.04	48.05	31.97	5.90	.57	.14
Mechanics and Repairmen		4.06	13.69	47.00	28.28	5.99	.74	.21

EXAMPLE OF OCCUPATION DISTRIBUTION FOR VARIOUS COUNTRIES USED
AS CHECK RATIOS IN GUAYANA MANPOWER PLANNING STUDY

All Industries *Percentage Distribution*	*Canada 1951 Parnes pp. 96–97*	*U.K. 1957 pp. 98–99*	*U.S. 1950 pp. 102–10/*	*Chile 1960 census (Davis Tables)*	*Chile 1970 Proj. (Davis Table)*	*Venezuela 1951*	*Caroni District Proj. 1975*
Professionals	7.2	6.3	8.7	4.9	6.2	6.1	5.7
Administrators	7.8	2.3	8.8	1.9	2.1	3.8	4.6
Clerical	10.8	10.8	12.3	6.8	6.6	18.7	10.9
Sales	6.5	10.2	7.0	7.0	6.0	6.5	7.0
Farmers	18.8	5.4	12.0	27.5	33.9	.8	2.9
Miners	1.3	3.0		2.3	2.1	3.5	3.8
Transportation & Communications	7.9	10.5		3.3	2.9	7.7	10.3
Skilled Trades and Operators	29.7	40.0	39.7	26.6	25.5	44.5	40.2
Service workers	8.5	11.0	10.3	13.5	9.7	8.4	11.8
Not Otherwise Classified	1.2	0.5	1.3	6.2	4.9	.1	2.7

SOURCE: Columns 1–3: Parnes, Herbert, S. *Forecasting Educational Needs for Economic and Social Development* (Paris: OECD, 1962).

Columns 4–5: Platt, William J. Al. M. Loeb and Russel G. Davis, *Manpower and Educational Planning in Chile* (Santiago: Chile-California Project, 1964).

Columns 6–7: Venezuelan data and projections.

Notes on Appendices P and Q

Appendix P is a building survey form devised for application in a developing country. It is handy as a basis for conducting a survey of existing school facilities. In any given country, the planner would probably wish to make modifications on this basic form.

Appendix Q is the format used for detailing school building costs in the United States. It has some handy standards and unit measures that may be useful for planners in developing countries, but it also has some elaborations that are not necessary for the school buildings of countries with very limited resources. It can be used as the basis for designing a more adequate instrument for analyzing the costs of various construction components. As with all check lists and forms, it should be modified to fit the reality of the specific country to which it is to be applied.

Both Appendix P and Appendix Q are useful for the kind of component cost analysis described in Chapter VI.

BUILDING SURVEY FORM

Serial Number_____

Date _____

Name of School_____No. Students (a) enrolled _____
(b) attending
this day _____

Location of school (e.g. name of town)_____No. rooms_____

Grade levels taught_____No. teachers_____

Name and position of respondent_____

Does your school have more than one session? If so, how many?_____

> Note: Please answer every question. If a question is inapplicable, indicate so by "n/a". If you feel your answer needs explanation, please write on the reverse of this sheet.

I. Site

   1. Accessibility—what % of students live within two miles of school?_____

   2. Safety (a) are there any unfenced natural hazards adjacent? (e.g. river)

   _____

      (b) are there any unfenced man-made hazards adjacent? (e.g. highway) _____

   3. Sanitation—are there health hazards adjacent? (swamps, dumps)_____

II. Lot

   1. Drainage: no. of school days lost last year due to flooding_____

   2. Is the lot reasonably level?_____

   3. Size—give square meter measurement_____

   4. Other—are there any other unsatisfactory conditions?_____
      (explain on reverse)

III. Outside area

   1. Is there a play area?_____ If so give square meter dimension_____

   2. Is there a garden area?_____ If so give square meter dimension_____

IV. Maintenance
    1. Do you have regular maintenance repairs?_____
    2. Do you have regular janitor service?_____

V. Administrative facilities
    1. Are such facilities adequate?_____(if not, explain on reverse)

VI. Instructional facilities use
Name of school_____Location_____
No. of classrooms_____
    Note: Use one of these forms for each and every classroom or laboratory
    in your school.

I Room Schedule

Hours	Monday	Tuesday	Wednesday	Thursday	Friday	Saturday	Sunday
	(1) Subj. Atten.						
7–8							
8–9							
9–10							
10–11							
11–12							
12–1							
1–2							
2–3							
3–4							
4–5							
5–6							
eve							

    (1) For attendance figures use students in attendance in each class on
    each day last week.

VII. Structure
    A. Materials
        1. walls made of outside _____
                       inside _____
        2. floor made of _____
        3. roof made of _____
        4. ceiling _____

5. windows _____

*6. sound proofing _____

B. Size
1. floor   square meter _____

2. ceiling height _____

3. windows   square meter _____
Are they adequate for illumination and
ventilation_____. If not comment on
reverse.

C. Facilities
1. storage square feet_____adequate_____

2. heating: type_____adequate_____

3. artificial illumination: type_____adequate_____

4. potable water: source_____

5. meal facilities: type_____adequate_____

6. sanitary facilities: type_____location_____
separate_____

*7. lab water supply: source_____adequate_____

*8. lab heat supply: source_____adequate_____

D. Equipment
1. blackboard—square mt. _____

2. display board—square mt. _____

3. bookshelves—number, mt. _____

4. number student seats available_____

5. number student writing spaces_____

6. teachers desk_____and chair_____

*7. lab tables. number_____adequate_____

8. other lab or shop fixtures (specify)_____

E. Boarding School
Please use appropriate sections to describe dorms. Please supply the
following as well:
1. number of beds_____

2. number of meals provided per day per student_____
(enclose last week menu)

3. location of cooking area_____

4. where do students eat_____

VIII. Summary
1. Indicate nature of school: (1) government owned_____
     (check appropriate)   (2) government rented_____

(3) loaned to government_____

(4) private school_____

_____

2. Age of structure   _____
3. Rank facility overall:

Class 1 Priority:	Both building and site wholly inadequate must be replaced in different location_____
Class 2	Building wholly inadequate. Replace on same site_____
Class 3	Major remodeling and expansion required _____
Class 4	Major remodeling only_____
Class 5	Expansion only_____
Class 6	Some repairs necessary_____
Class 7	Currently adequate_____

SOURCE: Charleson, William, Davis, Russell G., and Williams, David, Harvard University Center for Studies in Education and Development

SCHOOL-BUILDING COSTS

School-Building Costs: Controls, Economy and Comparisons

1. Components of Total Cost

Land purchase price	$_____	Stage lighting	$_____
Site development		Laboratory tables	_____
Grading	$_____	Chairs and desks	_____
Drainage	_____	Kitchen and dining	_____
Roads	_____	Equipment subtotal	_____
Paved play areas	_____	*Professional fees*	
Paved parking	_____	Architect	$_____
Athletic fields	_____	Consultant	_____
Fencing	_____	Clerk of works	_____
Water supply	_____	Engineer	_____
Sewage system	_____	Other	_____
Electric and gas service	_____	Fees subtotal	_____
Outdoor equipment	_____	*Administrative costs*	
Landscaping	_____	Board attorney	$_____
Site subtotal	_____	Bond attorney	_____
Equipment		Advertising	_____
Auditorium seats	_____	Other	_____
Bleachers	_____	Administrative subtotal	_____
Movable partitions	_____		
Draperies	_____		

SOURCE: Englehardt, N. L. Jr. "School Building Costs: Controls, Economy and Comparisons". American School and University—1958–59. Vol. 1. New York. American School Publishing Corp., 1958. p. 294–95

Building construction

Exclude all costs except:

		Region	Index
General construction $_____		I	1.06
Plumbing _____		II	1.33
Heating & Ventilating _____		III	.83
Electrical work _____		IV	.66
Cabinet work _____		V	1.15
Painting _____		VI	1.00
Elevator _____		VII	.86
Building construction cost $_____		VIII	.93
(Total actual cost $_____)		IX	1.22

2. CORRECTION FACTORS

External influences on construction costs represented by three indices.

Time	Index
1949	1.00
1950	1.07
1951	1.14
1952	1.18
1953	1.22
1954	1.27
1955	1.33
1956	1.39
1957 (Sept.)	1.47

Type of community

Rural	.90
Suburban	1.00
Metropolitan	1.10

Composite index

Time $\times$ Region $\times$ Type

_____ $\times$ _____ $\times$ _____ = _____

Corrected cost =

Building construction costs

$$\frac{\text{Composite index (Cost)}}{\text{(Index)}} =$$

Corrected cost $_____

3. COST PER PUPIL

Pupil capacity

Type of space	No. of units	Unit capacity	Total capacity
Classroom	_____	27	_____
Kindergarten (on double sessions)	_____	40	_____
Science laboratory	_____	25	_____
Commercial education	_____	25	_____
Home economics	_____	25	_____
Art	_____	25	_____
Shop	_____	20	_____
Band or chorus rooms	_____	35	_____
Gymnasium or playroom	_____	35	_____
with partition	_____	70	_____
Swimming pool	_____	25	_____
General education laboratory or study hall	_____	35	_____
Total No. of Pupils			_____

Index sources: Unit capacities (above) are those currently considered good practice. They must be used (regardless of actual capacities) if school comparisons are to be valid. Regional indices are developed from average square-foot costs of elementary and secondary schools from July, 1952 to September, 1952. Medium average: North Central region. Time index is *Engineering News-Record* Building Cost Index.

$$Adjusted\ cost\ per\ pupil = \frac{Corrected\ cost}{Total\ No.\ of\ pupils}$$

$$\frac{(Cost)}{(Pupils)} = Adjusted\ cost\ per\ pupil\ \$\underline{\hspace{2cm}}$$

Costs per Square Foot

4. GROSS AREA

This is the total square foot area of the floors, including stairways and developed basement areas, plus one-half the total square-foot area of the other areas listed below:

Floor areas (incl. stairs):
Developed basements _____

First floor _____

Second floor _____

Third floor _____

Porticoes _____

Bicycle sheds _____

Porches _____

Open, covered play areas _____

Passages _____

Sheltered bus loading
platforms _____

Subtotal,
divided by 2 _____
                2

Gross area _____

$$Adjusted\ cost\ per\ gross\ square\ foot = \frac{Corrected\ cost}{Gross\ area\ (sq.\ ft.)}$$

$$\frac{(Cost)}{(Gross\ area)} = Adjusted\ cost\ per\ gross\ sq.\ ft.\ \$\underline{\hspace{2cm}}$$

5. NET EDUCATIONAL AREA

This is the total square-foot area (inside dimensions, wall to wall, including cabinet space) of all spaces listed below:

Classroom	_____	Cafeteria seating area not kitchen and auxiliary spaces	_____
Kindergarten	_____		
Science laboratory	_____	Library reading rooms	_____
Commercial education	_____		
Home economics	_____	Gymnasium locker and shower rooms	_____
Art	_____	Administrative offices health suite, guidance and con-ference rooms, teachers' workrooms, student organization rooms	
Shop	_____		
Band or chorus room	_____		
Gymnasium or playroom	_____		_____
Swimming pool	_____	Net educational area	_____
General education laboratory or study hall	_____		
Auditorium seating area, stage, stagecraft rooms, dressing rooms—not lobby	_____		
Music practice rooms	_____		

Note: for comparison of educational programs divide each area by total pupil capacity (sec. 3). This will indicate the difference between schools in availability of educational facilities.

$$\textit{Adjusted cost per net square foot} = \frac{\text{Corrected cost}}{\text{Net educational area (sq. ft.)}}$$

$$\frac{\text{(Cost)}}{\text{(Net area)}} = \text{Adjusted cost per net sq. ft. \$_____}$$

6. PROGRAM AND MATERIALS

In comparing two or more schools, the unit cost per pupil per gross or net square foot may vary because of differences in any or all of the following factors:

Extent of educational program

Make separate comparisons of space in each category:
Regular classrooms, science laboratories, physical education, music, etc.

Character of plan and site

Size of site, number of buildings, number of stories.

Character of structure and materials

Fire and earthquake resistance

Framing: wood, steel, concrete

Exterior walls: brick-block, block alone, steel, aluminum

Interior: floor finish, wainscot, walls, ceiling, toilet room walls, locker room floors.

Lighting: fluorescent, incandescent

Heating

Ventilating

Note: the factors in 6 are not now reducible to dollar index figures, for comparative purposes. It may soon be possible to work out some broad quality classifications based on (a) completeness of facilities, and (b) standard of quality in materials and equipment. For example, a school with science laboratory rooms, art and music rooms, separate gym, auditorium, and cafeteria might be called Class A educationally; one with separate gym, auditorium, cafeteria, Class B; with multipurpose room embracing two of the above functions, Class C; classrooms only, Class D. (Nothing invidious is meant; for example, a new wing with classrooms only may make great sense, but it would still be unfair to compare its cost index with that of a complete new school.)

At some time a similar rating by construction groups, as A, B, C, or D, may be worked out.

Design efficiency ratio=

$$\frac{Net\ education\ area}{Gross\ area}$$

Workable plans range from 50 to 80%

Good average for closed plan is 65 to 70%

Good average for campus plan is 75 to 80%

$$\frac{(Net\ area)}{(Gross\ area)}$$

Design efficiency ————————%

BIBLIOGRAPHY

Adelman, Irma, *A Linear Programming Model of Educational Planning: A Case Study of Argentina* (Preliminary Draft) 1965.

American Association of School Administrators, *Planning America's School Buildings*. Washington, D.C.: AASA, 1960.

American Library Association, *Planning a Library Building: The Major Steps,* (ed. Hoyt R. Galvin.) Chicago: 1955.

American Standards Association, *American Standard Methods of Determining Areas in School Buildings,* Document Z65. 2-1958. New York City: ASA, 1958.

Anderson, C. (Arnold and Mary Jean Bowman, eds.). *Education and Economic Development*. Chicago: Aldine, 1965.

Archer, J. N. *Educational Development in Nigeria 1961–1970*. Lagos: Ministry of Education, 1961.

Armstrong, Charles M. and Mary S. Harris, *A Method of Predicting School-Age Population*. Albany: University of the State of New York, 1949.

Babigan, G. R. "The Use of the Critical Path Method in Building Schools," *School Board Journal,* August, 1965, pp. 26–27.

Banco de Mexico, *Tendencias de Crecimiento de la Industria de Transformación en Mexico—1950–1958*. Mexico, D. F. 1961.

Barclay, George W., *Techniques of Population Analysis*. New York: Wiley, 1958.

Barzun, Jacques, *The House of Intellect*. New York: Harper, 1959.

Baumol, William J., *Economic Theory and Operations Analysis,* Englewood Cliffs, New Jersey: Prentice-Hall, 1961.

Becker, Gary S., *Human Capital: A Theoretical and Empirical Analysis* (with special reference to education). National Bureau of Economic Research, 1964.

Beeby, C. E., "Stages in the Growth of a Primary Education System," *Comparative Education Review,* 6 (1), 1962, 2–11.

Beeby, C. E., *The Quality of Education in Developing Countries.* Cambridge: Harvard University Press, 1966.

Benham, Frederic, *The National Income of Malaya (1947–49).* Singapore: Government Printing Office, 1951.

Bennis, Warren G., Kenneth D. Benne, and Robert Chin (eds.). *The Planning of Change.* New York: Holt, Rinehart and Winston, 1964.

Benson, Charles S., *The Economics of Public Education,* Boston: Houghton Mifflin, 1961.

Bereday, George Z. F., *Comparative Method in Education,* New York: Holt, Rinehart, 1964.

Berg, Elliot, "Education and Manpower in Senegal, Guinea and the Ivory Coast," *Manpower and Education in Developing Countries* (F. H. Harbison and C. A. Meyers, editors). New York: McGraw-Hill, 1964.

Bernanos, George, *Les Grandes Cimetières sous la lune.* Paris: Plon, 1938.

Bestor, Arthur E., *Educational · Wastelands,* Urbana: University of Illinois Press, 1953.

Biological Sciences Curriculum Study (Schwab, Joseph J., Supervisor) *Biology Teachers' Handbook.* New York: Wiley, 1963.

Blot, Daniel, "Les Deperditions D'Effectifs Scolaires: Analyse Theorique Et Applications," *Tiers-Monde,* Tome VI, No. 22, pp. 479–510 (Avril-juin, 1965).

Books in Print, *An author-title series index to the Publishers Trade List Annual* (ed. Sarah L. Prakken.) New York: Bowker, 1962.

Bowles, Samuel. "A Planning Model for Efficient Allocation of Resources in Education". (Unpublished doctoral dissertation, Department of Economics, Harvard University, Cambridge, 1965).

Bowen, William G., *Economic Aspects of Education.* Princeton, New Jersey: Industrial Relations Section, Princeton University, 1964.

Brand, Willem, *"New Directions for Education and Centralized versus Decentralized Systems."* Paper circulated to participants attending 4–6th Nov. 1963 meeting of the Study Group in the Economics of Education, (Université de Paris.)

Brand, Willem, *Planning for Balanced Social and Economic Development in the Netherlands with Particular Reference to the Post-War Years.* United Nations Economic and Social Council. E/CN.5/346/Add.6 1961.

Brandwein, Paul F., Fletcher G. Watson and Paul E. Blackwood, *Teaching High School Science: A Book of Methods,* New York: Harcourt, Brace, 1958.

Brubaker, Charles William and Lawrence B. Perkins, *Sketch Book: Space for Individual Learning.* New York: School Executive and Educational Business, 1959.

Brown, Byron W., Jr. and I. Richard Savage. *Methodological Studies in Educational Attendance Prediction.* Minneapolis: University of Minnesota, Department of Statistics, 1960.

Bruner, Jerome S., *The Process of Education.* Cambridge: Harvard University Press, 1960.

California Association of Public School Building Officials and California Council of Architects, *Recommended Procedures for Uniform Cost Reporting and Comparison.* School Building Committee, 1950–51.

Carroll, John B. *Programmed Self-Instruction in Mandarin Chinese: Observations of Student Progress with an Automated Audio-Visual Instructional Device.* Wellesley: Language Testing Fund, 1963.

CCSSO, *Purchase Guide for Programs in Science, Mathematics, Modern Foreign Languages.* Boston: Ginn, 1959.

Cochran, William G., *Sampling Techniques,* New York: Wiley, 1953.

Committee on Higher Education (Lord Robbins, Chairman) *Higher Education: Administrative, Financial and Economic Aspects of Higher Education.* London: Her Majesty's Stationery Office, 1963. (Report and five volumes of Appendices.)

Commonwealth of Puerto Rico-Committee on Human Resources, *Puerto Rico's Manpower Needs and Supply,* San Juan; 1957.

Conant, James B., *The American High School Today,* New York: McGraw-Hill, 1959.

Cooley, William W. and Paul R. Lohnes, *Multivariate Procedures for the Behavioral Sciences,* New York: Wiley, 1962.

Cook, Desmond L. "An Introduction to PERT," Occasional Papers, 64–156, Columbus, Ohio: The Bureau of Educational Research and Service, Ohio State University, 1964.

Cooke, Lot H. *Lowell Massachusetts: A Case Study for Proposed Research in Manpower Analysis and Training Systems Planning.* (A special paper submitted to the Committee on the Degree of Doctor of Education), Cambridge: The Harvard Graduate School of Education, 1966.

Correa, Hector. *Educational Planning: Its Quantitative Aspects and Integration with Economic Planning.* Paris: International Institute for Educational Planning, 1965 (Working Draft).

Correa, Hector, and Tinbergen, Jan, "Quantitative Adaptation of Education to Accelerated Growth." *Kyklos,* 15 (11), 1962.

Correa, Hector, *The Economics of Human Resources.* Amsterdam: North-Holland Publishing Company, 1963.

Curle, Adam, *Educational Strategy for Developing Societies.* London: Travistock, 1963.

Curle, Adam, *World Campaign for Universal Literacy,* Center for Studies in Education and Development, Harvard University, Paper No. 1, 1964.

Curle, Adam, *Planning for Education in Pakistan: A Personal Case Study.* Cambridge: Harvard University Press, 1966.

Davis, Russell G., Lot H. Cooke Jr. Oriol Pi-Sunyer and Richard Bolin, *A Study of Scientific and Technical Education in Mexico and a Strategy for Developmental Assistance,* Mexico, D. F.: Ford Foundation Document, 1964. (150 pp., prepared for limited circulation.)

Danière, André. "The Rate of Return in Educational Planning: A Post Mortem" (Paper presented to Harvard Center for Studies in Education and Development Seminar, 1965).

Dill, W. R., D. P. Gaver and W. L. Weber, *Models and Modeling for Manpower Planning.* Pittsburgh: Carnegie Institute of Technology, 1965.

Dodge Corporation, *Schools for the New Needs: An Architectural Record Book,* 1956.

Domar, Evsey D., *Essay on the Theory of Economic Growth.* New York: Oxford University Press, 1957.

Doob, Leonard W., *Becoming More Civilized.* New Haven: Yale University Press, 1960.

Dorfman, Robert, Paul A. Samuelson and Robert M. Solow, *Linear Programming and Economic Analysis.* New York: McGraw-Hill, 1958.

Educational Facilities Laboratories, *Relocatable School Facilities.* New York: EFL, 1964.

Ellena, William J., *A Technique for Predicting Pupil Yield by Types of Dwelling Units.* (Doctoral Dissertation) College Park: University of Maryland, 1959.

Englehardt, N. L., "School Building Costs: Controls, Economy and Comparisons," *American School and University—1958–59.* Volume I. New York: American School Publishing Corporation, 1958.

Enriques, Ernesto, *Estimacion del Progreso obtenido en la ejecucion del plan nacional para el mejoramiento y la expansion de la educacion primaria en México.* Mexico: Ministerio de Education Publica, 1963.

Fitzroy, Dariel and John Lyon Reid, *Accoustical Environment of School Buildings.* New York: Educational Facilities Laboratories, Technical Report 1, 1963.

Frankel, S. Herbert. The Economic Impact on Under-Developed Societies. Cambridge: Harvard Press, 1953.

Gass, Saul I., *Linear Programming: Methods and Applications.* New York: McGraw-Hill, 1958.

Getzels, Jacob W. and Phillip W. Jackson, Creativity and Intelligence. New York: Wiley, 1962.

Ginsburg, Norton. *Atlas of Economic Development.* Chicago: University of Chicago Press, 1961.

Gordon, Margaret S., *Retraining and Labor Market Adjustment in Western Europe.* Washington, D.C.: U.S. Department of Labor, Manpower Automation Research Monograph, No. 4 (1965).

Guilford, J. P., *A factor analystic study of creative thinking: Reports from the Psychology Laboratory.* Los Angeles: University of Southern California, 1952, No. 8 (also Report no. 11).

Hansen, Morris H., William N. Hurwitz and William G. Madow, *Sample Survey Methods and Theory,* Vols. I, II. New York: John Wiley, 1953.

Harbison, Frederick and Charles A. Meyers, *Education, Manpower and Economic Growth.* New York: McGraw-Hill, 1964.

Harris, Seymour E., *Higher Education: Resources and Finance.* New York: McGraw-Hill, 1962.

Higher Education in the United States, The Economic Problem (edited and with an introduction by Seymour E. Harris.) Cambridge: Harvard University Press, 1960.

Herskowits, Melville J., *The Human Factor in Changing Africa.* New York: Knopf, 1962.

Houthakker, H. S., "Education and Income," *Review of Economics and Statistics.* February, 1959.

Hurd, P. D., *Science Facilities for the Modern High School,* Education Monograph No. 2. Stanford: Stanford University Press, 1954.

IIME (Guatemala: Instituto de Investigacións y Mejoramiento Educativo) *Formacion del Personal para la ensenanza media: Estimacion de Costos.* 1964.

India, *The National Sample Survey,* Technical Paper No. 70 on Sample Design. Calcutta: The Cabinet Secretariat, 1962.

International Cooperation Administration, *U.S. Industry Fact Sheets. Industry Profiles.* Washington: Technical Aid Branch.

International Labour Office, *International Standard Classification of Occupations.* Geneva: ILO, 1962.

Iowa Educational Information Center. *Computer Concepts and Educational Administration.* Iowa City: The University of Iowa and the University Council for Educational Administration, 1966.

Irons, Gerald E. and Willis P. Kern, *A Survey of Population, School Enrollment and School Building Program in Willoughby-Eastlake School District.* Lake County, Ohio. Willoughby-Eastlake District: Board of Education, 1953.

Jacoby, E. G., *Methods of School Enrollment Projections.* UNESCO, Educational Studies and Documents, No. 32, Paris, 1959.

Jaffe, A. J., *Handbook of Statistical Methods for Demographers.* U.S. Department of Commerce, Bureau of the Census. Washington, D.C.: U.S. Government Printing Office, 1951.

Johnson, P., *Science Facilities for Secondary Schools.* U.S. Office of Education, Misc. Bull. No. 17, Washington, D.C.: U.S. Government Printing Office, 1952.

Johnson, R., F. Kast and J. Rosenzweig, *The Theory and Management of Systems.* New York: McGraw-Hill, 1960.

Joseph, Alexander, Paul F. Brandwein, Evelyn Morhold, Harvey Pollack, Joseph F. Castka, *Teaching High School Science: A Sourcebook for the Physical Sciences.* New York: Harcourt, Brace, 1961.

Kerr, Clark, *The Uses of the University.* Cambridge: Harvard University Press, 1963.

Kershaw, J. A. and R. N. McKean, *System Analysis and Education* (RM-2473-FF). Santa Monica: RAND Corporation, 1959.

Klaus, D. J. and A. A. Lumsdaine, "Some Economic Realities of Teaching Machine Instruction," in *Applied Program Instruction.* (Editors Marguiles, Stuart and Lewis D. Eigen.) New York: Wiley, 1962.

Kopstein, Felix F. and R. T. Cave, *Preliminary Cost Comparison of Technical Training by Conventional and Programmed Learning Methods.* Technical Documentary Report No. MRL-TDR-62-79, Wright-Patterson Air Force Base, Ohio, July, 1962.

Leff, Nathaniel H. "The Brazilian Capital Goods Industry". (Unpublished doctoral dissertation, Massachusetts Institute of Technology, Cambridge, 1966.)

Leon, Alberto, *An Annotated Bibliography on Optimization.* Ann Arbor: Mental Health Research Institute, The University of Michigan (Preprint 162), July, 1965.

Levin, Lowell S. and Ann M. Martin. *Study of Manpower Needs in the Basic Health Sciences: The Development of Functional Criterion Analysis for Studies of Manpower Problems.* Washington, D.C.: Federation of American Societies for Experimental Biology, 1963.

Lewis, W. Arthur, *The Theory of Economic Growth.* Homewood, Illinois: Richard D. Irwin, Inc., 1955.

Lindquist, E. F. (ed.) *Educational Measurement.* Washington: American Council on Education, 1951.

Marshall, Alfred, *Principles of Economics.* London: Macmillan (4th ed.), 1908.

Martin, C. J. "World Population Kaleidoscope," *Finance and Development,* Vol. III, No. 1, pp. 1–8, (March, 1966).

McClelland, David C., *The Achieving Society.* Princeton: Van Nostrand, 1961.

McCusker, Henry F., *An Approach for Educational Planning in the Developing Countries.* Menlo Park: Stanford Research Institute, 1963.

McDonald, John S., "Development Decisions and Cost-Benefit Analysis." *Society for International Development; Development Seminar,* June, 1964.

Miles, Matthew B. (ed.). *Innovation in Education.* New York: Teachers College, Columbia University, 1964.

Miller, R. W. "How to Plan and Control With PERT," *Harvard Business Review,* Vol. 40, No. 2, pp. 93–104 (March–April, 1962).

Mincer, Jacob. "On-the-Job Training: Costs, Returns, and Some Implications" *The Journal of Political Economy,* LXX (5) (Supplement: October, 1962).

Moberg, Sven, "Methods and Techniques for Forecasting Specialized Manpower Requirements," *Forecasting Manpower Needs for the Age of Science.* Office for Scientific and Technical Personnel, Organization for European Economic Co-operation, September, 1960.

Moore, Carl L. and Robert K. Jaedicke, *Managerial Accounting.* Cincinnati: South Western, 1963.

Moser, C. A. and P. Redfern, *Education and Manpower: Some Current Research.* (unpublished paper.) London, 1964.

Myers, Charles N. Jr., *Education and National Development in Mexico,* Princeton, N.J.: Industrial Relations Section, Princeton University, 1964.

National Bureau of Economic Research, *The Rate and Direction of Inventive Activity: Economic and Social Factors.* Princeton: University Press, 1962.

National Council on Schoolhouse Construction, *Guide for Planning School Plants*. Nashville: NCSC, 1958.

Nigeria, Government of, *Investment in Education, the Report of the Commission on Post-School Certificate and Higher Education in Nigeria.* (The Report of the Ashby Commission.) Lagos: Government Printing Office, 1960.

OECD. *Econometric Models of Education: Some Applications.* Paris: OECD Education and Development, Technical Reports, 1965.

Orcutt, Guy H., M. Greenberger, J. Korbel and A. Rivlin, *Microanalysis of Socioeconomic Systems: A Simulation Study.* New York: Harper and Brothers, 1961.

Ovsiew, L. and W. Castetter, *Budgeting for Better Schools.* Englewood Cliffs: Prentice Hall, 1960.

Parnes, Herbert S., *Forecasting Educational Needs for Economic and Social Development.* Paris: OECD, the Mediterranean Regional Project, 1962.

Parnes, Herbert S., *Planning Education for Economic and Social Development.* Paris: OECD, the Mediterranean Regional Project, 1963.

Piaget, Jean. *Logic and Psychology.* Manchester: Manchester University Press, 1953.

Platt, William J., Al M. Loeb and Russell G. Davis, *Manpower and Educational Planning in Chile,* Chile-California Program of Technical Cooperation. Vol. 1. Santiago, Chile: June, 1964.

Polya, G. *How to Solve It: A New Aspect of Mathematical Methods.* (2nd ed.) Garden City: Doubleday, 1957.

Reed, Lowell and Margaret Merrell, "A Short Method for Constructing an Abridged Life Table," in A. J. Jaffe, *Handbook of Statistical Methods for Demographers.* Washington, U.S. Bureau of the Census, 1951, pp. 12–27.

Reid, John Lyon and Archibald B. Shaw, "The Random Falls Idea," *School Executive* 75, March, 1956, 47–86.

Reinfeld, Nyles and William R. Vogel, *Mathematical Programming.* Englewood Cliffs, New Jersey: Prentice Hall, 1958.

Rickover, H. G., *Education and Freedom.* New York: Dutton, 1960.

Ruggles, Richard and Nancy D. Ruggles, *National Income Accounts and Income Analysis.* New York: McGraw-Hill, 1956.

Sardie, Johannes L., *Población y Mano de Obra en Chile, 1930–1975.* Santiago de Chile: Centro Latinoamericano de Demografia D. 6/2, 1962.

Sattinger, I. J. "Systems Analysis in Development Programs," *International Development Review,* Vol. V, No. 3, pp. 20–25 (September, 1963).

Schultz, Theodore W., "Capital Formation by Education," *Journal of Political Economy,* LXVII, (6), 1960.

Schultz, Theodore W., *The Economic Value of Education.* New York: Columbia University Press, 1963.

Schumpeter, Joseph, *Capitalism, Socialism and Democracy,* (2nd.Ed) New York: Harper, 1947.

Smith, Adam, *The Wealth of Nations,* 5th Ed. London: Ed. Edwin Canaan, 1930.

Stanbery, Van Beuren, *Some New Techniques for Area Population Projections.* Los Angeles: John Randolph Haynes and Dora Haynes Foundation, 1960.

Stanford Institute for Communication Research. *Occasional Papers on Programmed Instruction: Programmed Instruction in Other Countries.* Stanford: Institute for Communication Research, 1963.

Stanford Research Institute: Research Information Center, *Growth Factors: Compound Interest Tables.* Menlo Park, California: SRI, 1963.

Stone, Beverly S. and John M. Bahner, *The Teaching Team Project.* Lexington, Massachusetts: SUPRAD document, Harvard, 1962.

Stone, Richard. "A Model of the Educational System." *Minerva,* 3 (2), Winter 1965, 172–186.

Svenlinson, Ingvar, in association with Friedrich Edding and Lionel Elvin, *Targets for Education in Europe in 1970,* OECD Policy Conference on Economic Growth, 16–20 October, 1961, Paper II. Washington: OECD, 1962.

Tarver, James D. *A Component Method of Estimating and Projecting State and Subdivisional Populations.* Stillwater Oklahoma: State University, Miscellaneous Publication MP—54, 1959.

Tatsuoka, Maurice M. *Joint Probability of Membership and Success in a Group: An Index which Combines the Information from Discriminant and Regression Analyses as Applied to the Guidance Problem.* Cambridge: Harvard Studies in Career Development No. 6, 1957.

Tinbergen, Jan. *The Design of Development.* Baltimore: The Johns Hopkins Press, 1958.

Tinbergen, Jan and H. C. Bos. *Econometric Models of Education: Some Applications.* Paris, OECD, 1965.

———. *Mathematical Models of Economic Growth.* New York: McGraw-Hill, 1964.

Thompson, Ronald B. "Numbers of College-Age Youths and College Enrollment Projected to 1975." *The College Blue Book,* (9th Ed.), September 1st, 1959.

UNESCO, *Literacy Campaign Data.* 12 C/Prg/3, Paris, October 10, 1962.

United Nations, *Demographic Aspects of Manpower: Report: Sex and Age Patterns of Participation in Economic Activities.* Populations Studies No. 33, New York, 1962.

United Nations, *Handbook of Population Census Methods. Volume 1: General Aspects of a Population Census. Volume II: Economic Characteristics of the Population.* Studies in Methods, Series F. No. 5, Rev. 1 New York: United Nations, 1958.

United Nations, *International Standard Industrial Classification of All Economic Activities,* Statistical Papers, Series M, No. 4. Rev. 1, New York: United Nations Organization.

United Nations, *Principles and Recommendations for National Population Censuses* (ST/STAT/Ser.,/27).

United Nations, ST/SO/Series A. *Population Studies* (Nos. 3,4,5,6,7, 10,20,22,23,25).

U.S. Department of Commerce. Bureau of the Census. *Florencia: A Case Study in Economic Census, Vol. 1: Documents. Vols. 2 and 3: Exhibits.* Washington, D.C. 1964.

U.S. Department of Commerce. Bureau of the Census. *Providencia: A Case Study in Economic Census, Vol 1: Documents. Vols 2 and 3: Exhibits.* Washington, D.C. 1964.

U.S. Department of Commerce, Bureau of the Census. *Illustrative Projections to 1980 of School and College Enrollment in the United States.* Series P-25, No. 232, 1961 (Also P-20, P-23, P-25, P-27 series generally, various numbers.)

U.S. Department of Defense. *PERT Cost System Design* (guide). Washington, D.C.: NASA, 1961.

U.S. Department of Health, Education and Welfare, OE-50027, *Bulletin 1962, No. 5. Economics of Higher Education,* ed., Selma J. Mushkin; Bowman, Mary Jane, "Human Capital: Concepts and Measures." pp. 69–92; Schultz, Theodore, "Rise in the Capital Stock Represented by Education in the United States." pp. 93–101.

Dictionary of Occupational Titles 1965, 3rd ed., Vols. I and II, U.S. Dept. of Labor: Washington, D.C., 1965.

U.S. Department of Labor, *Occupational Outlook Handbook,* Bulletin No. 1375, Washington, D.C.: Bureau of Labor Statistics, 1963, 1966.

U.S. Department of Labor: Bureau of Labor and Statistics. *Economic Forces in the U.S.A. in Facts and Figures.* 6th Ed., May, 1960.

U.S. Department of Labor, *The Skilled Labor Force,* Bureau of Apprenticeship: April, 1954

U.S. Department of Labor, United States Employment Service. *Estimates of Worker Trait Requirements for 4,000 Jobs, as defined in the Dictionary of Occupational Titles,* Washington: Bureau of Employment Security, 1956.

U.S. Department of Labor. *Area Skill Survey: Employment Security Job Market Research Methods* (handbook). Washington, D.C.: Bureau of Employment Security, 1965.

U.S. Department of Labor. *Manpower Research Programs* (reprinted from the 1966 Report of the Secretary of Labor). Washington, D.C.: D. O. L., 1966.

U.S. Office of Education, *Financial Accounting Handbook.* Washington, D.C.

U.S. Office of Education, *The Cost of Library Materials,* Washington, D.C. 1961.

U.S. Office of Education, *Financial Accounting for Local and State School Systems,* Washington, D.C. 1957.

Vaizey, John, *The Economics of Education.* London: Glencoe Press, 1962.

Vaizey, John. *The Costs of Education.* London: Allen and Unwin, 1958.

Venn, Grant. *Man, Education and Work: Postsecondary Vocational and Technical Education.* Washington, D.C.: American Council of Education, 1964.

Wagner, H. M. "A Linear Programming Solution to Dynamic Leontief Type Models," RAND Report P-609, Santa Monica: Rand Corporation, 1954.

Wall, W. D., F. J. Schonell and Willard D. Olson. *Failure in School.* Hamburg: UNESCO Institute for Education, 1962.

Ward, Joe H. "Hierarchical Grouping to Optimize an Objective Function," *Journal of American Statistics Association,* 1963, 58, 236–244.

Wasserman, William, *Education Price and Quantity Indexes, The Economics and Politics of Public Education,* XII, Syracuse: Syracuse University Press, 1963.

Waterston, Albert. "A Hard Look at Development Planning," *Finance and Development,* Vol. 3, No. 2, pp. 85–91 (June, 1966).

Weisbrod, Burton A., *External Benefits of Public Education: An Economic Analysis,* Princeton, New Jersey: Princeton University, 1964.

Whitla, Dean. *On the Prediction of School Enrollment.* Special Paper (Mimeo) Cambridge: Harvard Graduate School of Education, December, 1954.

Whitla, Dean. *Meeting Present and Future School Housing Needs: Waltham.* A Report of the Center for Field Studies. Cambridge: Harvard Graduate School of Education, 1951.

Whorf, Benjamin L., "Four Articles on Metalinguistics" (Reprinted from *Technology Review and Language, Culture and Personality.*) Washington: Foreign Service Institute, 1950.

Zymelman, Manuel, *Skill Requirements in Manufacturing Industries* (paper prepared for the Inter-Regional Symposium on Industrial Project Evaluation). Prague: Czechoslovakia, 1965.

Index

Printed in U.S.A.